Bill Saiff's

Rod & Reel

Recipes for
Hookin' & Cookin'

In Appreciation to the Viewers of Bill Saiff's Rod & Reel

To the many loyal viewers of our program, I would like to express my deep appreciation, for it has been their letters of encouragement to me and support for Public Television that have allowed the series to grow in the past twelve years.

This cookbook represents participation by individuals from all around the Country — both the United States and Canada — who shared their favorite recipes in order to make this first cookbook a success.

To them — my heartfelt thanks.

And, in addition, to my personal Secretary, Barb Kellogg, for her patience in gently pushing and prodding me into the project, and for the many hours of hard work in helping me put this book together — I thank her.

This cookbook is a collection of our favorite recipes which are not necessarily original recipes.

Published by Favorite Recipes® Press
P.O. Box 305142
Nashville, Tennessee 37230

© Rod & Reel of WNPE-TV, Channel 16
1056 Arsenal Street
Watertown, New York 13601

ISBN: 0-87197-264-6
Library of Congress Number: 89-27495

Manufactured in the United States of America
First Printing: 1990, 15,000 copies

Contents

Rod & Reel—A History 5

Dedication 7

Let's Talk Hookin' 10

Appetizers, Soups & Salads 19

Seafood 45

Main Dishes 79

Game 113

Vegetables & Side Dishes 131

Breads 149

Desserts 167

Substitution Chart 197

Equivalent Chart 198

Herb Chart 200

Index 202

Order Information 207

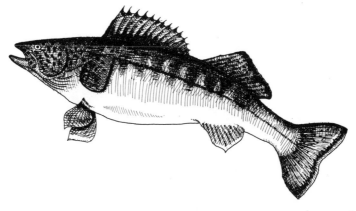

Nutritional Analysis Guidelines

The editors have attempted to present these family recipes in a form that allows approximate nutritional values to be computed. Persons with dietary or health problems or whose diets require close monitoring should not rely solely on the nutritional information provided. They should consult their physicians or a registered dietitian for specific information.

Abbreviations for Nutritional Analysis

Cal — Calories	Chol — Cholesterol	Potas — Potassium
Prot — Protein	Carbo — Carbohydrates	gr — gram
T Fat — Total Fat	Sod — Sodium	mg — milligram

Nutritional information for recipes is computed from values furnished by the United States Department of Agriculture Handbook. Many specialty items and new products now available on the market are not included in this handbook. However, producers of new products frequently publish nutritional information on each product's packaging and that information may be added, as applicable, for a more complete analysis. If the nutritional analysis notes the exclusion of a particular ingredient, check the package information.

Unless otherwise specified, the nutritional analysis of these recipes is based on the following guidelines. All measurements are level.

- Artificial sweeteners vary in use and strength so should be used "to taste," using the recipe ingredients as a guideline.
- Artificial sweeteners using aspertame (NutraSweet and Equal) should not be used as a sweetener in recipes involving prolonged heating which reduces the sweet taste. For further information on the use of these sweeteners, refer to package information.
- Alcoholic ingredients have been analyzed for the basic ingredients, although cooking causes the evaporation of alcohol thus decreasing caloric content.
- Buttermilk, sour cream and yogurt are the types available commercially.
- Chicken, cooked for boning and chopping, has been roasted; this method yields the lowest caloric values.
- Cottage cheese is cream-style with 4.2% creaming mixture. Dry-curd cottage cheese has no creaming mixture.
- Eggs are all large.
- Flour is unsifted all-purpose flour.
- Garnishes, serving suggestions and other optional additions and variations are not included in the analysis.
- Margarine and butter are regular, not whipped or presoftened.
- Milk is whole milk, 3.5% butterfat. Lowfat milk is 1% butterfat. Evaporated milk is produced by removing 60% of the water from whole milk.
- Oil is any type of vegetable cooking oil. Shortening is hydrogenated vegetable shortening.
- Salt to taste as noted in the method has not been included in the nutritional analysis.
- If a choice of ingredients has been given, the nutritional analysis reflects the first option.

Rod & Reel—A History

In 1973, I moved from commercial to Public Television (then known as educational television), bringing with me a background in production.

I was anxious to broaden the viewing audience of our Station, and with knowledge of a new salmon and lake trout fisheries emerging in Lake Ontario, the idea of a local fishing show intrigued me.

What to name it? Why not *ROD & REEL*? After researching titles and receiving trademark rights, a fishing series called *ROD & REEL* was born to Public Television.

Because I had been a fisherman all my life, I had the basic elements with which to start the show—a 14-foot cartop boat, an 18 horse motor, a couple of bass rods, a tackle box, and a net! With the addition of a small trailer, I soon became mobile.

The first *ROD & REEL* programs, which were shot on 16mm film, processed locally, and edited hastily, sometimes came off as pretty good "home movies." Let's face it—some were downright primitive.

Joining me on those early shoots was cameraman Wink Whitney, and together we made the transition from 16mm film to videotape. The production was polished under the keen eye of our editor, Ross Ney, and thirteen years later the team is still together.

From the very beginning, we decided to do an honest fishing show with no "canned" fishing, nothing caught and re-hooked, replayed, or re-netted. If we made an error, we showed it—all fisherman make them.

The concept caught on, and I soon realized that the program was becoming quite popular in our local market. Little did I know the appeal it would have for the 400,000 Canadians in our viewing audience. They flocked across the border to fish Lake Ontario on the U.S. side, and many of them have contributed to the contents of this book.

The trout and salmon populations were growing, and big fish in large numbers were caught. Henderson Harbor, home port of the *Rod & Reel*, had about nine charter boat captains in 1977. The surge of new tourists wanting to fish led many weekend fisherman to test for their guide's license and to take advantage of the demand for more boats and fishing expertise. Today, that harbor is home to over seventy guide boats.

In 1984, the Eastern Educational Network, based in Boston, was organizing the Interregional Program Service. This service supplies programs to Public Television stations all over the country.

At the urging of Art Gillick, my good friend, and then-Program Director of the Syracuse, New York, Public Television Station, I was encouraged to release fifteen programs of *ROD & REEL* as a trial balloon to the network. It took twenty-three stations for network acceptance, and on the very first vote, we picked up fifty-four markets—and *ROD & REEL* became a national program.

At the time of this publication, we are entering our seventh year of national release and are the longest continuous-playing series on the Interregional Program Service, carried on over two hundred Public Television stations across the U.S.

As the years went by and the series became more popular, so, too, did the boat grow—from the 14-foot cartop to a 16-foot pike pro boat, then to a 22-foot center console to the present-day film platforms which consist of a 19-foot Starcraft bass boat and a 24-foot center console Blue Water Starcraft built to handle both fresh water and ocean fishing.

My fear all along was that we would become too big, too electronic, leaving behind the bank fisherman, the wader, and the small boater who had been so loyal to the program when it was first broadcast.

A couple of years after the initial success of *ROD & REEL* on national television, we created the companion program, *ROD & REEL STREAMSIDE*, to speak to the needs of that group of fisherman who couldn't afford the big boats and electronics to fish big waters.

STREAMSIDE followed close on the heels of *ROD & REEL*, and together they make up fifty-two weeks of fishing on most Public Television stations.

Where it all ends is only a guess. We recently signed a contract for European release of the series, and here we are writing the foreword for our first cookbook!

All this I could never have envisioned when we set forth on Lake Ontario in that 14-foot cartop to do our first local fishing show.

Dedication

I dedicate this book to my mom and dad, Helen T. Saiff and William J. Saiff, Sr., for they are most responsible for my love of the outdoors and, in particular, my interest in fishing.

Thanks to them, I have never known a time when I didn't have a fishing rod in my hands or the opportunity to go fishing. I can remember fishing with my dad as a very young boy with cane pole and bobber. Our quarry was usually bullheads that frequent the streams off Lake Ontario in the early springtime.

I first fished from a boat while it was tied at the family dock in Chaumont Bay, New York, in the eastern end of Lake Ontario. At age seven, or maybe eight, my mom allowed me to row the boat out in front of our dock and anchor it in a weed bed to fish bass and perch.

Being a parent now myself, I understand the worry that both my parents must have experienced as they allowed my brother, Bob, and me to try our wings on the water.

About this stage of my life, my dad taught me some of his techniques for trolling—many of which are still successful today.

One day, while trolling a live pike minnow, a large northern grabbed it (the first northern, incidentally, I had ever hooked), and my Dad insisted I was just caught in the weeds! I was still fighting the big fish as he pulled the boat up on the ramp, and, when he realized I wasn't kidding, it was too late—the northern broke my line, and I was heartbroken. I can remember Dad trolling with me three to four more hours in an effort to hook up with another big fish.

My disappointment was short-lived, however, because a couple of days later my brother and I hooked big northerns within a half hour of each other. While we sat on the first fish so it wouldn't jump out of the row boat, we hollered to our mother on shore to come and see what we'd caught. Naturally, she made a fuss over it.

In those years Dad worked for the local newspaper and, of course, our picture with our big fish got into the paper.

And the heartache of the big one that "got away" was soon forgotten.

From that row boat, Dad turned me loose with a horse and a quarter Evinrude-Elto engine. I can still remember winding the rope on the flywheel and the exhilaration I felt when, with feet braced, I was able to start the engine myself!

And I really thought I'd progressed when he allowed me to use his old 2-cylinder, 4-horse—then, we were really starting to move.

But the ultimate fishing engine came when he let me buy (with my paper money) a 9.7, 4-cylinder Evinrude with an honest-to-goodness ratchet re-wind. I was in hog heaven because there was no fish in Chaumont Bay that was safe from the Saiff brothers!

We were having a ball running our boat and fishing, with never a thought about what Mom and Dad were going through as they watched us test our wings on the water.

I recall how tolerant they were when, as I grew older, I showed interest in high speed boats and power boat racing. For sixteen years they drove all over the country to watch me compete in my quest for a national title. When I was discouraged and ready to hang it all up, it was my mother's insistence that I give it "one more try," along with support of colleagues at work, that led me to capture a national power boat title in 1961.

Even today, friends of mine who board the *Rod & Reel* say that during the first few minutes of the ride, the old power boat racer still comes out in me.

Many times I've thought about how my parents questioned the sport and kept their fingers crossed that I would never be injured. Never wavering in their support, they were always there urging me on and, I guess, I took them for granted because that's what parents were "supposed to do."

Only after becoming a parent myself did I thoroughly understand what they went through and what they gave me.

I can't pay them back for all that support, but I can take this opportunity to say, "Thanks!"

Rod & Reel's Number One fans,
Bill's parents William J. Saiff, Sr. and
Helen T. Saiff, aboard the **Rod & Reel**

Let's Talk Hookin'

In the next couple of pages, I would like to discuss spoon and plug compatibility as they relate to trolling, and hopefully, give you some recipes for hookin' some of the wonderful fighting fish we have in our rivers and lakes.

SPOONS

Let me say, first of all, that I may mention in the following few paragraphs some spoon brand names. Please understand that I have not fished with every spoon made, but that the information I'm sharing with you applies to *all* spoons regardless of manufacturer.

The key word in trolling spoons is "speed compatibility."

In my opinion, spoons fall into three categories:

Slow Trolled — They include most flutter lites, such as the Sutton and Luhr-Jensen flutter spoons. They tend to work very well up to speeds of about 1.3 knots. Over that speed, they begin to spin, losing their darting motion and effectiveness, usually twisting the angler's line.

However, they are extremely effective when trolled correctly on finicky fish such as lake trout, especially when the fish are not very active and hesitate to bite.

Moderate Speeds — These operate well between 1.4 and 2.5 knots. Spoons such as Southport Slammers, Evil Eye in No. 3 and No. 5, the Attacker Spoon, the Hookster, the Stinger, and other such moderate weight flutter type spoons. They give you the broadest range of trolling speed, working pretty well from the low end at about 1.4 knots and normally operating well up to 2.5 before they begin to spin out.

High Speed Trolling Spoons — This group operates from 2.6 to 3.5, and sometimes 4 knots, and is normally made of heavier spoon stock. They require a high trolling speed to make them work efficiently. A few that I use and have a great deal of respect for are Luhr-Jensen Loco Spoons, No. 3 and 4, and No. 4 Luhr-Jensen Diamond Kings. The Monarch by Red Eye and the Northern King, produced in New York State will tolerate speeds to 4 knots before they begin to spin out. Trolling faster has an advantage — the bait can be presented to many more fish on a wider area of the lake.

Some fish, like the steelhead, require a speed of at least 2.7 knots to agitate them into striking, while a lake trout requires a slower speed around 1.3 to 1.9. They are noted for following lures for long periods of time before being enticed to nip at the bait.

Speeds in knots or in miles-per-hour will vary from boat to boat, depending on which trolling speed indicator you are using. The best way is to test these spoons along side your boat against your speed indicator, keeping a log of their performance. This will help you better match speeds.

I personally installed on my trolling line a small plastic keel, or rudder, and swivel six feet up from the lure. Les Davis and Luhr-Jensen make these, and you can obtain them in most tackle shops around the Great Lakes, particularly in the northwest where they are manufactured. They prevent your trolling line from twisting if your boat speed is too high and the spoon starts to spin out.

The small swivel behind the keel will relax the twist in the line, saving your main trolling line from twisting on the reel.

Try to avoid mixing spoons of various speeds. Mix your colors, but be sure to stay speed compatible.

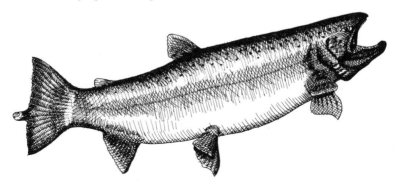

PLUGS

Stick and Jointed Minnows — For the troller who uses planer board or flat line techniques, there are three categories of plugs that I like to work with.

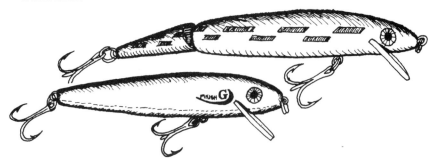

Let's class them as, "The Shallow Diver," "The Medium Diver," and "The Deep Diver."

My favorite shallow trolling plugs are the J20 Rebel in the jointed floater variety and the J15 Long (A) Bomber. Both are 4 1/2 inches long, 3/8 ounces, and have very similar tracking characteristics.

Whether flat lining or trolling from planer boards, they will normally run three to four feet below the surface of the water, and they are excellent baits in the early springtime and late fall when big fish are high and near the surface.

I like to remove the split ring and tune them by bending the nose loop a little to the left or right until they track correctly.

In the springtime I often use these models for brown trout. The fall finds me using one size larger — the J30 Rebel and the Bomber Long (A) Magnum, 5 1/2 to 7 inches. These become my top salmon surface presentations at that time.

In medium diving plugs, Rapalas such as the No. 9 and 11 reach depths of about seven to nine feet. I sometimes mix the Rebel and Rapala to cover a broader range of depths when using a planer board, or whenever I want to vary my depth flat lining.

The J20 Rebel, the Long "A" Bomber, and the Rapala are very close as they relate to speed and can be trolled successfully together.

In the deep divers, you might want to try a DJ20S jointed spoonbill Rebel, or the Bomber Long (A), Model 25A. These lures, compatible in speed, will allow you to get down from seven to fifteen feet. They work well when the fish are suspended well below the surface.

For the high speed troller, I must suggest two additional models — the FTJ20SS and the FTJ30SS in the Fastrac jointed Rebel. They have a new and innovative plastic lip which allows them to be trolled successfully over a 4-knot speed if you are hankering to go that fast.

They will work well at slow speeds and are extremely forgiving when speeds are increased. They have a depth range of about seven to nine feet which puts them in the upper range of the deep diving plugs. The above named plugs, tuned correctly, are responsible for many fish being taken across the Great Lakes in the months of April, May and June. July and August will see the fish go deep to avoid the warm surface water.

However, in September and October, as the surface water cools, these planer board and flat line techniques again come into play.

The presentations I have outlined will vary somewhat from lake to lake depending on water clarity and the predominant forage fish available. Try to match colors as best you can to closely simulate the target's natural bait.

On the following pages, I will attempt to give you some "recipes" for catching fish in specific situations.

Be sure to keep your hooks sharp, your lines tight, and your mind ever creative. Good luck.

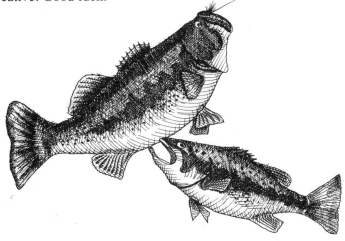

TROLLING

FALL SALMON

LOCATION/METHOD: Determine rivers that are stocked or known to be spawning waters for returning Chinook or Coho salmon.

SITUATION: Boat in 5 to 30 feet of water in the mouth of known salmon rivers.

TARGET: Chinook and Coho salmon seen porpoising and jumping at first light or at sunset.

INGREDIENTS

4 Cannon downriggers (electric or manual) or equivalent brands (Walker, Penn, Proo's, etc.)	4 Daiwa 8 to 8$^{1}/_{2}$ foot downrigger rods with 47SH reels or their equivalent (Shimano, Garcia, or Penn)

MIX . . . . . speed between 2.5 and 3.5 knots. Higher speeds will agitate salmon.

PLACE . . . . . Rebel J30SS jointed minnow/floater in the following color patterns: 92 chartreuse/orange back/orange bars; 93 chartreuse/green back/green bars; or FTJH30SS Fastrac jointed minnow in No. 14 green/silver, or No. 15 chrome blue/silver. There are five glow-in-the-dark colors which work well in first light—165, 166, 167, 168 and 169. Attach plugs with 20 pound test monofilament 6 feet behind plastic keel and swivel.

DROP . . . . . 4 presentations 70 to 100 feet behind the downrigger release, varying them no deeper than 1 to 4 feet. Make your troll into, and away from, the rising or setting sum, minimizing the reflection of your trolling line.

BLEND . . . . . the ingredients of a violent strike and a screaming reel—for this fish cannot easily be ladled in and must be played carefully, keeping the rod tip high.

SEAL SECURELY . . . . . once dropped on the deck, place in large cooler; let stand and allow to chill for best results.

SERVE IMMEDIATELY . . . . . using recipes from the following pages.

DEEP WATER STEELHEAD

LOCATION/METHOD: Lowrance X16 paper graph or equivalent-liquid crystal display (LCD) or cathode ray tube sounder (CRT). Note: depth flashers will not give enough detail—size, fish activity, etc.

SITUATION: Boat in 220 feet of water. Graph is printing occasional fish marks between 20 feet and the surface.

TARGET: Marks are suspected to be steelhead or rainbow trout which normally feed on trash lines or surface bugs and minnows.

INGREDIENTS

4 Cannon downriggers (electric or manual) or equivalent brands (Walker, Penn, Proo's, etc.) Super Ski Planner Boards and retrievals	10 Daiwa 8 foot downrigger rods matched with 27SH reels, loaded with 15-pound test monofilament line with 2 dozen Visi-Grip planer board releases

MIX . . . . . speed between 2.7 and 4 knots. You are hunting one of the fastest swimming fresh water fish.

PLACE . . . . . J20S Rebel jointed minnow in colors 99 and 15, along with FTJ20SS Fastrac jointed minnow in colors 14 and 15 (refer to Rebel Catalog acquired through your local sporting goods store). Pattern on planer boards as in Spring Brown Trout recipe, Page 15.

ADD . . . . . to your downriggers 4 Luhr-Jensen Diamond King, No. 4, or Northern King, No. 28, high speed spoons, concentrating on colors of silver/red or silver/orange. Steelhead prefer red and orange to any other color.

DROP . . . . . planer boards out 100 feet and set 3 plugs in the Visi-Grip releases, and pattern 100, 90 and 80 feet. Set downriggers from 5 to 15 feet below the surface and concentrate on bird activity, trash lines, thermal breaks, and floating bugs, at no slower than 2.7 knots.

SOAK . . . . . baits at high speeds, concentrating your efforts in the top 15 feet of water. Allow steelhead to rise and take the bait. Be prepared for a fight that is aquatic, acrobatic and aerial.

WHISK IN . . . . . your quarry, using very light reel drag, with rod tip held high. Most fish will be lost while in the air, so yield the rod on the jump.

SEAL SECURELY . . . . . . upon capture in large cooler; let stand and allow to chill for best results.

SERVE IMMEDIATELY . . . . . using recipes from the following pages.

SUMMER SALMON

LOCATION/METHOD: Lowrance X16 paper graph or equivalent-liquid crystal display (LCD) or cathode ray tube sounder (CRT). Note: depth flashers will not give enough detail—size, fish activity, etc.

SITUATION: Boat in 150 to 190 feet of water, large marks in two's and three's appearing at 45 to 65 feet. Your temperature probe shows water temperature 45 feet down to be 55 degrees (salmon's preferred temperature). Many other fish located below 120 feet.

TARGET: Suspected salmon at 45 to 65 feet. Fish at 120 feet most probably are lake trout. Temperature probe can confirm this if it shows 43 to 47-degree water.

INGREDIENTS

4 Cannon downriggers (electric or manual) or equivalent brands (Walker, Penn, Proo's, etc.)

4 $8^{1}/_{2}$ foot Daiwa downrigger rods with matching 47SH reels, or equivalent, loaded with 20-pound test monofilament line

MIX . . . . . speeds between 2.5 and 3.5 knots.

PLACE . . . . . 4 high-speed spoons such as Diamond King, No. 4, Northern King, 28's, Red Eye's Monarch spoon, or No. 4 Loco. Select blacks, purples, greens, chartreuse, or other known-to-be successful colors. Secure each spoon 6 feet down from the plastic keel and swivel and attach to downrigger release, leaving only 8 feet between the release and the spoon.

GARNISH . . . . . spoon with fish scent, if desired, or neutralize human scent with anise paste or oil.

DROP . . . . . downriggers to depths of 45 to 65 feet and begin to troll, watching your graph carefully. Your downrigger weight will displace water, salmon will sense this, and will investigate. Your lure presentation 8 feet behind your downrigger weight will be positioned correctly.

BLEND . . . . . the ingredients of a violent strike and a screaming reel—for this fish cannot easily be ladled in and must be played carefully, keeping the rod tip high.

SEAL SECURELY . . . . . once dropped on the deck, place in large cooler; let stand and allow to chill for best results.

SERVE IMMEDIATELY . . . . . using recipes from the following pages.

SUMMER LAKE TROUT

LOCATION/METHOD: Lowrance X16 paper graph or equivalent-liquid crystal display (LCD) or cathode ray tube sounder (CRT). Note: depth flashers will not give enough detail—size, fish activity, etc.

SITUATION: Boat in 150 feet of water, large numbers of fish are viewed, layered at 120 feet with some suspended 85 to 105 feet.

TARGET: Preferred fish are suspended 85 to 105 feet as layered fish are normally dormant and inactive. Suspended fish often are feeding and more aggressive.

INGREDIENTS

4 Cannon downriggers (electric or manual) or equivalent brands (Walker, Penn, Proo's, etc.)

Daiwa 8 to 8¹/₂ foot downrigger rods and matching reels (27SH or 47SH) or their equivalents (Shimano, Garcia, or Penn)

MIX . . . . . speed between 1.3 and 1.9 knots—most preferred speed for suspended lake trout.

PLACE . . . . . medium speed spoon, such as Southport Slammer, Evil Eye, Attacker, etc., 6 feet behind the plastic keel and swivel using 12 to 15-pound test monofilament line. Use colors known to work in your lake. Colors may vary, but be sure to stay speed compatible with your spoon.

GARNISH . . . . . spoon with fish scent, if desired, or run clean (spoon washed free of human scent). A good neutralizer is anise paste or oil.

ADD . . . . . monofilament line with keel and spoon to the downrigger release, keeping spoon within 6 to 12 feet of the release. The reason for this is that downrigger weights move through the water creating vibrations that fish sense through their lateral line. They are curious and will come to investigate, and your spoon will be presented right behind the curious disturbance.

DROP . . . . . downrigger weight and release to fish suspended 85 to 105 feet, ignoring layered fish and staying 1 to 2 feet above the target, and allow the fish to rise to the bait.

WHISK IN . . . . . upon release of the rod, set the hook crisply and whisk in your trout being careful to ladle it safely in the landing net head first.

SEAL SECURELY . . . . . in large cooler; let stand and allow to chill for best results.

SERVE IMMEDIATELY . . . . . using recipes from the following pages.

SPRING BROWN TROUT

LOCATION/METHOD: As the ice recedes from the lake and sunlight penetrates and warms the near-shore water, bait fish and brown trout move in looking for their preferred temperature of 52 to 57 degrees. This makes the shoreline our target area for this recipe.

SITUATION: Boat in 10 feet of water close to shoreline. Stir in points and structure.

TARGET: Brown trout are suspected in 10 feet or less of warmer in-shore water placed between the boat and shoreline.

INGREDIENTS

One set of Super Ski Planer Boards with retrievals of their equivalent

4 or 5 rod holders–both port and starboard

8 to 10 Daiwa 8 foot downrigger rods with 27SH reels or equivalent with 2 dozen Visi-Grip planer board releases

MIX . . . . . speed between 2 and 3 knots. Brown trout will strike a fast moving bait.

PLACE . . . . . Rebel J20 jointed, or equivalent in Bomber or Rapala, 6 feet behind the plastic keel and swivel using 12 to 15-pound test monofilament line to the keel and 10-pound from the keel to the plug. Some Rebel color suggestions—No. 15 chrome blue/silver; No. 70, brown trout; No. 71, rainbow trout; and No. 98, white/red head and belly.

ADD . . . . . planer boards in full extended position, letting the first plug out 100 feet. Place line on Visi-Grip releases. Attach release to planer board line and let slide to within 1 foot of the board. Place the second line 95 feet, layering that release 10 feet above line 1. Place line 3 at 90 feet, line 4 at 85 feet, and line 5 at 80 feet. Repeat the process, layering ever 10 feet. Using known bait fish colors, vary your presentation and adjust as "kneaded."

DROP . . . . . planer board presentation close to shore in 3 feet of water or less. Troll quickly along the shoreline's contour and structure, and wait for the fish to strike.

WHISK IN . . . . . . when the strike occurs, set the hook crisply, playing the fish over the transom, being sure to whisk it into the net head first.

SEAL SECURELY . . . . . in large cooler; let stand and allow to chill for best results.

SERVE IMMEDIATELY . . . . . using recipes from the following pages.

FIRST LIGHT

Appetizers, Soups and Salads

First Light

This is a time of day that most people miss—the sun as it breaks over the horizon sending its first rays of daylight across the placid waters of Lake Ontario. A scene many times viewed from the deck of the Rod & Reel—sunrise over Stoney Island with a big fish on.

Dockside Cocktail Party

Baked Brie
page 22

Asparagus Roll-Ups
page 21

Spinach Dip in a Bread Bowl
page 26

Salmon Log
page 27

Chicken Bits with Horseradish Sauce
pages 23 and 148

Peppered Beef Brisket on
Mashed Potato Rolls
pages 81 and 165

Lemon Cheese Bars
page 191

ARTICHOKE SQUARES

2 6-ounce jars
   marinated artichoke
   hearts
1 onion, chopped
1 clove of garlic, minced
4 eggs, beaten
1/4 cup bread crumbs
Dash of Tabasco sauce
1/2 teaspoon oregano
2 cups shredded Cheddar
   cheese

Drain and chop artichokes, reserving half the marinade. Sauté onion and garlic in reserved marinade in skillet. Combine eggs, bread crumbs, Tabasco sauce, oregano and salt and pepper to taste in bowl; mix well. Stir in sautéed vegetables, artichokes and cheese. Spoon into greased 9x13-inch baking pan. Bake at 325 degrees for 30 minutes. Cut into squares. Serve hot.
Yield: 30 squares.

Approx Per Square: Cal 57; Prot 3.1 g; Carbo 2.1 g; T Fat 4.2 g; Chol 44.5 mg; Potas 55.2 mg; Sod 122.0 mg.

ASPARAGUS ROLL-UPS

20 large fresh asparagus
   spears
2 tablespoons water
8 ounces cream cheese,
   softened
2 ounces blue cheese,
   crumbled
10 slices bread
2 tablespoons melted
   butter
1/4 cup Parmesan cheese

Microwave asparagus with water in covered glass dish on High for 7 minutes or until tender-crisp; drain. Blend cream cheese and blue cheese in bowl until smooth. Trim crusts from bread; cut slices into halves. Flatten each half with rolling pin. Spread with cheese mixture. Place asparagus spear on each slice; roll to enclose asparagus. Place seam side down on lightly greased baking sheet. Brush with melted butter; sprinkle with Parmesan cheese. Chill in refrigerator until serving time if desired. Broil until light brown. Drain on paper towel. Serve hot or cold. Yield: 20 servings.

Approx Per Serving: Cal 105; Prot 3.5 g; Carbo 7.8 g; T Fat 6.8 g; Chol 18.4 mg; Potas 78.4 mg; Sod 174.0 mg.

BAKED BRIE

**6 sheets frozen phyllo
dough, thawed**
**2 tablespoons melted
butter**
8 ounces brie cheese
**2 tablespoons apricot
preserves**

Cut phyllo sheets into halves crosswise. Brush melted butter on 1 sheet. Place cheese in center. Spread preserves on top of cheese. Fold dough over cheese from each side, buttering all exposed dough. Repeat with next 5 phyllo sheets, turning cheese to wrap alternately over top and bottom and buttering all exposed dough. Place on ungreased baking sheet. Bake at 350 degrees for 15 minutes or until golden brown. Let stand until set before slicing. Place on serving plate. Garnish with red seedless grapes and parsley. Keep unused dough covered until ready to use.
Yield: 6 servings.

Approx Per Serving: Cal 178; Prot 7.9 g; Carbo 4.8 g; T Fat 14.3 g; Chol 47.6 mg; Potas 64.5 mg; Sod 270.0 mg.
Nutritional information does not include phyllo dough.

THREE-CHEESE BALLS

**8 ounces cream cheese,
softened**
**8 ounces sharp Cheddar
cheese, shredded**
4 ounces blue cheese
1 tablespoon grated onion
**1/8 teaspoon
Worcestershire sauce**
1 teaspoon lemon juice
1 teaspoon sugar
**1/4 cup finely chopped
pecans**
**1 teaspoon chopped
parsley**
**3 tablespoons chopped
pecans**
**2 teaspoons chopped
parsley**

Combine cream cheese, Cheddar cheese, blue cheese, onion, Worcestershire sauce, lemon juice, sugar, 1/4 cup pecans and 1 teaspoon parsley in mixer bowl; beat until well mixed. Shape into 2 balls. Roll in mixture of 3 tablespoons pecans and 2 teaspoons parsley. Chill until serving time.
Yield: 48 tablespoons.

Approx Per Tablespoon: Cal 52; Prot 2.1 g; Carbo 0.6 g; T Fat 4.6 g; Chol 11.9 mg; Potas 21.6 mg; Sod 76.4 mg.

TACO BALL

1 envelope taco seasoning
  mix
8 ounces cream cheese,
  softened
8 ounces small curd
  cottage cheese
1 tomato, finely chopped
1 onion, minced
1/4 cup finely chopped
  black olives
1 green bell pepper,
  finely chopped
1/2 cup shredded Cheddar
  cheese

Combine seasoning mix, cream cheese and cottage cheese in mixer bowl; beat until well mixed. Shape into ball. Press mixture of tomato, onion, olives and green pepper over cheese ball. Coat with Cheddar cheese. Serve with chips. Yield: 12 servings.

    Approx Per Serving: Cal 150; Prot 6.0 g; Carbo 9.6 g; T Fat 10.0 g;
      Chol 28.4 mg; Potas 154.3 mg; Sod 882.3 mg.

CHICKEN BITS

8 chicken breast filets
3 eggs
1 cup milk
1/4 cup soy sauce
1 tablespoon onion salt
1 tablespoon garlic salt
2 cups (about) flour
Oil for frying

Cut chicken into bite-sized pieces. Combine eggs, milk, soy sauce, onion salt and garlic salt in bowl; mix well. Add chicken. Marinate in refrigerator for 6 hours or longer. Drain chicken. Roll in mixture of flour and salt and pepper to taste, coating well. Heat 1 inch oil in skillet. Add chicken a few pieces at a time. Fry until golden brown on all sides. Drain on paper towels. May substitute fish for chicken if preferred. Yield: 16 servings.

    Approx Per Serving: Cal 181; Prot 15.3 g; Carbo 13.1 g; T Fat 7.0 g;
      Chol 89.4 mg; Potas 180.0 mg; Sod 1112.0 mg.
      Nutritional information does not include oil for frying.

Yvonne Schriock
Carthage, New York

PEANUTTY CHICKEN WINGS

3 pounds chicken wings
6 tablespoons chunky
   peanut butter
3 tablespoons lime juice
3/4 teaspoon Kitchen
   Bouquet
3 tablespoons oil
3/4 teaspoon soy sauce
3/4 teaspoon chili powder
3/4 teaspoon salt
Garlic powder to taste

Separate wings at joints, discarding tips. Combine peanut butter, lime juice, Kitchen Bouquet, oil, soy sauce, chili powder, salt and garlic powder in bowl; mix well. Add wings. Marinate in refrigerator overnight, turning occasionally; drain. Arrange in single layer on baking sheet; do not allow wings to touch. Bake at 325 degrees for 45 to 60 minutes; do not turn. May be frozen before baking. Yield: 8 servings.

Approx Per Serving: Cal 497; Prot 34.7 g; Carbo 2.5 g; T Fat 38.4 g; Chol 132.0 mg; Potas 354.0 mg; Sod 406.0 mg.

CRAB MUFFIN TOASTIES

8 ounces cooked crab meat
5 ounces Old English
   cheese spread
1 1/2 tablespoons
   mayonnaise
1/2 cup butter, softened
1/4 teaspoon onion salt
1/8 teaspoon garlic salt
6 English muffins, split

Combine crab meat, cheese spread, mayonnaise, butter, onion salt and garlic salt in bowl; mix well. Spread on muffin halves. Cut each into 6 wedges. Arrange on baking sheet. Broil until brown. Serve immediately. Yield: 72 toasties.

Approx Per Toastie: Cal 34; Prot 1.4 g; Carbo 2.4 g; T Fat 2.1 g; Chol 7.5 mg; Potas 44.7 mg; Sod 91.9 mg.

COCKTAIL SAUCE

Catsup
Prepared horseradish
Lemon juice to taste

Combine desired amounts of catsup and horseradish in bowl; mix well. Stir in lemon juice to taste. Serve with fish.

Nutritional information for this recipe is not available.

S.W. Carr
Watertown, New York

CHEESY HOT CRAB DIP

1 pound crab meat
16 ounces cream cheese,
   softened
1 cup sour cream
1/4 cup (rounded)
   mayonnaise
Juice of 1/2 lemon
2 teaspoons
   Worcestershire sauce
1 teaspoon mustard
1/4 teaspoon garlic powder
1 cup shredded Cheddar
   cheese

Combine crab meat, cream cheese, sour cream, mayonnaise, lemon juice, Worcestershire sauce, mustard, garlic powder and salt to taste in bowl; mix well. Stir in half the cheese. Spoon into greased 2-quart baking dish. Top with remaining cheese. Bake at 350 degrees for 30 to 40 minutes or until bubbly. Serve with crackers. Yield: 48 ounces.

    Approx Per Ounce: Cal 59; Prot 2.8 g; Carbo 0.5 g; T Fat 5.1 g;
       Chol 20.7 mg; Potas 45.2 mg; Sod 86.5 mg.

DILL DIP

2 cups mayonnaise
2 cups sour cream
1 tablespoon Salad
   Supreme seasoning
1 tablespoon dillweed
2 tablespoons onion flakes
1/4 cup chopped parsley

Combine mayonnaise, sour cream, Salad Supreme seasoning, dillweed, onion flakes and parsley in bowl; mix well. Chill for several hours. Serve with assorted bite-sized fresh vegetables. Yield: 72 tablespoons.

    Approx Per Tablespoon: Cal 58; Prot 0.3 g; Carbo 0.6 g; T Fat 6.2 g;
       Chol 6.4 mg; Potas 15.6 mg; Sod 38.3 mg.
       Nutritional information does not include Salad Supreme seasoning.

TROPICAL FRUIT DIP

1 8-ounce can crushed
   pineapple
3/4 cup milk
1/2 cup sour cream
1 3-ounce package
   coconut instant
   pudding mix

Combine pineapple, milk, sour cream and pudding mix in blender container. Process until smooth. Chill, covered, overnight. Pour into serving bowl. Serve with fresh fruit. Yield: 32 tablespoons.

    Approx Per Tablespoon: Cal 27; Prot 0.3 g; Carbo 4.4 g; T Fat 1.0 g;
       Chol 2.4 mg; Potas 20.3 mg; Sod 22.2 mg.

LAYERED FIESTA DIP

1 16-ounce can bean dip
1 8-ounce container
   avocado dip
1 4-ounce can chopped
   black olives
1 tomato, chopped
1 4-ounce can chopped
   green chilies, drained
2 green onions, chopped
1 cup sour cream
1 cup shredded Monterey
   Jack cheese

Layer bean dip and avocado dip in shallow serving dish. Sprinkle with black olives, tomato, green chilies and green onions. Dot with sour cream. Top with cheese. Chill until serving time. Serve with tortilla chips. Yield: 20 servings.

> **Approx Per Serving:** Cal 101; Prot 3.6 g; Carbo 6.6 g; T Fat 7.4 g; Chol 10.3 mg; Potas 215.0 mg; Sod 177.0 mg.

SALMON DIP

1 6¹/₂-ounce can salmon,
   drained, flaked
5 ounces buttermilk salad
   dressing
8 ounces ranch salad
   dressing
¹/₄ cup mayonnaise
¹/₄ to ¹/₂ teaspoon dillweed
Onion powder to taste

Combine salmon, salad dressings, mayonnaise, dillweed and onion powder in bowl; mix well. Chill until serving time. Serve with sesame crackers, onion rounds or vegetables. Yield: 32 tablespoons.

> **Approx Per Tablespoon:** Cal 51; Prot 1.8 g; Carbo 0.4 g; T Fat 4.7 g; Chol 8.8 mg; Potas 31.6 mg; Sod 44.6 mg.

Barbara Alcamo
Houston, Texas

SPINACH DIP

1 10-ounce package
   frozen chopped spinach
1¹/₂ cups sour cream
1 cup mayonnaise
1 package dry vegetable
   soup mix
1 8-ounce can sliced
   water chestnuts, drained

Thaw spinach. Drain, pressing to remove excess liquid. Combine with sour cream, mayonnaise, soup mix and water chestnuts in bowl; mix well. Chill until serving time. May serve in hollowed-out loaf of bread with bread pieces reserved for dipping. Yield: 20 servings.

> **Approx Per Serving:** Cal 139; Prot 1.7 g; Carbo 5.8 g; T Fat 12.6 g; Chol 14.4 mg; Potas 110.0 mg; Sod 371.0 mg.

SALMON LOG

2 7½-ounce cans salmon
8 ounces cream cheese,
  softened
1 tablespoon chopped
  onion
2 tablespoons prepared
  horseradish
1 tablespoon lemon juice
½ teaspoon Tabasco sauce
¼ teaspoon
  Worcestershire sauce
¼ teaspoon salt
Pepper to taste
½ cup chopped pecans
3 tablespoons chopped
  parsley

Drain salmon and flake into bowl. Add cream cheese, onion, horseradish, lemon juice, Tabasco sauce, Worcestershire sauce, salt and pepper in large bowl; mix well. Chill for several hours. Shape into log. Roll in mixture of pecans and parsley. Chill until serving time. Serve with crackers. Yield: 48 tablespoons.

Approx Per Tablespoon: Cal 37; Prot 2.0 g; Carbo 0.5 g; T Fat 3.0 g; Chol 10.5 mg; Potas 53.6 mg; Sod 29.9 mg.

Lee Sipes
Iroquois, Ontario, Canada

SALMON PÂTÉ

1 7-ounce can red
  salmon, drained
2 tablespoons mayonnaise
½ cup melted butter
1 teaspoon minced fresh
  dill or ¼ teaspoon dried
  dillweed

Combine salmon, mayonnaise, butter, dill and salt and pepper to taste in blender container. Process until smooth. Spoon into oiled mold. Chill until firm. Unmold onto serving plate. Garnish with parsley and paper-thin slices of cucumber. Serve with crackers. Yield: 16 tablespoons.

Approx Per Tablespoon: Cal 79; Prot 2.3 g; Carbo 0.1 g; T Fat 7.8 g; Chol 24.0 mg; Potas 57.1 mg; Sod 63.0 mg.

Lee Sipes
Iroquois, Ontario, Canada

SEVICHE

Fillets of any white, non-oily fish such as perch, bass, walleye or northern pike
Fresh limes
1 onion, minced
4 jalapeño peppers, minced

Slice fish fillets crossways very, very thinly with very, very sharp knife. Place in dish. Combine enough lime juice to cover fillets with onion and jalapeño peppers in small bowl; mix well. Pour over fillets, stirring gently to coat. Let stand for 2 hours or longer. Serve with chopped parsley. Use scallops or octopus for a really exotic dish. The lime juice does the cooking.

Nutritional information for this recipe is not available.

D. Paige Gorham
Elbridge, New York

SWEET AND SOUR SAUSAGE BITES

1 pound smoked sausage links, cooked
1 cup packed brown sugar
3 tablespoons flour
2 teaspoons dry mustard
1 cup unsweetened pineapple juice
1/2 cup vinegar
2 teaspoons soy sauce

Place sausage links in baking dish. Mix brown sugar, flour, dry mustard and pineapple juice in small saucepan. Bring to a boil. Cook for 2 minutes, stirring constantly. Cool. Stir in vinegar and soy sauce. Pour over sausage. Chill until serving time. Bake at 300 degrees until bubbly. Serve warm. Yield: 8 servings.

Approx Per Serving: Cal 343; Prot 11.6 g; Carbo 34.6 g; T Fat 17.7 g; Chol 48.0 mg; Potas 362.0 mg; Sod 831.0 mg.

Toni Stanton
Carthage, New York

YUMMY SNACKS

1 cup wheat sprouts
1 cup sunflower seed
1 cup raisins
1 tablespoon honey
1/2 cup coconut

Combine wheat sprouts, sunflower seed and raisins in food processor container. Process until chopped. Combine with honey in bowl; mix well. Shape into 1-inch balls. Roll in coconut, coating well. Chill for 20 minutes or longer. Yield: 24 snacks.

Approx Per Snack: Cal 63; Prot 1.7 g; Carbo 7.6 g; T Fat 3.6 g; Chol 0.0 mg; Potas 99.3 mg; Sod 1.3 mg.
Nutritional information does not include wheat sprouts.

Marilyn K. Adams
Watertown, New York

BEAN SOUP

1 pound dried beans
2 pork chops
4 cups chopped potatoes
2 carrots, chopped
1 medium onion, chopped
2 tablespoons catsup
1/4 cup hot sauce
1 tablespoon
    Worcestershire sauce
1/4 cup packed
    brown sugar
1 teaspoon salt
1/2 teaspoon pepper

Rinse dried beans. Combine with pork chops, potatoes, carrots, onion, catsup, hot sauce, Worcestershire sauce, brown sugar, salt and pepper in 4-quart pressure cooker. Add enough water to fill cooker 3/4 full. Cook using manufacturer's directions for 11/2 hours. Yield: 16 cups.

Approx Per Cup: Cal 310; Prot 15.5 g; Carbo 30.3 g; T Fat 14.4 g; Chol 23.9 mg; Potas 757.0 mg; Sod 628.0 mg.

Randy L. Riley
Carthage, New York

COLD CARROT SOUP

2   10-ounce packages
    frozen carrots
1 cup chicken broth
1 tablespoon curry
    powder
1 tablespoon chopped
    fresh oregano
1 tablespoon chopped
    fresh coriander
1 cup whipping cream

Cook carrots using package directions. Drain, reserving half the cooking liquid. Combine carrots and liquid with chicken broth, curry powder, herbs and cream in blender container. Process until smooth. Chill until serving time. Yield: 4 servings.

Approx Per Serving: Cal 265; Prot 4.1 g; Carbo 13.6 g; T Fat 22.5 g; Chol 81.7 mg; Potas 321.0 mg; Sod 300.0 mg.

CHICKEN VEGETABLE SOUP

2   28-ounce cans whole
     tomatoes
2 large onions, chopped
2 to 3 cloves of garlic,
   minced
4 pounds chicken breasts
   and thighs
6 chicken bouillon cubes
3 tablespoons olive oil
10 carrots, sliced
4 stalks celery, sliced
1/3 head cabbage, chopped
6 ounces uncooked thin
   egg noodles
3 tablespoons olive oil

Purée undrained tomatoes, onions and garlic in blender or food processor container. Strain into bowl; discard pulp. Cook chicken in water to cover in large saucepan for 30 minutes. Remove and bone chicken, reserving broth. Add enough water to broth to measure 6 cups. Dissolve bouillon cubes in broth. Add 3 tablespoons olive oil and tomato purée. Bring to a boil over low heat. Add carrots, celery and cabbage. Simmer, covered, for 30 minutes or until tender. Sauté noodles in 3 tablespoons olive oil in skillet until golden brown. Add noodles and chicken to soup. Simmer for 5 to 10 minutes. Serve with shredded cheese and hot biscuits. Yield: 20 cups.

Approx Per Cup: Cal 194; Prot 15.3 g; Carbo 15.3 g; T Fat 8.1 g; Chol 37.9 mg; Potas 445.0 mg; Sod 518.0 mg.

Paula Anne Jay
Star Lake, New York

CLAM CHOWDER

4 potatoes, peeled,
   chopped
1 small onion, chopped
1 pound white fish,
   chopped, cooked
1   7-ounce can baby clams
1 tablespoon cornstarch
2 cups milk
1   16-ounce can cream-
   style corn

Cook potatoes in water to cover in saucepan for 15 minutes or until tender. Add onion, fish and undrained clams. Blend cornstarch with a small amount of milk. Add remaining milk to soup. Bring to a boil. Stir in cornstarch mixture. Simmer for 1 hour. Stir in corn. Yield: 6 servings.

Approx Per Serving: Cal 425; Prot 34.4 g; Carbo 55.6 g; T Fat 7.6 g; Chol 77.6 mg; Potas 1343.0 mg; Sod 351.0 mg.

Joy M. J. Karam
Ottawa, Ontario, Canada

FISH CHOWDER

2 cups ground potatoes
2 cups ground onions
1 pound fish fillets
2 teaspoons salt
4 cups cold water
1/2 cup butter
2 cups milk
1/4 teaspoon white pepper

Combine potatoes, onions, fish and salt with cold water in 4-quart saucepan. Bring to a boil; reduce heat. Simmer for 45 to 60 minutes, stirring every 5 minutes. Add butter, milk and white pepper. Heat to serving temperature; do not boil. Serve chowder with crackers. Yield: 4 servings.

> **Approx Per Serving:** Cal 595; Prot 37.2 g; Carbo 37.1 g; T Fat 33.0 g; Chol 150.0 mg; Potas 1258.0 mg; Sod 1407.0 mg.

William Cormier
Ontario, Canada

CREAMY FISH CHOWDER

4 cups chopped potatoes
1 cup chopped celery
1 small onion, chopped
2 1/2 teaspoons salt
1 teaspoon pepper
4 cups water
2 pounds fish fillets
2 cups water
1/4 teaspoon thyme
1 bay leaf
1 teaspoon salt
1/2 cup melted margarine
2/3 cup flour
4 cups milk
2 cups shredded Cheddar cheese
1   16-ounce can whole kernel corn, drained

Combine potatoes, celery, onion, 2 1/2 teaspoons salt and pepper with 4 cups water in saucepan. Cook until potatoes are tender. Combine fish fillets with 2 cups water, thyme, bay leaf and 1 teaspoon salt in saucepan. Cook until fish flakes easily. Strain broth into undrained vegetables. Flake fish. Add to soup. Blend margarine and flour in large saucepan. Cook for several minutes. Add milk. Cook until thickened, stirring constantly. Stir in cheese until melted. Add to soup. Stir in corn. Heat to serving temperature; do not boil. Yield: 10 servings.

> **Approx Per Serving:** Cal 506; Prot 31.2 g; Carbo 41.4 g; T Fat 24.4 g; Chol 90.6 mg; Potas 963.0 mg; Sod 1212.0 mg.

New York State Department of Environmental Conservation
Albany, New York

FISH AND VEGETABLE CHOWDER

3 cups chopped potatoes
2 cups chopped carrots
1¹/₂ cups chopped onions
2 cups chopped celery
6 cups water
1 can cream of mushroom
  soup
5¹/₂ ounces butter
2 pounds fish fillets,
  chopped
1 small bunch parsley,
  chopped

Combine potatoes, carrots, onions and celery with water in large saucepan. Cook until vegetables are tender. Add soup and butter. Simmer until flavors are blended. Add fish. Cook for 5 minutes. Stir in parsley. Yield: 6 servings.

Approx Per Serving: Cal 626; Prot 44.2 g; Carbo 37.7 g; T Fat 32.8 g; Chol 153.0 mg; Potas 1505.0 mg; Sod 764.0 mg.

Lydia Blancher
Athens, Ontario, Canada

MARITIME FISH CHOWDER

4 ounces salt pork,
  chopped
1 medium onion, chopped
3 cups chopped potatoes
2 cups water
2 pounds fish fillets, cut
  into bite-sized pieces
4 cups milk
²/₃ cup evaporated milk
8 crackers, crushed
3 tablespoons butter
3 tablespoons chopped
  parsley
Paprika to taste
2 teaspoons salt
Pepper to taste

Fry salt pork in large saucepan until crisp and brown. Remove salt pork and reserve for garnish. Sauté onion in pan drippings just until tender. Add potatoes and water. Cook until potatoes are tender. Add fish. Simmer for 5 to 10 minutes or until fish flakes easily. Combine milk, evaporated milk, cracker crumbs, butter, parsley, paprika, salt and pepper in saucepan. Bring just to the simmer; do not boil. Add to soup; mix well. Heat to serving temperature. Ladle into serving bowls; top with reserved salt pork. Yield: 8 servings.

Approx Per Serving: Cal 471; Prot 40.3 g; Carbo 30.6 g; T Fat 19.9 g; Chol 119.0 mg; Potas 1167.0 mg; Sod 977.0 mg.

F. Joyce Ralph
Lansdowne, Ontario, Canada

FISH SOUP

8 ounces bacon
1 cup chopped celery
1 cup chopped onion
1 cup chopped carrot
4 cups water
1 can tomato soup
1 cup flaked cooked fish

Fry bacon in saucepan until crisp; drain. Crumble bacon. Combine bacon, celery, onion, carrot and water in saucepan. Stir in soup and fish. Bring to a boil; reduce heat. Simmer until vegetables are tender. Yield: 4 servings.

Approx Per Serving: Cal 335; Prot 25.7 g; Carbo 17.0 g; T Fat 18.1 g; Chol 59.6 mg; Potas 804.0 mg; Sod 1062.0 mg.

Helen Saiff
Watertown, New York

EASY GAZPACHO

2 tomatoes, peeled
1 cucumber, peeled
1/4 cup chopped onion
1/4 cup chopped green bell pepper
1 cup tomato juice
2 tablespoons olive oil
1 1/2 tablespoons vinegar
1/8 teaspoon Tabasco sauce
1/4 teaspoon garlic salt

Combine vegetables in blender or food processor container. Add tomato juice, olive oil, vinegar, Tabasco sauce and garlic salt. Process until of desired consistency. Chill until serving time. Serve in frosty soup cups, garnished with lime slices. Yield: 4 servings.

Approx Per Serving: Cal 97; Prot 1.6 g; Carbo 8.8 g; T Fat 7.1 g; Chol 0.0 mg; Potas 407.0 mg; Sod 360.0 mg.

SOUR CREAM POTATO SOUP

3 cups chopped peeled potatoes
1/2 cup chopped celery
1/2 cup chopped onion
3 cups water
2 cups milk
1 tablespoon instant chicken bouillon
3 tablespoons butter
1 cup sour cream
1 tablespoon flour

Combine potatoes, celery, onion and water in large saucepan. Cook, covered, until potatoes are tender. Add milk, bouillon and butter. Bring soup to a simmer, stirring frequently. Blend sour cream and flour in small bowl. Stir into soup. Cook until thickened, stirring constantly; do not boil. Season with salt and pepper to taste. Yield: 6 servings.

Approx Per Serving: Cal 254; Prot 5.6 g; Carbo 21.4 g; T Fat 16.7 g; Chol 43.6 mg; Potas 442.0 mg; Sod 285.0 mg.

COLD STRAWBERRY SOUP

2 cups strawberries
1 cup plain yogurt
1 cup 2% milk
3 tablespoons brown
  sugar
1 teaspoon lemon juice
1 teaspoon Brandy extract
1 teaspoon vanilla extract

Combine strawberries, yogurt, milk, brown sugar, lemon juice and flavorings in blender container. Process until smooth. Chill until serving time. Ladle into soup bowls. Garnish with sliced fresh strawberries. Yield: 4 servings.

Approx Per Serving: Cal 132; Prot 5.3 g; Carbo 24.0 g; T Fat 2.2 g; Chol 9.0 mg; Potas 377.0 mg; Sod 76.3 mg.

Barbara H. Haller
Dexter, New York

OLD-FASHIONED TOMATO SOUP

5 large ripe tomatoes,
  peeled, chopped
1 tablespoon sugar
1 medium onion
5 to 6 cloves
3 cups milk
1 bay leaf
1 tablespoon butter
1/3 cup fine bread crumbs
1/8 teaspoon soda
1 1/4 teaspoons salt
1/4 teaspoon pepper

Cook tomatoes with sugar in heavy saucepan over low heat until tender. Stud onion with cloves. Combine with milk, bay leaf, butter and bread crumbs in saucepan. Bring to a simmer over low heat. Stir soda into tomatoes. Add tomatoes to soup. Heat to serving temperature. Season with salt and pepper. Remove onion and bay leaf. Yield: 6 servings.

Approx Per Serving: Cal 150; Prot 6.0 g; Carbo 18.2 g; T Fat 6.6 g; Chol 22.0 mg; Potas 426.0 mg; Sod 578.0 mg.

Phyllis Wendt
Constableville, New York

TURTLE CHOWDER

1 snapping turtle
1 pound bacon
6 medium potatoes,
   chopped
3 medium onions, chopped
1 cup chopped celery
4 carrots, chopped
1 cup chopped broccoli
1   16-ounce can cream-
   style corn
2 tablespoons
   Worcestershire sauce
2 tablespoons chopped
   parsley
1 teaspoon salt
1 teaspoon pepper

Clean turtle and chop meat into small cubes. Combine with bacon in saucepan. Fry until bacon is crisp, stirring to brown turtle meat. Remove bacon. Add enough water to turtle meat and drippings to cover by 3 inches. Add potatoes, onions, celery, carrots, broccoli, corn, Worcestershire sauce, parsley, salt and pepper. Simmer, covered, for 3 hours. Chill overnight and reheat for best flavor. Ladle into soup bowls. Crumble bacon over top. Yield: 8 servings.

Approx Per Serving: Cal 576; Prot 23.4 g; Carbo 58.8 g; T Fat 28.6 g; Chol 47.7 mg; Potas 1307.0 mg; Sod 1411.0 mg.

Marsha Morley
Heuvelton, New York

CRANBERRY FREEZE

1 pound cranberries,
   ground
1   8-ounce package
   miniature
   marshmallows
1   29-ounce can crushed
   pineapple, drained
1 1/2 cups sugar
1/2 cup chopped walnuts
1/2 cup sugar
1 pint whipping cream,
   whipped

Combine cranberries, marshmallows, pineapple and 1 1/2 cups sugar in bowl; mix well. Chill overnight. Add walnuts and 1/2 cup sugar; mix well. Fold in whipped cream. Pour into 9x13-inch dish. Freeze until firm. Cut into squares. Yield: 10 servings.

Approx Per Serving: Cal 436; Prot 2.4 g; Carbo 83.1 g; T Fat 12.7 g; Chol 32.6 mg; Potas 184.0 mg; Sod 36.9 mg.

FROZEN FRUIT CUP

1 12-ounce can frozen
   orange juice concentrate,
   thawed
1 12-ounce can water
2 tablespoons lemon juice
1 cup (scant) sugar
2 16-ounce cans
   apricots, drained,
   chopped
1 17-ounce can
   pineapple tidbits,
   drained
6 bananas, peeled, sliced

Blend orange juice concentrate, water, lemon juice and sugar in bowl. Add apricots, pineapple and bananas. Spoon into individual serving dishes. Freeze, covered with plastic wrap, until firm. Thaw at room temperature for 1 1/2 hours before serving. May microwave on Low for several seconds for quick thawing. Yield: 8 servings.

Approx Per Serving: Cal 362; Prot 2.7 g; Carbo 92.3 g; T Fat 0.6 g; Chol 0.0 mg; Potas 850.0 mg; Sod 7.8 mg.

POPPY SEED FRUIT SALAD

2 11-ounce cans
   mandarin oranges
1 16-ounce can freestone
   peaches
1 15-ounce can
   pineapple tidbits
4 bananas, peeled, sliced
1 10-ounce package
   frozen sweetened sliced
   strawberries
1 3-ounce package
   vanilla instant
   pudding mix
1 cup orange juice
1 teaspoon poppy seed

Drain oranges, peaches and pineapple. Combine drained fruit with bananas and strawberries in large bowl; mix gently. Combine pudding mix, orange juice and poppy seed in bowl; mix well. Pour over fruit; mix gently. Chill overnight. Yield: 12 servings.

Approx Per Serving: Cal 166; Prot 1.2 g; Carbo 43.0 g; T Fat 0.4 g; Chol 0.0 mg; Potas 339.0 mg; Sod 54.2 mg.

GRAPE RING WITH CREAMY DRESSING

2 cups seedless red grapes
2   3-ounce packages
   grape gelatin
2 cups boiling water
1   6-ounce can frozen
   grape juice concentrate
1/2 cup chopped pecans
5 tablespoons
   marshmallow creme
1   6-ounce jar pimento
   cream cheese spread

Cut grapes into halves. Dissolve gelatin in boiling water in bowl. Add grape juice concentrate and grapes; stir until grape juice concentrate is thawed. Chill until partially set. Stir in pecans. Pour into oiled ring mold. Chill until firm. Unmold onto serving plate. Blend marshmallow creme and cream cheese spread in bowl. Spoon into center of ring. Yield: 12 servings.

Approx Per Serving: Cal 205; Prot 5.2 g; Carbo 30.2 g; T Fat 8.0 g; Chol 13.5 mg; Potas 104.0 mg; Sod 253.0 mg.

PEACH SALAD

2   15-ounce cans peaches
1   3-ounce package peach
   gelatin
2   3-ounce packages
   vanilla tapioca pudding
   mix

Drain peaches, reserving juice. Add enough water to reserved juice to measure 3 cups. Combine with gelatin and pudding mix in saucepan. Bring to a boil, stirring to mix well. Cool. Stir in peaches. Chill in refrigerator. Yield: 8 servings.

Approx Per Serving: Cal 197; Prot 1.5 g; Carbo 50.5 g; T Fat 0.2 g; Chol 0.0 mg; Potas 98.5 mg; Sod 182.5 mg.

PINEAPPLE AND COTTAGE CHEESE SALAD

1   16-ounce can juice-
   pack crushed pineapple
1   3-ounce package lime
   gelatin
1   3-ounce package lemon
   gelatin
1/2 cup milk
3/4 cup cottage cheese
1/2 cup coarsely chopped
   pecans
1/4 cup maraschino
   cherries

Drain pineapple, reserving juice. Add enough water to measure 1 2/3 cups. Bring juice to a boil in saucepan. Pour over lime and lemon gelatins in bowl, stirring to dissolve completely. Chill for 30 minutes or until partially set. Stir in milk, pineapple, cottage cheese and pecans. Pour into mold. Decorate with cherries. Chill until firm. Yield: 8 servings.

Approx Per Serving: Cal 198; Prot 5.8 g; Carbo 31.8 g; T Fat 6.4 g; Chol 5.0 mg; Potas 142.0 mg; Sod 154.0 mg.

Toni Stanton
Carthage, New York

CONGEALED PINEAPPLE SALAD

1 15-ounce can crushed
  pineapple
1   3-ounce package lemon
  gelatin
8 ounces cream cheese,
  softened
1 cup chopped celery
1 small red bell pepper,
  chopped
1/2 cup chopped walnuts

Bring pineapple to a boil in small saucepan. Add gelatin, stirring to dissolve completely. Combine with cream cheese in bowl; mix well. Stir in celery, red pepper and walnuts. Spoon into mold. Chill until firm. Unmold onto serving plate. Yield: 6 servings.

Approx Per Serving: Cal 311; Prot 6.1 g; Carbo 31.3 g; T Fat 19.5 g;
Chol 41.3 mg; Potas 242.0 mg; Sod 177.0 mg.

Margaret E. Gardner
Ottawa, Ontario, Canada

CURRIED CHICKEN AND FRUIT SALAD

4 chicken breast filets
1/4 cup unsalted butter
1 cup plain yogurt
2 ounces (or more) curry
  powder
1 teaspoon salt
Freshly ground pepper to
  taste
8 ounces seedless green
  grapes
1 pound dried apricots,
  cut into strips
1   16-ounce can
  mandarin oranges,
  drained
8 ounces cashews
4 ounces apricot liqueur
  or apricot nectar
6 lettuce leaves

Cut chicken filets into 1-inch pieces. Cook in butter in skillet over medium-low heat for 7 to 10 minutes or until firm but not brown, turning frequently. Remove with slotted spoon to large bowl. Combine yogurt, curry powder, salt and pepper in bowl; mix well. Add to chicken; mix well. Add grapes, apricots, oranges, cashews and liqueur; toss gently. Chill, covered, for 1 hour or longer. Serve on lettuce-lined plates. Yield: 6 servings.

Approx Per Serving: Cal 705; Prot 34.8 g; Carbo 83.5 g; T Fat 29.8 g;
Chol 86.8 mg; Potas 1708.0 mg; Sod 696.0 mg.

HAM SALAD

1 package long grain and
  wild rice mix
1 envelope dry vinaigrette
  seasoning mix
1/2 cup sliced green olives
1 cup chopped celery
1/2 cup chopped cucumber
1 6-ounce jar artichoke
  hearts, drained, sliced
1/2 cup drained chopped
  tomato
1 cup chopped ham
1/2 cup (about) reduced-
  calorie mayonnaise
Onion powder to taste

Cook rice using package directions. Prepare vinaigrette mix using package directions. Stir vinaigrette into rice in bowl. Add olives, celery, cucumber, artichoke hearts, tomato and ham. Add enough mayonnaise to moisten well. Season with onion powder and salt and pepper to taste. Yield: 12 servings.

Approx Per Serving: Cal 151; Prot 4.3 g; Carbo 19.5 g; T Fat 6.3 g; Chol 10.8 mg; Potas 136.0 mg; Sod 337.0 mg.

SALMON SALAD

4 medium potatoes, peeled
2 tomatoes
2 cups flaked cooked
  salmon
4 hard-boiled eggs, sliced
1/2 cup chopped celery
1/2 cup chopped green
  onions
1/4 cup sliced black olives
1/4 cup sliced green olives
1/4 cup Italian salad
  dressing
1/4 cup mayonnaise
1/4 cup chopped parsley

Cut potatoes into wedges. Cook in a small amount of water in large saucepan until tender; drain. Cut tomatoes into wedges. Spoon salmon into center of large serving platter. Arrange potatoes, tomatoes and eggs around salmon. Combine celery, green onions, olives, salad dressing, mayonnaise and parsley in bowl; mix well. Spoon over salad. Yield: 6 servings.

Approx Per Serving: Cal 356; Prot 26.1 g; Carbo 11.0 g; T Fat 24.8 g; Chol 251.0 mg; Potas 558.0 mg; Sod 523.0 mg.

SHRIMP LOUIS

1 cup mayonnaise
1/4 cup chili sauce
2 teaspoons lemon juice
2 tablespoons grated onion
1 cup whipping cream,
   whipped
1 head lettuce, shredded
2 pounds shrimp, cooked,
   peeled
12 black olives
3 hard-boiled eggs, cut
   into quarters
3 large tomatoes, cut into
   quarters
2 avocados, peeled, sliced

Combine mayonnaise, chili sauce, lemon juice and onion in bowl; mix well. Fold in whipped cream. Chill in refrigerator. Place shredded lettuce on 6 chilled serving plates. Arrange shrimp in centers of plates. Arrange black olives, eggs, tomatoes and avocados around shrimp. Spoon sauce over top. Serve immediately. Yield: 6 servings.

Approx Per Serving: Cal 677; Prot 38.3 g; Carbo 14.1 g; T Fat 53.6 g; Chol 481.0 mg; Potas 1005.0 mg; Sod 829.0 mg.

TORTELINI SALAD

1 pound tortelini
1/4 cup vinegar
1 teaspoon Dijon mustard
1/2 cup (about) olive oil
2 cloves of garlic, chopped
1 green bell pepper, cut
   into julienne strips
1 bunch scallions, chopped
2 tomatoes, peeled,
   seeded, chopped
1/4 cup chopped fresh
   parsley
1/2 cup sliced pepperoni
1/4 cup freshly grated
   Parmesan cheese

Cook tortelini *al dente* in water to cover in saucepan; rinse with cold water. Whisk vinegar and mustard in large bowl until blended. Add olive oil, garlic and salt and pepper to taste, whisking to mix well. Add green pepper, scallions, tomatoes, parsley and pepperoni; mix well. Add tortelini and cheese; mix gently. Chill, covered, for several hours to overnight.
Yield: 8 servings.

Approx Per Serving: Cal 456; Prot 10.6 g; Carbo 46.5 g; T Fat 25.5 g; Chol 4.8 mg; Potas 298.0 mg; Sod 229.0 mg.

TUNA SALAD SUPREME

2 hard-boiled eggs
1/2 cup low-fat yogurt
1/2 teaspoon mustard
1/2 teaspoon Old Bay spice
1/4 teaspoon pepper
1   7-ounce can
    water-pack tuna,
    drained
1/2 cup chopped apple
1/2 cup chopped celery
1/4 cup chopped green
    onions
1 tablespoon minced onion
1 tablespoon chopped
    parsley

Mash egg yolks in bowl. Stir in yogurt, mustard, Old Bay spice and pepper. Add chopped egg whites, tuna, apple, celery, green onions, onion and parsley; mix well. Chill for 1 hour. Serve with crackers, bagels or toast. Yield: 6 servings.

Approx Per Serving: Cal 91; Prot 13.0 g; Carbo 3.7 g; T Fat 2.4 g; Chol 111.0 mg; Potas 226.0 mg; Sod 169.0 mg.

GARDEN SALAD LOAF

2 green bell peppers, cut
    into strips
4 green onions, chopped
10 radishes, thinly sliced
2 carrots, thinly sliced
4 small tomatoes, cut into
    thin wedges
3/4 cup French salad
    dressing
2 envelopes unflavored
    gelatin
1/2 cup red wine vinegar
2 tablespoons lemon juice
1/4 cup sugar
1 teaspoon salt
2 2/3 cups boiling water
2 cups finely shredded
    lettuce
1 cup torn spinach
6 thick tomato wedges

Combine green peppers, green onions, radishes, carrots and 4 tomatoes with salad dressing in bowl; mix well. Let stand for 15 minutes or longer. Soften gelatin in vinegar and lemon juice in bowl. Add sugar, salt and boiling water; stir until sugar and gelatin are dissolved. Chill until partially set. Drain vegetables well. Fold marinated vegetables, lettuce and spinach into gelatin mixture. Pour into oiled 4x8-inch loaf pan. Chill until set. Unmold onto serving plate. Top with thick tomato wedges. Cut into slices to serve. Yield: 6 servings.

Approx Per Serving: Cal 253; Prot 4.2 g; Carbo 21.5 g; T Fat 18.1 g; Chol 0.0 mg; Potas 482.0 mg; Sod 753.0 mg.

PEANUTTY PEA SALAD

2 20-ounce packages
   frozen green peas,
   thawed
1 1/2 pounds dry roasted
   salted peanuts
3 green onions, sliced
1 12-ounce bottle of
   ranch salad dressing
1/2 2-ounce bottle of
   poppy seed

Combine peas with peanuts and green onions in bowl. Add salad dressing and poppy seed; mix well. Let stand for 3 1/2 to 4 hours before serving. Yield: 20 servings.

Approx Per Serving: Cal 243; Prot 10.1 g; Carbo 12.0 g; T Fat 18.7 g; Chol 5.3 mg; Potas 282.0 mg; Sod 228.0 mg.

CONFETTI POTATO SALAD

2 1/2 pounds potatoes,
   peeled, cooked, sliced
1 cup chopped red bell
   pepper
1 cup sliced black olives
1 cup green peas
2 tablespoons chopped
   red onion
1 cup mayonnaise
1/3 cup cider vinegar
2 tablespoons Dijon
   mustard
3/4 teaspoon celery seed
1/2 teaspoon salt
1/8 teaspoon pepper

Combine potatoes, red pepper, olives and peas in large bowl; mix well. Mix onion, mayonnaise, vinegar, mustard, celery seed, salt and pepper in small bowl. Add to potatoes; mix gently. Chill, covered, for several hours to blend flavors.
Yield: 8 servings.

Approx Per Serving: Cal 390; Prot 5.0 g; Carbo 41.3 g; T Fat 24.3 g; Chol 16.3 mg; Potas 681.0 mg; Sod 434.0 mg.

LAYERED SPINACH SALAD

1 medium red onion,
 chopped
6 hard-boiled eggs,
 chopped
1/2 cup crumbled crisp-
 fried bacon
1 pound fresh spinach,
 torn
1 10-ounce package
 ' frozen peas
1 large head lettuce, torn
2 cups mayonnaise
1 cup sour cream
1 cup shredded Swiss
 cheese

Toss onion, eggs and bacon in bowl to mix well. Layer half the spinach and half the onion mixture in 3-quart salad bowl. Spread peas over top. Layer remaining spinach, lettuce and remaining onion mixture over peas. Mix mayonnaise and sour cream in bowl. Spread over salad, sealing to edge of bowl. Top with cheese. Chill until serving time. Yield: 10 servings.

Approx Per Serving: Cal 516; Prot 12.3 g; Carbo 11.5 g; T Fat 47.9 g; Chol 213.0 mg; Potas 511.0 mg; Sod 445.0 mg.

COLD RICE SALAD

3 cups cooked rice, chilled
1/2 cup peas
1/2 cup corn
1/3 cup sultana raisins
1/4 cup chopped green bell
 pepper
1/4 cup chopped red bell
 pepper
4 slices bacon, crisp-fried,
 crumbled
1/3 cup olive oil

Combine rice, peas, corn, raisins, green pepper, red pepper and bacon in bowl; mix well. Add olive oil and salt and pepper to taste; toss to mix well. Chill for 12 hours or longer. Yield: 8 servings.

Approx Per Serving: Cal 222; Prot 3.7 g; Carbo 28.5 g; T Fat 10.8 g; Chol 2.7 mg; Potas 153.0 mg; Sod 53.5 mg.

F. Joyce Ralph
Lansdowne, Ontario, Canada

FAVORITE SLAW

1 2-pound head cabbage,
   shredded
3/4 cup mayonnaise
1 1/2 tablespoons fresh
   lemon juice
1/2 teaspoon salt
1/4 teaspoon white pepper
1/4 teaspoon dry mustard
1/2 teaspoon sugar

Soak cabbage in ice water to cover in large bowl until crisp; drain well. Combine mayonnaise, lemon juice, salt, pepper, dry mustard and sugar in small bowl. Pour over cabbage; toss to mix. Chill for 1 hour or longer. Yield: 8 servings.

   Approx Per Serving: Cal 113; Prot 1.6 g; Carbo 11.7 g; T Fat 7.6 g;
      Chol 5.6 mg; Potas 282.0 mg; Sod 309.0 mg.

SUMMER SALAD

1 bunch broccoli, chopped
1 head cauliflower,
   chopped
2 cups sliced mushrooms
1 8-ounce can black
   olives
1 tablespoon chopped
   pimento
1 8-ounce bottle of
   oil-free Italian dressing

Combine broccoli, cauliflower, mushrooms, black olives and pimento in salad bowl. Add dressing; toss lightly. Yield: 12 servings.

   Approx Per Serving: Cal 64; Prot 2.3 g; Carbo 5.8 g; T Fat 5.2 g;
      Chol 1.1 mg; Potas 308.0 mg; Sod 308.0 mg.

MARINATED TOMATOES

6 tomatoes, sliced
2 4-ounce cans
   mushrooms, drained
1/4 cup wine vinegar
3/4 cup safflower oil
1 tablespoon chopped
   parsley
1 clove of garlic, minced
1/2 teaspoon salt
1/8 teaspoon pepper

Place tomatoes and mushrooms in serving dish. Combine vinegar, oil, parsley, garlic, salt and pepper in bowl; mix well. Pour over vegetables. Marinate in refrigerator for 1 hour or longer. Yield: 6 servings.

   Approx Per Serving: Cal 276; Prot 1.8 g; Carbo 8.0 g; T Fat 27.6 g;
      Chol 0.0 mg; Potas 319.0 mg; Sod 349.0 mg.

BOUNTY
FROM THE SEA

Seafood

Bounty from the Sea

Lake Ontario, like many of the Great Lakes, is home to a number of big fish that are hatchery-raised and released to forage and grow. The newest inhabitant of the Lake is the Skamania Steelhead, preferred by many an angler for its aerial acrobatics. My daughter, Tisha Rae, holds a typical Lake Ontario Skamania.

Great Lakes Treasures

Creamy Fish Chowder
page 31

Layered Spinach Salad
page 43

Salmon with Lemon-Mushroom Sauce
page 59

Carrot and Rice Bake
page 136

Jalapeño Corn Bread
page 153

Lemon Lush or
page 174

Easy Wonderful Cheesecake Pie
page 195

BAKED FISH

1 onion, chopped
1 tablespoon shortening
1 can tomato soup
1 soup can milk
1   16-ounce can sliced
   carrots, drained
Dillweed to taste
6 fish fillets
2 tablespoons margarine

Sauté onion in shortening in skillet until golden brown. Combine with tomato soup, milk, carrots and dillweed in bowl; mix well. Place fish fillets in greased baking pan. Pour sauce over top. Dot with margarine. Bake at 350 to 375 degrees for 1 hour. May add vegetables of your choice to sauce. Yield: 6 servings.

Approx Per Serving: Cal 386; Prot 43.0 g; Carbo 15.3 g; T Fat 16.2 g; Chol 102.0 mg; Potas 1075.0 mg; Sod 718.0 mg.

Ruth Oot
Watertown, New York

BAKED FISH FRY

2 eggs
2 tablespoons flour
1 teaspoon oil
1 teaspoon soy sauce
4 fish fillets
1 cup bread crumbs
3 onions, sliced
1/4 teaspoon celery seed
1 tablespoon butter
1 tablespoon oil
Paprika to taste

Combine eggs, flour, 1 teaspoon oil and soy sauce in bowl; mix well. Dip fish fillets in egg mixture; coat well with crumbs. Place on plate. Chill until baking time. Place onion slices in 7x14-inch baking dish. Sprinkle with celery seed; dot with butter. Arrange breaded fish in prepared dish. Sprinkle with 1 tablespoon oil and paprika. Bake at 425 to 450 degrees for 20 minutes or until fish flakes easily and breading is crisp and brown. Garnish with lemon slices and parsley sprigs. Yield: 4 servings.

Approx Per Serving: Cal 528; Prot 52.8 g; Carbo 30.4 g; T Fat 20.3 g; Chol 253.0 mg; Potas 1075.0 mg; Sod 462.0 mg.

Mrs. Arch Brick
Watertown, New York

COTTAGE FISH BAKE

1/2 cup finely chopped
   onion
1/2 cup finely chopped
   celery
1/2 cup finely chopped
   green bell pepper
2 tablespoons butter
1   28-ounce can
   Italian-style tomato
   sauce
1/2 teaspoon basil
1/2 teaspoon garlic powder
3 cups cooked long grain
   rice
11/2 pounds fillets of
   walleye, pike or bass
2 cups shredded
   Monterey Jack cheese

Sauté onion, celery and green pepper in butter in skillet. Add tomato sauce, basil, garlic powder and salt and pepper to taste; mix well. Layer rice and fish fillets in 9x13-inch baking dish. Pour sauce over fish. Top with cheese. Bake at 350 degrees for 45 to 50 minutes or until fish flakes easily. Yield: 6 servings.

Approx Per Serving: Cal 523; Prot 44.0 g; Carbo 36.5 g; T Fat 21.2 g; Chol 116.0 mg; Potas 1132.0 mg; Sod 1661.0 mg.

Denise Belair
Ottawa, Ontario, Canada

STUFFED BAKED FISH

1   61/2-ounce can crab
   meat
2 eggs, slightly beaten
1/2 cup chopped onion
3/4 cup chopped celery
2 slices bacon, minced
1 cup fresh bread crumbs
2 tablespoons butter
1 tablespoon
   Worcestershire sauce
1/2 teaspoon grated lemon
   rind
Paprika to taste
2 whole trout

Mix crab meat with eggs in bowl. Sauté onion, celery, bacon and bread crumbs in butter in skillet. Add to crab meat; mix well. Season with Worcestershire sauce, lemon rind, paprika and salt and pepper to taste. Rinse fish inside and out; pat dry. Stuff cavities with crab mixture. Place in baking dish sprayed with nonstick cooking spray. Bake at 400 to 425 degrees until fish flakes easily. Yield: 2 servings.

Approx Per Serving: Cal 710; Prot 64.2 g; Carbo 43.1 g; T Fat 29.7 g; Chol 466.0 mg; Potas 1311.0 mg; Sod 1143.0 mg.

Mrs. Arch Brick
Watertown, New York

SIMPLY DELICIOUS BAKED FISH

4 fish fillets or steaks
1/2 cup butter
2 cloves of garlic, minced
Juice of 1 fresh lemon

Place fish fillets in 9x13-inch baking dish. Bake at 400 to 425 degrees until fish flakes easily. Combine butter, garlic and lemon juice in saucepan. Heat until butter is melted. Place fish fillets in individual serving dishes. Serve with butter sauce. Garnish with sprigs of fresh parsley. Yield: 4 servings.

Approx Per Serving: Cal 388; Prot 30.1 g; Carbo 1.5 g; T Fat 28.7 g; Chol 134.0 mg; Potas 568.0 mg; Sod 281.0 mg.

Mrs. Arch Brick
Watertown, New York

BONELESS FISH FILLETS

1/2 cup flour
1/2 cup cornmeal
1 teaspoon paprika
1 1/2 pounds fish fillets
Oil for frying

Mix flour, cornmeal, paprika and salt and pepper to taste in plastic bag. Place moist fillets in bag; shake to coat well. Fry in hot oil in skillet until fish flakes easily. May deep-fry, broil or bake fillets if preferred. Yield: 4 servings.

Approx Per Serving: Cal 390; Prot 47.6 g; Carbo 25.4 g; T Fat 8.9 g; Chol 107.0 mg; Potas 847.0 mg; Sod 131.0 mg.
Nutritional information does not include oil for frying.

New York State Department of Environmental Conservation
Albany, New York

DEEP-FRIED FISH

Peanut oil
Fish fillets
1 or 2 eggs
1/2 to 1 cup milk
Finely crushed cornflakes

Preheat enough peanut oil in deep-fryer to cover fish fillets. Dip fillets into mixture of eggs and milk; coat well with cornflakes. Place in single layer in hot oil. Deep-fry for 4 to 6 minutes or until fish flakes easily. Serve immediately.

Nutritional information for this recipe is not available.

Mr. and Mrs. B. McCallan
Kingston, Ontario, Canada

FISH FRITTERS

1 pound fish fillets
2 stalks celery, chopped
1 green bell pepper
2 small onions, chopped
2 cups flour
1 teaspoon baking powder
1 egg
1¹/₂ cups water

Put fish fillets, celery, green pepper and onions through meat grinder. Combine with flour, baking powder, egg, water and salt and pepper to taste in bowl; mix well. Drop by teaspoonfuls into hot oil. Deep-fry until golden brown. Drain on paper towels. Serve with mixture of catsup, mayonnaise and Tabasco sauce or horseradish to taste. Yield: 4 servings.

Approx Per Serving: Cal 452; Prot 38.6 g; Carbo 52.9 g; T Fat 7.9 g; Chol 140.0 mg; Potas 786.0 mg; Sod 207.0 mg.
Nutritional information does not include oil for deep frying or sauce.

Mattie Bicknell
Watertown, New York

FISH LOAF

¹/₂ cup rice
1 chicken bouillon cube
1 cup water
1 cup chopped mushrooms
2 tablespoons butter
2¹/₂ pounds fish fillets
1 medium onion, chopped
3 hard-boiled eggs, finely
  chopped
¹/₂ cup chopped green
  bell pepper
6 tablespoons melted
  butter
1¹/₂ teaspoons dillweed
4 cups flour
1 teaspoon salt
1¹/₄ cups butter, chilled
10 to 12 tablespoons cold
  water
1 tablespoon melted
  butter
1 egg yolk, beaten
1 tablespoon milk

Cook rice with bouillon cube in 1 cup water until tender. Sauté mushrooms in 2 tablespoons butter. Put fish fillets and onion through meat grinder fitted with finest blade. Combine with rice, mushrooms, chopped eggs, green pepper, 6 tablespoons butter and dillweed in bowl; mix well. Set aside. Mix flour and salt in bowl. Cut in 1¹/₄ cups butter until crumbly. Add enough cold water to form dough. Divide into 2 portions. Roll 1 portion into 7x16-inch rectangle on floured surface. Place on greased baking sheet. Spoon fish mixture over pastry, leaving 1-inch border. Roll remaining pastry into 9x18-inch rectangle. Place over filling; seal edges. Cut 1-inch circle from center of pastry. Pour 1 tablespoon melted butter into opening. Brush pastry with mixture of egg yolk and milk. Bake at 400 degrees for 1 hour. Serve with sour cream or tartar sauce. Yield: 8 servings.

Approx Per Serving: Cal 861; Prot 47.6 g; Carbo 53.3 g; T Fat 49.6 g; Chol 331.0 mg; Potas 859.0 mg; Sod 871.0 mg.

New York State Department of Environmental Conservation
Albany, New York

FISH PATTIES

2¹/2 pounds fish fillets
1 medium onion, chopped
6 bread slices, cubed
1 egg
1¹/2 teaspoons salt
¹/2 cup flour
6 tablespoons melted
   margarine

Grind fish and onion finely. Combine with bread cubes, egg, salt and pepper to taste in bowl; mix well. Shape into 12 patties. Coat lightly with flour. Arrange in melted margarine in shallow baking pan; turn to coat. Bake at 400 degrees for 15 minutes or until brown, turning once. Yield: 12 patties.

Approx Per Patty: Cal 288; Prot 28.0 g; Carbo 15.9 g; T Fat 11.5 g; Chol 82.4 mg; Potas 505.0 mg; Sod 484.0 mg.

New York State Department of Environmental Conservation
Albany, New York

LIVELY LEMON FISH ROLL-UPS

¹/3 cup butter
¹/3 cup lemon juice
2 teaspoons salt
¹/4 teaspoon pepper
1 cup cooked rice
1   10-ounce package
   frozen chopped
   broccoli, thawed
1 cup shredded sharp
   Cheddar cheese
8   4-ounce fish fillets

Melt butter with lemon juice, salt and pepper in small saucepan. Combine ¹/4 cup lemon butter with rice, broccoli and cheese in bowl; mix well. Spoon mixture onto centers of fish fillets. Roll to enclose filling. Place seam side down in shallow baking dish. Pour remaining lemon butter over rolls. Bake at 375 degrees for 25 minutes or until fish flakes easily. Place roll-ups on serving plate. Spoon cooking juices over top; garnish with paprika. Yield: 8 servings.

Approx Per Serving: Cal 339; Prot 34.3 g; Carbo 8.0 g; T Fat 18.0 g; Chol 107.0 mg; Potas 602.0 mg; Sod 775.0 mg.

FISH IN SOUR CREAM

2 pounds fish fillets
2 small onions, thinly
   sliced
1 green bell pepper,
   thinly sliced
2 tablespoons butter
2 cups sour cream

Arrange fish fillets in single layer in 9x13-inch baking pan. Sprinkle with salt and pepper to taste. Sauté onions and green pepper in butter in skillet until tender. Spoon over fish. Top with sour cream. Bake at 350 degrees for 15 minutes or until fish flakes easily. Yield: 6 servings.

Approx Per Serving: Cal 452; Prot 42.5 g; Carbo 6.1 g; T Fat 27.6 g; Chol 140.0 mg; Potas 907.0 mg; Sod 191.0 mg.

Mabel I. Huck
Watertown, New York

FISH IN WINE SAUCE

12 large mushrooms,
  sliced
1 tablespoon butter
1¹/₂ pounds fish fillets
1 cup white wine
2 tablespoons lemon juice
2 egg yolks
1 cup heavy cream
3 tablespoons butter
1 tablespoon chopped
  parsley
³/₄ teaspoon salt
¹/₈ teaspoon pepper

Sauté mushrooms in 1 tablespoon butter in saucepan; set aside. Poach fish fillets in wine and lemon juice in saucepan until tender. Remove fillets to heated platter; keep warm. Bring pan juices to a boil. Cook for 10 minutes. Beat egg yolks with cream in bowl. Stir a small amount of hot liquid into egg mixture; stir eggs into hot liquid. Add 3 tablespoons butter, sautéed mushrooms, parsley, salt and pepper. Cook mixture until thickened, stirring constantly. Spoon over fish. Serve immediately. Yield: 6 servings.

Approx Per Serving: Cal 436; Prot 31.8 g; Carbo 2.3 g; T Fat 29.9 g; Chol 237.0 mg; Potas 652.0 mg; Sod 438.0 mg.

Suzanne Acres
Finch, Ontario, Canada

BAKED FILLETS WITH TOMATO

1 pound fish fillets
1 medium tomato,
  chopped
2 tablespoons chopped
  green bell pepper
2 tablespoons chopped
  onion
1 tablespoon lemon juice
¹/₄ teaspoon thyme

Arrange fish fillets in single layer in lightly greased 9x9-inch baking pan. Combine tomato, green pepper, onion, lemon juice and thyme in small bowl; mix well. Pour over fillets. Bake at 400 degrees for 20 minutes or until fish flakes easily. Serve with parslied potatoes and green salad. Yield: 4 servings.

Approx Per Serving: Cal 190; Prot 30.1 g; Carbo 2.2 g; T Fat 5.8 g; Chol 71.4 mg; Potas 623.0 mg; Sod 90.1 mg.

Rena L. Hough
Watertown, New York

CARP FISH CAKES

1 6-pound carp
1 cup coarse salt
4 cups water
2 cups sauerkraut
8 eggs, beaten
1 large yellow onion,
   chopped
1/2 teaspoon thyme
1/2 teaspoon basil
1/2 teaspoon tarragon
1/2 cup oil
1/2 cup butter

Clean and rinse fish, discarding skin; pat dry. Cut into pieces. Combine with salt in bowl. Refrigerate overnight. Rinse and drain fish. Combine with water in saucepan. Cook until tender. Flake fish, discarding large bones. Mix with sauerkraut in bowl; press down lightly. Let stand for 2 hours. Put fish and sauerkraut through meat grinder. Combine with eggs, onion and seasonings in bowl; mix well. Shape into cakes. Fry in mixture of oil and butter in skillet until brown on both sides. Drain on paper towels. May bake fish cakes at 375 degrees until brown if preferred. Yield: 35 fish cakes.

Approx Per Fish Cake: Cal 197; Prot 22.0 g; Carbo 1.1 g; T Fat 10.9 g; Chol 119.0 mg; Potas 417.0 mg; Sod 3111.0 mg.

Mrs. Marguerite Fortier
Cornwall, Ontario, Canada

NORWEGIAN BASS

3 cups heavy whipping
   cream
1 tablespoon lemon juice
Whole bass
Potatoes, thickly sliced
3 or 4 tiny onions per
   person
Milk
1/4 cup flour

Combine cream with lemon juice in bowl. Let stand for 1 hour or until soured. Clean and rinse fish cavity; pat dry. Split fish or leave whole; do not fillet. Spoon enough soured cream into glass baking dish to cover bottom. Layer fish, potatoes and onions in dish. Pour remaining soured cream over layers. Add milk if necessary to cover layers. Sprinkle with salt and pepper to taste. Sift flour over top. Bake at 325 degrees for 3 hours. Do not substitute commercial sour cream for soured whipping cream.

Nutritional information for this recipe is not available.

Persis E. Boyesen
Ogdensburg, New York

BAKED HADDOCK

1 pound haddock fillets
Juice of 2 lemons
3 tablespoons melted
butter
3/4 cup sour cream
1 medium onion, sliced
into rings
1 green bell pepper

Arrange fillets in lightly buttered 9x13-inch baking dish. Drizzle with lemon juice and butter. Bake at 350 degrees for 10 minutes. Spread with sour cream. Top with onion and green pepper rings. Bake for 10 minutes or until fish flakes easily. Garnish with paprika. Serve with lemon wedges and sprigs of fresh parsley. Yield: 3 servings.

Approx Per Serving: Cal 503; Prot 42.9 g; Carbo 11.7 g; T Fat 31.5 g; Chol 152.0 mg; Potas 1009.0 mg; Sod 247.0 mg.

Marion J. Pickette
Chaumont, New York

BAKED PERCH

1 pound perch fillets
3 tablespoons minced
green onions
2 tomatoes, quartered
1/4 teaspoon basil
1/2 teaspoon sugar
1/4 cup melted butter

Arrange skinned fillets in single layer in buttered shallow oven-proof serving dish. Sprinkle with green onions and salt and pepper to taste. Mix tomatoes with basil and sugar in bowl. Spoon over fillets. Drizzle with melted butter. Bake at 450 degrees for 10 minutes. Yield: 2 servings.

Approx Per Serving: Cal 594; Prot 60.9 g; Carbo 6.9 g; T Fat 34.6 g; Chol 205.0 mg; Potas 1368.0 mg; Sod 379.0 mg.

Coleen Holder-barry
Morrisburg, Ontario, Canada

ITALIAN OVEN-BAKED PERCH

2 cups flour
1/4 cup Seafood Seasoning
Mix (see page 77)
2 eggs, beaten
1 cup milk
2 pounds perch fillets
3 cups Italian bread
crumbs
1/4 cup butter

Combine flour and Seafood Seasoning Mix in shallow dish; mix well. Combine eggs and milk in shallow dish. Coat fillets with flour mixture. Dip in egg mixture; coat with crumbs. Brush butter on large baking sheet. Place fillets on baking sheet. Bake at 350 degrees for 15 minutes or until golden brown. Garnish with lemon wedges and parsley. Yield: 4 servings.

Approx Per Serving: Cal 927; Prot 64.3 g; Carbo 107.8 g; T Fat 25.0 g; Chol 275.0 mg; Potas 1007.4 mg; Sod 2166.0 mg.

Chef Bob Smith
Akron, Ohio

PERCH NUGGETS

1/2 cup white wine
2 cups 7-Up
2 cups pancake mix
1/2 cup 7-Up
2 pounds perch fillets
Oil for deep frying

Combine wine and 2 cups 7-Up in bowl. Add pancake mix; mix well. Add remaining 1/2 cup 7-Up if necessary to form a sticky batter. Cut perch fillets into 1-inch pieces, discarding bones. Dip into batter, coating well. Deep-fry in hot oil until golden brown. Serve with cocktail sauce. Yield: 4 servings.

Approx Per Serving: Cal 443; Prot 59.5 g; Carbo 16.2 g; T Fat 11.3 g; Chol 143.0 mg; Potas 1102.0 mg; Sod 182.0 mg.
Nutritional information does not include pancake mix or oil for deep frying.

Robert D. Robert
Canton, New York

PERCH PIZZA

1/4 package dry yeast
3/4 cup water
2 tablespoons warm (110 to 115-degree) water
3 to 3 1/4 cups sifted flour
3 perch fillets
1 clove of garlic, minced
2 tablespoons olive oil
2 cups shredded mozzarella cheese

Dissolve yeast in 3/4 cup water. Add 2 tablespoons warm water. Combine with flour in bowl; mix to form dough. Knead on floured surface until smooth. Place in greased bowl, turning to grease surface. Let stand in warm (85-degree) place for 1 1/2 hours or until doubled in bulk. Cook perch fillets in water to cover in skillet until fish flakes easily. Chop into small pieces. Combine with garlic in bowl. Press dough into greased 10x14-inch baking pan. Brush with olive oil. Sprinkle fish over dough. Top with cheese. Bake at 425 degrees for 15 to 30 minutes or until crust is brown.
Yield: 6 servings.

Approx Per Serving: Cal 575; Prot 44.3 g; Carbo 52.6 g; T Fat 18.5 g; Chol 101.0 mg; Potas 638.0 mg; Sod 230.0 mg.

S.W. Carr
Watertown, New York

BROILED NORTHERN PIKE

4 4-ounce northern pike
  fillets, 1/2 inch thick
2 tablespoons melted
  butter
2 tablespoons
  Worcestershire sauce

Place fish fillets on rack in broiler pan. Pour mixture of butter and Worcestershire sauce over fillets, turning to coat both sides. Broil 3 to 7 inches from heat source for 2 1/2 minutes on each side or until fish flakes easily. Yield: 4 servings.

Approx Per Serving: Cal 237; Prot 29.9 g; Carbo 1.4 g; T Fat 11.4 g; Chol 87.0 mg; Potas 603.0 mg; Sod 209.0 mg.

DILLED PIKE AND PEA PODS

8 pike fillets, 1/2 to 1 inch
  thick
2 teaspoons flour
1/3 cup plain yogurt
1/4 cup milk
1 teaspoon instant
  chicken bouillon
1/4 teaspoon dillweed
1 medium carrot, cut into
  thin diagonal slices
1 cup pea pods
1 tablespoon oil

Cut fish into 1-inch pieces, discarding bones and skin. Blend flour and yogurt in small bowl. Stir in milk, bouillon and dillweed. Spray wok or skillet with nonstick cooking spray. Preheat to medium-hot. Stir-fry carrot for 2 minutes. Add pea pods. Stir-fry for 2 to 3 minutes or until tender-crisp. Remove to bowl. Pour oil into wok. Add fish. Stir-fry for 3 to 6 minutes or until cooked through, taking care not to break up pieces. Remove gently to bowl. Reduce heat. Add yogurt mixture. Cook until thickened and bubbly, stirring constantly. Cook for 1 minute longer. Add vegetables and fish; toss lightly to coat. Heat to serving temperature.
Yield: 2 servings.

Approx Per Serving: Cal 344; Prot 35.8 g; Carbo 15.9 g; T Fat 14.5 g; Chol 77.9 mg; Potas 953.0 mg; Sod 212.0 mg.

Diane Hiles
Watertown, New York

LORIE'S SALMON FILLET BAKE

1 recipe favorite turkey
  stuffing
Salmon fillets
Lemon pepper

Spoon stuffing into large baking dish. Press salmon into stuffing until just the top is showing. Sprinkle with seasoning. Bake at 350 degrees for 20 to 25 minutes or until fish flakes easily.

Nutritional information for this recipe is not available.

Lorie Stanic
Henderson Harbor, New York

BAKED KING SALMON

1 onion, chopped
8 ounces mushrooms,
   chopped
1/2 cup virgin olive oil
3 tablespoons chopped
   parsley
3 cups bread crumbs
1 cup croutons
1/4 cup chopped black
   olives
1 whole salmon
4 slices bacon
1 lemon, sliced
1 small apple, sliced
2 maraschino cherries

Sauté onion and mushrooms in 1/2 cup hot olive oil in skillet for 3 to 5 minutes or until tender. Add parsley, bread crumbs, croutons, black olives and salt and pepper to taste; mix well. Cool to room temperature. Wash salmon inside and out; pat dry. Spoon stuffing into cavity. Spoon remaining stuffing into oiled baking dish. Place stuffed salmon on top. Layer bacon over salmon. Top with lemon slices, apple slices, cherries and salt and pepper to taste. Bake at 350 degrees for 1 1/4 hours or until fish flakes easily. Yield: 6 servings.

Approx Per Serving: Cal 892; Prot 69.7 g; Carbo 48.5 g; T Fat 45.9 g; Chol 172.0 mg; Potas 1820.0 mg; Sod 685.0 mg.

D. Paige Gorham
Elbridge, New York

SALMON IN HERB SAUCE

1/4 cup butter
1 onion, chopped
Chopped parsley
2 teaspoons capers
1 anchovy, chopped
Juice of 1 lemon
4 salmon steaks

Melt butter in skillet. Add onion, parsley, capers and anchovy. Cook, covered, for several minutes. Stir in lemon juice. Add salmon steaks. Cook, covered, over low heat until salmon flakes easily. Serve with potatoes. Yield: 4 servings.

Approx Per Serving: Cal 288; Prot 24.5 g; Carbo 3.9 g; T Fat 19.2 g; Chol 98.3 mg; Potas 663.0 mg; Sod 155.0 mg.

A. Bruchhauser
Ottawa, Ontario, Canada

BARBECUED SALMON

1 large salmon
2 teaspoons lemon juice
2 tablespoons butter,
   softened

Wash salmon and pat dry. Brush cavity with lemon juice. Rub with butter. Sprinkle with salt and pepper to taste. Wrap tightly in foil, sealing well. Wrap with damp newspaper and second layer of foil. Place on grill over medium coals. Bake for 30 minutes on each side. Skin will stick to foil; salmon will be very moist. May bake salmon in 375-degree oven for 1 hour if preferred.
Yield: 8 servings.

Approx Per Serving: Cal 428; Prot 56.2 g; Carbo 0.1 g; T Fat 20.9 g; Chol 164.0 mg; Potas 1392.0 mg; Sod 149.0 mg.

Lydia Blancher
Athens, Ontario, Canada

CANNED SALMON

Fresh salmon
Canning salt
Olive oil
White vinegar

Wash salmon and pat dry. Cut into pieces. Pack into 1-pint jars, leaving 1 inch headspace. Add 1 teaspoon canning salt, 1 teaspoon olive oil and 2 tablespoons vinegar to each jar. Seal with 2-piece lids. Process in pressure cooker at 10 pounds pressure for 1 hour and 40 minutes. Use only pint jars.

Nutritional information for this recipe is not available.

Mrs. Ken (Sly Fox) Hollister
Owego, New York

POOR MAN'S SHRIMP

Salt
2 quarts cold water
2 pounds salmon, cut into
   1-inch cubes

Add enough salt to cold water in 4-quart saucepan to float an egg in the shell. Stir in 1/4 cup additional salt. Bring water to a boil. Add salmon. Bring to a boil again; drain. Serve hot with favorite sauce.

Nutritional information for this recipe is not available.

Randy L. Riley
Carthage, New York

SALMON BALLS

2 cups flaked canned
  salmon
1 egg
2/3 cup milk
1/4 cup minced onion
1 tablespoon chopped
  parsley
1 teaspoon
  Worcestershire sauce
13/4 cups Italian bread
  crumbs
1 teaspoon salt
1/2 teaspoon pepper

Combine salmon, egg, milk, onion, parsley, Worcestershire sauce, bread crumbs, salt and pepper in bowl; mix well. Shape into balls. Fry in hot oil in skillet until brown on all sides. Drain on paper towels. May shape into patties if preferred. Yield: 24 salmon balls.

Approx Per Salmon Ball: Cal 84; Prot 7.7 g; Carbo 5.8 g; T Fat 3.1 g; Chol 26.1 mg; Potas 144.0 mg; Sod 316.0 mg.

Mrs. Ken (Sly Fox) Hollister
Owego, New York

SALMON WITH LEMON-MUSHROOM SAUCE

1   16-ounce can salmon
1/4 cup (about) milk
1/4 cup chopped onion
1/4 cup butter
2 cups fine dry bread
  crumbs
3 eggs, slightly beaten
1/4 cup minced parsley
1/4 teaspoon poultry
  seasoning
Dash of nutmeg
1/4 teaspoon salt
4 Spanish olives, sliced
1/2 cup milk
1 can cream of mushroom
  soup
1 tablespoon lemon juice
1/2 teaspoon paprika

Drain salmon, reserving liquid. Add enough milk to liquid to measure 1/2 cup. Sauté onion in hot butter in skillet until golden brown. Add salmon, bread crumbs, eggs, reserved liquid mixture, parsley, poultry seasoning, nutmeg and salt; mix well. Shape into 4 mounds in shallow baking dish. Top with olive slices. Combine 1/2 cup milk, soup, lemon juice and paprika in bowl; mix well. Pour into baking dish around salmon mounds. Bake at 350 degrees for 30 minutes. Serve with buttered green beans or cold asparagus salad and hot biscuits. May substitute two 7-ounce cans tuna for salmon. Yield: 4 servings.

Approx Per Serving: Cal 627; Prot 34.9 g; Carbo 46.9 g; T Fat 33.1 g; Chol 316.0 mg; Potas 804.0 mg; Sod 1432.0 mg.

Amy Semenick
Manville, New Jersey

SALMON LOAF

1 16-ounce can salmon,
   drained
1 can cream of celery soup
2 cups bread crumbs
2 eggs, slightly beaten
1 tablespoon melted
   butter
1 teaspoon salt
1/2 teaspoon pepper

Combine salmon, soup, bread crumbs, eggs, butter, salt and pepper in large bowl; mix well. Shape into loaf. Place in baking dish. Bake at 350 degrees for 45 minutes. Remove to serving plate. Yield: 4 servings.

Approx Per Serving: Cal 459; Prot 30.8 g; Carbo 42.2 g; T Fat 18.1 g; Chol 224.0 mg; Potas 684.0 mg; Sod 1581.0 mg.

Randy L. Riley
Carthage, New York

SALMON AND POTATO PIE

1 11-ounce package
   pastry mix
2 pounds potatoes, peeled,
   sliced
4 carrots, peeled, sliced
3 onions, sliced
2 tablespoons butter
1/4 cup butter
1/3 cup flour
1/8 teaspoon paprika
1 1/2 teaspoons salt
1/4 teaspoon pepper
2 cups milk
1 pound cooked or canned
   salmon
2 tablespoons butter
1 egg yolk
1 tablespoon water

Prepare pastry mix using package directions. Roll on floured surface. Cut out circle to fit top of 2-quart baking dish. Cut three 2 1/2-inch circles from remaining pastry. Set aside. Cook potatoes and carrots in water to cover in large saucepan for 10 minutes; drain. Saute onions in 2 tablespoons butter in skillet for 5 minutes or until golden brown. Melt 1/4 cup butter in small saucepan. Stir in flour, paprika, salt and pepper. Blend in milk. Cook over medium heat until thickened and smooth, stirring constantly. Layer potatoes, carrots, salmon and white sauce 1/2 at a time in greased baking dish. Dot with 2 tablespoons butter. Top with pastry, sealing edges. Brush with mixture of egg yolk and water. Cut pastry circles into halves. Arrange on top of pie. Bake at 350 degrees for 30 to 40 minutes or until crust is brown. Yield: 8 servings.

Approx Per Serving: Cal 592; Prot 19.2 g; Carbo 60.6 g; T Fat 30.9 g; Chol 107.0 mg; Potas 1045.0 mg; Sod 806.0 mg.

Ruth M. Morse
Henderson, New York

PLANKED SALMON

Cured oak plank
Peanut oil
1 whole salmon, cleaned
1/4 cup melted butter
Salt and freshly ground
  pepper to taste
1/8 teaspoon Old Bay
  seasoning
Juice of 1 lemon

Rub plank with peanut oil. Preheat in 350-degree oven until warm. Remove head and tail of fish if desired. Place salmon back side down on plank; spread open, cutting underside of backbone if necessary. Tuck excess meat under salmon. Brush generously with mixture of butter, seasonings and lemon juice. Broil for 8 to 14 minutes or until fish flakes easily. Serve on plank, brushing with remaining butter mixture just before serving.

Nutritional information for this recipe is not available.

D. Paige Gorham
Elbridge, New York

POACHED SALMON

1 pound salmon fillets
Juice of 1/2 lemon
1/4 teaspoon garlic
  powder with parsley
1/2 teaspoon seasoned salt
1/2 onion, thinly sliced

Place salmon fillets on 12-inch circle of foil. Drizzle with lemon juice. Sprinkle with seasonings. Top with onion. Place 10-inch circle of foil on top; seal edges of foil. Place packet in 1/2-inch simmering water in skillet. Cook, covered, for 15 minutes or until fish flakes easily. Yield: 3 servings.

Approx Per Serving: Cal 227; Prot 30.4 g; Carbo 2.9 g; T Fat 9.7 g; Chol 83.2 mg; Potas 796.0 mg; Sod 423.0 mg.

Barbara Alcamo
Houston, Texas

TERIYAKI SALMON STEAKS

1 cup teriyaki sauce
1 tablespoon peanut oil
3 tablespoons chopped
  parsley
1 clove of garlic, crushed
1/2 teaspoon freshly
  ground pepper
6 salmon steaks

Mix first 5 ingredients in bowl. Add salmon steaks. Let stand for 1 to 2 hours, turning steaks every 20 to 30 minutes. Place steaks on sheet of heavy foil. Grill for 4 to 5 minutes, basting with sauce. Turn steaks. Grill for 3 minutes or until fish flakes easily, basting with sauce. Serve hot or cold. Yield: 6 servings.

Approx Per Serving: Cal 705; Prot 92.7 g; Carbo 8.0 g; T Fat 31.7 g; Chol 249.5 mg; Potas 2344.0 mg; Sod 2040.5 mg.

D. Paige Gorham
Elbridge, New York

CRUNCHY SALMON SCALLOP

1 cup cornflake crumbs
1 16-ounce can salmon
1 tablespoon lemon juice
2 hard-boiled eggs, sliced
2 tablespoons chopped
   onion
1/4 cup finely chopped
   green bell pepper
3 tablespoons butter
3 tablespoons flour
1 teaspoon salt
1/4 teaspoon pepper
2 cups milk
11/2 cups cornflake crumbs

Sprinkle 1 cup cornflake crumbs in greased 1-quart baking dish. Drain and flake salmon, discarding skin and bones. Place in prepared baking dish. Sprinkle with lemon juice; top with sliced eggs. Sauté onion and green pepper in butter in small saucepan until tender. Stir in flour, salt and pepper. Add milk gradually. Cook until thickened, stirring constantly. Pour over salmon. Sprinkle with 11/2 cups cornflake crumbs. Bake at 350 degrees for 25 minutes. May serve reheated leftovers on toast. Yield: 6 servings.

Approx Per Serving: Cal 277; Prot 19.5 g; Carbo 15.8 g; T Fat 14.8 g; Chol 163.0 mg; Potas 495.0 mg; Sod 608.0 mg.

Helen Pawlak
Ottawa, Ontario, Canada

SAVORY LAKE TROUT

4 lake trout fillets
1 sweet onion, sliced
1 lemon, sliced
1 potato, sliced
3 tablespoons butter
1/4 cup wine
3 tablespoons chopped
   parsley

Layer fillets, onion, lemon slices and potato slices on large double fold of foil. Dot with butter. Pour wine over top; sprinkle with parsley. Season with salt and freshly ground pepper to taste. Seal foil tightly. Grill over hot coals until fish flakes easily. May wrap individual servings in foil and bake in moderate oven if preferred.
Yield: 4 servings.

Approx Per Serving: Cal 550; Prot 61.5 g; Carbo 17.6 g; T Fat 20.2 g; Chol 166.3 mg; Potas 1429.3 mg; Sod 255.8 mg.

D. Paige Gorham
Elbridge, New York

BAKED TROUT IN CREAM

4 whole 1-pound rainbow
  trout
2 tablespoons lemon juice
1 teaspoon dillweed
1 teaspoon salt
1/4 teaspoon white pepper
2 cups whipping cream
2 tablespoons fine dry
  bread crumbs

Wash fish and pat dry. Brush inside and out with lemon juice; sprinkle with dillweed, salt and white pepper. Place in lightly buttered baking dish. Pour cream over top; sprinkle with bread crumbs. Bake at 400 degrees for 15 minutes or until fish flakes easily. Bake frozen fillets for 20 to 25 minutes. Serve with green salad made with Boston lettuce, buttered and herbed new potatoes and asparagus or tiny green peas. Yield: 4 servings.

Approx Per Serving: Cal 650; Prot 40.0 g; Carbo 6.3 g; T Fat 51.3 g; Chol 252.0 mg; Potas 780.0 mg; Sod 710.0 mg.

Amy Semenick
Manville, New Jersey

GARLIC TROUT

2 pounds lake trout fillets
3/4 cup extra virgin olive
  oil
3 to 4 cloves of garlic,
  finely chopped
1 lemon, thinly sliced
1 onion, thinly sliced
1/2 pint cherry tomatoes,
  cut into halves
11/2 cups chopped parsley

Cut trout into 2-inch pieces. Heat olive oil in large skillet over medium heat. Add garlic, lemon slices, onion slices, cherry tomatoes and parsley. Cook, covered, for 5 minutes or until oil has absorbed garlic flavor. Add trout. Cook, covered, for 5 minutes. Turn trout pieces. Cook for 30 seconds longer. Remove to serving plate. Spoon sauce over top. Yield: 6 servings.

Approx Per Serving: Cal 541; Prot 40.7 g; Carbo 5.2 g; T Fat 39.3 g; Chol 95.3 mg; Potas 947.0 mg; Sod 128.0 mg.

D. Paige Gorham
Elbridge, New York

CRISPY BROWN TROUT

Fillets of brown trout
New Hope Mills pancake
   flour
1 teaspoon freshly ground
   pepper
1 teaspoon Old Bay
   seasoning
1/2 cup (about) peanut oil

Soak fillets in ice water for 5 minutes; drain and pat dry. Combine pancake flour and seasonings in shallow dish. Coat fillets with pancake flour mixture. Fry in very hot but not smoking oil for 3 1/2 minutes; turn. Cook for 2 1/2 minutes or until golden, crispy and fish flakes easily. Drain on paper towels. Garnish with lemon and lime wedges and parsley sprigs. Serve with spicy seafood sauce or tartar sauce. You better keep on cooking, however, because this is one dish that folks will want more and more. This is such a fantastic taste treat that even the most finicky kid will ask for seconds and want to start cooking and catching his own. And he can because it's so easy and quick!

Nutritional information for this recipe is not available.

D. Paige Gorham
Elbridge, New York

PAN-FRIED BROWN TROUT

2 pounds brown trout
   fillets
1 1/2 cups pancake flour
1 teaspoon salt
1 1/2 teaspoons freshly
   ground pepper
1/2 cup peanut oil

Cut trout fillets into 2 to 3-inch pieces. Roll in mixture of pancake flour, salt and pepper, coating well. Place in hot peanut oil in large skillet over medium-high heat. Cook for 1 1/2 to 2 minutes or until golden brown. Turn fish. Cook for 1 1/2 minutes or until outside is crisp and fish flakes easily. Serve immediately on bed of watercress or parsley; garnish with lemon wedges. Yield: 6 servings.

Approx Per Serving: Cal 513; Prot 42.9 g; Carbo 23.8 g; T Fat 25.9 g; Chol 95.3 mg; Potas 751.0 mg; Sod 472.0 mg.

D. Paige Gorham
Elbridge, New York

TROUT QUICHE

4 1-pound trout
1/4 cup lemon juice
3/4 teaspoon sea salt
1 unbaked 9-inch pie shell
5 eggs, beaten
1 cup milk
2 tablespoons flour
1/4 teaspoon tarragon
1/4 teaspoon oregano
1/4 teaspoon basil
1/4 teaspoon pepper
1 1/4 cups shredded
   Swiss cheese

Cook trout with lemon juice and sea salt in water to cover in saucepan for 4 minutes; drain. Flake fish, discarding skin and bones. Sprinkle into pie shell. Combine eggs, milk, flour, tarragon, oregano, basil and pepper in bowl; mix until smooth. Stir in cheese. Pour over fish. Bake at 350 degrees for 45 minutes. Yield: 6 servings.

Approx Per Serving: Cal 823; Prot 94.5 g; Carbo 19.2 g; T Fat 37.7 g; Chol 446.0 mg; Potas 1607.0 mg; Sod 819.0 mg.

Mrs. Marguerite Fortier
Cornwall, Ontario, Canada

LIME AND WINE WALLEYE

2 1/2 pounds walleye fillets
2 cups good white wine
1/2 cup lime juice
1/4 cup butter, softened
Seafood Seasoning Mix to
   taste (see page 77)

Place fillets in bowl. Add mixture of wine and lime juice. Marinate in refrigerator for 2 hours, turning fillets 2 to 4 times. Place in 9x13-inch baking dish spread with butter. Sprinkle with Seafood Seasoning Mix. Broil for 5 to 10 minutes or until fish flakes easily. Garnish with lime slices and parsley. Yield: 4 servings.

Approx Per Serving: Cal 540; Prot 57.1 g; Carbo 3.5 g; T Fat 23.6 g; Chol 198.0 mg; Potas 1165.0 mg; Sod 272.0 mg.
Nutritional information does not include Seafood Seasoning Mix.

Chef Bob Smith
Akron, Ohio

CLAM SPAGHETTI

1 medium onion, chopped
2 cloves of garlic, minced
1/2 cup butter
1/2 cup oil
1/4 cup chopped parsley
8 ounces mushrooms,
  sliced
Juice of 1 lemon
1/2 cup white wine
2   10-ounce cans baby
  clams
1 pound thin spaghetti,
  cooked

Sauté onion and garlic in butter and oil in skillet. Add parsley and mushrooms. Cook until vegetables are tender. Add lemon juice, wine and undrained clams; mix well. Spoon hot spaghetti onto serving plate. Top with clam sauce. Serve with Parmesan cheese. Yield: 8 servings.

Approx Per Serving: Cal 437; Prot 22.0 g; Carbo 24.5 g; T Fat 27.0 g; Chol 78.5 mg; Potas 656.1 mg; Sod 179.8 mg.

RISOTTO WITH CLAMS

2 cups clams
3/4 cup chopped onion
4 cups sliced mushrooms
1 tablespoon chopped
  garlic
1/3 cup olive oil
1 1/4 cups crushed tomatoes
1 teaspoon saffron threads
1/2 teaspoon oregano
1/2 teaspoon hot pepper
  flakes
1/4 teaspoon salt
1/4 teaspoon pepper
6 cups water
1 cup uncooked rice
1/2 cup chopped parsley
6 tablespoons butter

Steam clams just until tender. Drain, reserving cooking liquid. Sauté onion, mushrooms and garlic in olive oil in saucepan for 3 minutes. Stir in tomatoes, saffron, oregano, pepper flakes, salt and pepper. Add water and reserved clam liquid. Bring to a simmer. Add rice. Cook for 4 minutes. Stir mixture. Cook for 25 minutes longer. Add clams, parsley and butter. Heat to serving temperature. Yield: 4 servings.

Approx Per Serving: Cal 499; Prot 26.2 g; Carbo 49.5 g; T Fat 21.8 g; Chol 100.0 mg; Potas 993.0 mg; Sod 380.0 mg.

Lydia Q. Peters
Watertown, New York

CRAB CAKES

3 slices soft bread,
trimmed, cubed
1 egg, slightly beaten
1/4 cup finely chopped
onion
2 tablespoons finely
chopped green bell
pepper
1 tablespoon finely
chopped parsley
1/4 cup mayonnaise
1 teaspoon horseradish
1/2 teaspoon
Worcestershire sauce
1/2 teaspoon soy sauce
1/2 teaspoon salt
1/4 teaspoon pepper
1 pound back-fin crab
meat
1/2 cup (about) butter

Combine 1/3 of the bread cubes, egg, onion, green pepper, parsley, mayonnaise, horseradish, Worcestershire sauce, soy sauce, salt and pepper in bowl; mix well. Add crab meat; mix lightly. Shape into 6 patties. Sauté remaining bread cubes in 1/4 cup butter in skillet. Coat crab cakes with sautéed crumbs. Brown in remaining 1/4 cup butter in skillet for 5 minutes on each side. Yield: 6 servings.

Approx Per Serving: Cal 332; Prot 17.9 g; Carbo 7.9 g; T Fat 25.5 g; Chol 168.0 mg; Potas 298.0 mg; Sod 686.0 mg.

CRAB MEAT DIVAN

1   10-ounce package
frozen broccoli, cooked,
drained
1   61/2-ounce can king
crab meat, drained
1/3 cup mayonnaise
1/2 teaspoon prepared
mustard
11/2 teaspoons lemon juice
1 teaspoon grated onion
1/2 cup shredded Cheddar
cheese

Layer broccoli and crab meat in baking dish. Mix mayonnaise, mustard, lemon juice and onion in bowl. Spoon over crab meat. Top with cheese. Bake at 350 degrees for 20 minutes. Yield: 4 servings.

Approx Per Serving: Cal 253; Prot 15.4 g; Carbo 4.7 g; T Fat 19.8 g; Chol 66.5 mg; Potas 323.0 mg; Sod 369.0 mg.

EASY CRAB IMPERIAL

2 cups flaked crab meat
1 cup mayonnaise
4 egg whites, stiffly beaten
1/4 teaspoon salt
1/8 teaspoon pepper
1/2 cup bread crumbs

Mix crab meat and mayonnaise in bowl. Fold in egg whites, salt and pepper. Pour into greased baking dish. Sprinkle with crumbs. Bake at 350 degrees for 45 minutes. Yield: 4 servings.

Approx Per Serving: Cal 625; Prot 22.5 g; Carbo 29.3 g; T Fat 46.8 g; Chol 102.0 mg; Potas 340.0 mg; Sod 960.0 mg.

LOBSTER CANTONESE

2 tablespoons preserved
   black beans
2 cloves of garlic, finely
   chopped
1 tablespoon soy sauce
1 cup ground pork
1/2 teaspoon salt
1/2 teaspoon sugar
1 teaspoon soy sauce
2 tablespoons oil
1 teaspoon salt
1/8 teaspoon pepper
2 pounds large lobster
   tails, cut into 1/2-inch
   slices
2 green onions, cut into
   1-inch pieces
1 cup chicken broth
2 tablespoons cornstarch
2 tablespoons water
2 eggs, beaten

Mash black beans with garlic in bowl. Add 1 tablespoon soy sauce. Combine pork, 1/2 teaspoon salt, sugar and 1 teaspoon soy sauce in bowl. Let stand for 15 minutes. Heat oil in large skillet. Add 1 teaspoon salt, pepper and pork mixture. Stir-fry for 4 minutes. Add lobster. Stir-fry for 2 minutes or until heated through. Add green onions and black bean mixture; mix well. Stir in broth. Cook, covered, for 10 minutes. Add mixture of cornstarch and water. Cook until thickened, stirring constantly. Remove from heat. Stir in eggs. Yield: 8 servings.

Approx Per Serving: Cal 181; Prot 15.0 g; Carbo 4.2 g; T Fat 11.2 g; Chol 132.0 mg; Potas 253.0 mg; Sod 950.0 mg.

SPANISH LOBSTER

6 cloves of garlic, finely
  chopped
2 large onions, finely
  chopped
3 green bell peppers,
  finely chopped
1/2 cup olive oil
1/2 cup dry Sherry
2 pounds ripe tomatoes,
  chopped
1 pound eggplant,
  chopped
1 teaspoon paprika
3 pounds chopped cooked
  lobster
1 8-ounce can green
  peas, drained
1 20-ounce can chopped
  pimento, drained
8 cups cooked rice

Sauté garlic, onions and green peppers in olive oil in saucepan. Add Sherry, tomatoes, eggplant and paprika. Simmer for 30 to 40 minutes or until eggplant is tender. Add lobster. Heat to serving temperature. Heat peas and pimento in separate saucepans. Serve lobster over hot rice. Top with peas and pimento. Yield: 10 servings.

    Approx Per Serving: Cal 300; Prot 28.7 g; Carbo 15.3 g; T Fat 12.6 g; Chol 129.0 mg; Potas 805.0 mg; Sod 470.0 mg.

LOBSTER NEWBURG

4 cups chopped lobster
  meat
1/4 cup butter
1 teaspoon salt
1/4 teaspoon pepper
Dash of cayenne pepper
Dash of mace
1 cup whipping cream
3 egg yolks, beaten

Sauté lobster meat in butter in saucepan for 5 minutes. Add salt, pepper, cayenne pepper and mace. Cook for 5 minutes. Stir in cream and eggs. Cook until thickened, stirring constantly. May add Sherry to taste if desired. Yield: 4 servings.

    Approx Per Serving: Cal 558; Prot 46.1 g; Carbo 2.8 g; T Fat 39.7 g; Chol 532.0 mg; Potas 649.0 mg; Sod 1338.0 mg.

LOBSTER FLORENTINE

1¹/₂ pounds chopped
  lobster meat
3 tablespoons butter
3 tablespoons Brandy,
  heated
1 teaspoon flour
1 cup sour cream
1 10-ounce package
  frozen spinach, cooked,
  drained
¹/₂ cup cooked peas
¹/₄ cup chopped cooked
  carrots
1 cup Hollandaise sauce
¹/₄ cup Parmesan cheese

Sauté lobster in butter in large skillet. Add Brandy. Ignite; allow flames to die down. Stir in flour and sour cream. Add spinach, peas and carrots. Simmer for 10 minutes, stirring occasionally. Remove from heat. Stir in Hollandaise sauce. Pour into greased 1¹/₂-quart baking dish. Sprinkle with cheese. Bake at 450 degrees for 10 minutes. Serve with hot cooked rice. Yield: 4 servings.

Approx Per Serving: Cal 660; Prot 42.4 g; Carbo 16.1 g; T Fat 46.6 g; Chol 476.0 mg; Potas 851.0 mg; Sod 1248.0 mg.

OYSTERS CASINO

1 pint oysters, drained
1 tablespoon chopped
  onion
¹/₄ cup chopped green bell
  pepper
¹/₂ cup seasoned bread
  crumbs
2 slices bacon, chopped

Place oysters in buttered baking dish. Sprinkle with onion and green pepper. Top with bread crumbs and bacon. Bake at 350 degrees for 15 minutes. Broil for 5 to 10 minutes or until bacon is crisp. Yield: 4 servings.

Approx Per Serving: Cal 154; Prot 11.4 g; Carbo 14.5 g; T Fat 5.3 g; Chol 71.3 mg; Potas 334.0 mg; Sod 281.0 mg.

OYSTERS ROCKEFELLER

5 tablespoons melted
  butter
1/2 cup chopped cooked
  spinach
2 tablespoons minced
  onion
2 teaspoons minced celery
3 tablespoons fine dry
  bread crumbs
1/2 teaspoon salt
1/8 teaspoon pepper
24 oysters on the half shell
Rock salt

Combine butter, spinach, onion, celery, bread crumbs, salt and pepper in bowl; mix well. Arrange oysters in 4 pie plates filled with rock salt. Broil for 5 minutes. Spoon spinach over oysters. Broil until bubbly. Serve immediately. Yield: 4 servings.

Approx Per Serving: Cal 686; Prot 25.2 g; Carbo 36.1 g; T Fat 48.6 g; Chol 255.0 mg; Potas 788.0 mg; Sod 1434.0 mg.
Nutritional information does not include rock salt.

SCALLOP CASSEROLE

1/2 cup melted butter
1 cup butter cracker
  crumbs
2 cups scallops
2/3 cup whipping cream
1/2 cup soft bread crumbs

Mix melted butter with cracker crumbs in bowl. Layer crumb mixture, scallops and cream 1/2 at a time in buttered baking dish. Sprinkle with bread crumbs. Bake, covered, at 350 degrees for 20 to 25 minutes or until bubbly. Bake, uncovered, for 5 to 10 minutes or until brown. Yield: 4 servings.

Approx Per Serving: Cal 554; Prot 21.9 g; Carbo 20.6 g; T Fat 45.3 g; Chol 153.0 mg; Potas 434.0 mg; Sod 620.0 mg.

COQUILLES ST. JACQUES

2 cups dry white wine
2 pounds fresh scallops
1 cup sliced mushrooms
4 green onions, sliced
1 tablespoon minced
    parsley
1/4 cup butter
Pinch each of marjoram
    and thyme
1 1/2 tablespoons flour
2 tablespoons whipping
    cream
Paprika to taste
1 cup bread crumbs
2 tablespoons butter

Heat wine in large saucepan. Add scallops. Simmer for 10 minutes or until scallops are translucent. Drain, reserving liquid. Cut each scallop into 2 to 4 pieces; keep warm. Sauté mushrooms, green onions and parsley in butter in large skillet until tender. Stir in marjoram, thyme, flour and salt and pepper to taste. Add reserved liquid and cream gradually. Cook until thickened, stirring constantly. Add paprika and scallops; mix well. Cool slightly. Spoon into buttered baking shells. Sprinkle with bread crumbs; dot with butter. Broil until crusty and golden brown. Yield: 6 servings.

Approx Per Serving: Cal 383; Prot 28.5 g; Carbo 19.1 g; T Fat 15.4 g; Chol 88.6 mg; Potas 645.0 mg; Sod 469.0 mg.

SHRIMP CACCIATORE

1/2 cup minced onion
1/2 cup minced green bell
    pepper
2 cloves of garlic, minced
1/3 cup olive oil
1   20-ounce can tomatoes
1   8-ounce can tomato
    sauce
1/2 cup red wine
2 teaspoons salt
1/4 teaspoon pepper
1/2 teaspoon allspice
1 bay leaf, crumbled
1/4 teaspoon thyme
Cayenne pepper to taste
2 pounds peeled shrimp,
    cooked

Sauté onion, green pepper and garlic in olive oil in large skillet until tender. Stir in tomatoes, tomato sauce, wine, salt, pepper, allspice, crumbled bay leaf, thyme and cayenne pepper. Simmer for 20 minutes. Add shrimp. Heat to serving temperature. Yield: 6 servings.

Approx Per Serving: Cal 307; Prot 33.3 g; Carbo 8.9 g; T Fat 13.9 g; Chol 295.0 mg; Potas 687.0 mg; Sod 1433.0 mg.

SHRIMP CREOLE

1 cup flour
1 cup oil
2 cups chopped onions
1 cup chopped celery
1/2 cup chopped green bell
  pepper
2 cloves of garlic, chopped
1 tablespoon salt
1/2 teaspoon pepper
1   28-ounce can tomatoes
2   6-ounce cans tomato
  paste
6 cups water
3 pounds peeled shrimp

Brown flour in oil in skillet, stirring constantly. Add onions, celery, green pepper, garlic, salt and pepper. Sauté until vegetables are tender. Add tomatoes and tomato paste; mix well. Cook for 5 minutes. Stir in water. Simmer for 1 hour. Add shrimp. Cook for 15 minutes. Serve over hot cooked rice. Garnish with parsley and green onion tops. Yield: 10 servings.

Approx Per Serving: Cal 432; Prot 32.3 g; Carbo 22.6 g: T Fat 24.0 g; Chol 265.0 mg; Potas 848.0 mg; Sod 1107.0 mg.

SHRIMP CURRY

1 large onion, chopped
1 green bell pepper,
  chopped
3 apples, peeled, chopped
1 1/2 tablespoons curry
  powder
1/2 teaspoon dry mustard
1 teaspoon sugar
1/2 cup margarine
5 cups canned tomatoes
4 cups peeled shrimp

Sauté onion, green pepper, apples, curry powder, dry mustard and sugar in margarine in large skillet. Stir in tomatoes. Cook until thickened to desired consistency, stirring occasionally. Add shrimp. Simmer for 10 minutes, adding a small amount of hot water if necessary for desired consistency. Serve over hot cooked rice. Garnish with grated coconut, chutney, chopped egg yolk and peanuts. Yield: 6 servings.

Approx Per Serving: Cal 324; Prot 22.4 g; Carbo 22.8 g; T Fat 17.1 g; Chol 184.0 mg; Potas 774.0 mg; Sod 717.0 mg.

SHRIMP ETOUFFÉE

¹/₂ cup butter
3 tablespoons flour
1 cup chopped onion
³/₄ cup chopped green
  onion tops
1 cup chopped celery
1 teaspoon paprika
1¹/₂ cups water
2 chicken bouillon cubes
1 pound shrimp, peeled
Black pepper to taste
Cayenne pepper to taste

Blend butter and flour in heavy skillet. Cook over low heat until dark brown, stirring constantly. Stir in onion, green onion tops and celery. Cook until vegetables are tender, stirring occasionally. Add paprika, water and bouillon cubes. Simmer for 20 minutes, stirring occasionally. Add shrimp, black pepper and cayenne pepper. Simmer for 20 minutes longer. Serve over hot cooked rice. Yield: 6 servings.

Approx Per Serving: Cal 251; Prot 16.9 g; Carbo 7.4 g; T Fat 17.1 g; Chol 157.0 mg; Potas 285.0 mg; Sod 631.0 mg.

SHRIMP PUNJABI

4 cups sliced mushrooms
1 cup finely chopped
  onion
2 cloves of garlic, crushed
¹/₄ cup oil
4 medium tomatoes,
  peeled, chopped
1 tablespoon curry
  powder
1 teaspoon chili powder
2 pounds shrimp, peeled
2 tablespoons cornstarch
1 tablespoon water
1 cup yogurt
2 cups cooked rice

Sauté mushrooms, onion and garlic in oil in large skillet for 3 to 5 minutes or until tender. Stir in tomatoes, curry powder, chili powder and salt and pepper to taste. Simmer for 10 to 12 minutes, stirring occasionally. Add shrimp. Cook, covered, for 7 minutes or until shrimp are pink. Dissolve cornstarch in water in bowl. Stir into shrimp mixture. Cook until thickened, stirring constantly; remove from heat. Stir in yogurt. Heat to serving temperature; do not boil. Serve over hot rice. Yield: 6 servings.

Approx Per Serving: Cal 376; Prot 37.0 g; Carbo 29.5 g; T Fat 11.8 g; Chol 297.0 mg; Potas 772.0 mg; Sod 374.0 mg.

SHRIMP AND RED RICE

6 cups long grain rice
3/4 cup oil
3 green bell peppers,
  chopped
3 onions, finely chopped
3 cloves of garlic, chopped
1 1/2 tablespoons salt
3/4 teaspoon cumin
1 teaspoon pepper
1 teaspoon basil
1 teaspoon rosemary
1 teaspoon chopped
  parsley
6 cups chicken broth
2 1/2 cups chopped peeled
  tomatoes
1 cup frozen mixed
  vegetables
6 cups chopped cooked
  shrimp

Brown rice in oil in large skillet, stirring constantly. Add chopped green peppers and onion. Sauté until vegetables are tender. Mash garlic with salt. Mix with cumin, pepper, basil, rosemary and parsley in small bowl. Add to rice mixture with broth, tomatoes, mixed vegetables and shrimp. Simmer, covered, for 45 minutes or until broth is absorbed and rice is tender. Garnish with green pepper and onion rings.
Yield: 18 servings.

> **Approx Per Serving:** Cal 240; Prot 12.7 g; Carbo 23.3 g; T Fat 10.2 g; Chol 74.0 mg; Potas 311.0 mg; Sod 1237.0 mg.

SHRIMP AND PASTA CASSEROLE

1 1/2 cups uncooked pasta
  shells
1 6-ounce can shrimp,
  drained
8 ounces cottage cheese
1/2 cup mayonnaise-type
  salad dressing
1/4 cup fine bread crumbs
1/4 cup chopped onion
1 tablespoon chopped
  parsley
1/4 cup Parmesan cheese
1 tablespoon melted
  margarine

Cook pasta shells in saucepan using package directions; rinse with cold water. Spoon half the pasta shells into greased medium baking dish. Combine shrimp, cottage cheese and salad dressing in bowl. Spoon into prepared dish. Top with remaining pasta shells. Mix bread crumbs, onion, parsley, Parmesan cheese and margarine in small bowl. Sprinkle over casserole. Bake at 350 degrees for 30 minutes or until bubbly.
Yield: 4 servings.

> **Approx Per Serving:** Cal 614; Prot 30.9 g; Carbo 78.5 g; T Fat 18.8 g; Chol 93.9 mg; Potas 364.0 mg; Sod 686.0 mg.

Joy M.J. Karam
Ottawa, Ontario, Canada

SHRIMP AND RICE SPECIAL

2   12-ounce packages
     frozen white and wild
     rice
1 cup sliced celery
1   4-ounce can
     mushrooms
2 tablespoons butter
1/4 teaspoon pepper
1/2 cup sliced green onions
2 tablespoons chopped
     pimento
1 pound cooked peeled
     shrimp
1   10-ounce can cream of
     mushroom soup
11/3 cups sour cream
2/3 cup dry bread crumbs
2 tablespoons chopped
     parsley
2 tablespoons melted
     butter

Cook rice using package directions. Sauté celery and mushrooms in butter in skillet until celery is tender-crisp. Stir in pepper, green onions, pimento, rice and shrimp. Spoon into greased 2-quart baking dish. Top with mixture of soup and sour cream. Toss bread crumbs and parsley with butter in bowl. Sprinkle over casserole. Bake at 325 degrees for 30 minutes or until brown. Garnish with parsley sprigs. Yield: 6 servings.

Approx Per Serving: Cal 810; Prot 31.8 g; Carbo 111.0 g; T Fat 23.4 g; Chol 192.0 mg; Potas 382.0 mg; Sod 2836.0 mg.

SEAFOOD PAELLA

1 large onion, chopped
2 cloves of garlic, chopped
1/4 cup oil
11/2 cups uncooked rice
1/8 teaspoon saffron
1 bay leaf
3 cups (or more) chicken
     broth
1 pound peeled shrimp
18 clams, washed
18 mussels, washed
2 tablespoons chopped
     pimento
1 cup green peas

Sauté onion and garlic in oil in skillet until tender. Add rice and saffron. Sauté for 5 minutes. Stir in bay leaf and 2 cups broth. Simmer, covered, for 10 minutes. Add remaining 1 cup broth and shrimp. Simmer, covered, for 5 minutes. Add clams, mussels and additional broth if necessary. Cook for 10 minutes or until shells open. Discard unopened shells and bay leaf. Add pimento, peas and salt and pepper to taste. Heat to serving temperature. Yield: 6 servings.

Approx Per Serving: Cal 449; Prot 33.3 g; Carbo 46.7 g; T Fat 23.7 g; Chol 158.0 mg; Potas 675.0 mg; Sod 649.0 mg.

LINGUINE WITH SEAFOOD SAUCE

1 clove of garlic, crushed
1/4 cup butter
1/2 cup dry white wine
4 ounces chopped cooked
  lobster
4 ounces peeled shrimp
4 ounces scallops
4 ounces cooked crab meat
1 cup whipping cream
1 tomato, peeled, chopped
3/4 cup Parmesan cheese
1/2 teaspoon cayenne
  pepper
Pinch of nutmeg
1/2 teaspoon salt
1/4 cup minced fresh
  parsley
1 pound linguine, cooked,
  drained

Sauté garlic in butter in skillet for 5 minutes. Add wine. Cook until reduced to 1/3 cup. Add seafood. Cook over medium heat for 2 to 3 minutes or until scallops are white and shrimp are pink. Add cream and tomato. Simmer for 2 to 3 minutes. Add cheese, cayenne pepper, nutmeg, salt and parsley; mix well. Serve over linguine. Yield: 6 servings.

Approx Per Serving: Cal 620; Prot 29.3 g; Carbo 60.3 g; T Fat 27.2 g; Chol 163.0 mg; Potas 489.0 mg; Sod 633.0 mg.

SEAFOOD SEASONING MIX

2 cups paprika
1 cup salt
1/2 cup ground celery seed
1/2 cup ground garlic
  cloves
1/4 cup oregano
1/4 cup chili powder
1/4 cup coriander
2 teaspoons black pepper
2 teaspoons onion powder
2 teaspoons thyme
1 teaspoon nutmeg
1/2 teaspoon cayenne
  pepper

Combine paprika, salt, celery seed, garlic, oregano, chili powder, coriander, black pepper, onion powder, thyme, nutmeg and cayenne pepper in bowl; mix well. Store in airtight container. This is a good seasoning for broiling, baking or seasoning flour for coating fish. For a cajun flavor, omit salt and add 2 additional teaspoons cayenne pepper. Yield: 80 tablespoons.

Approx Per Tablespoon: Cal 15.4; Prot 0.7 g; Carbo 2.8 g; T Fat 0.6 g; Chol 0.0 mg; Potas 96.4 mg; Sod 1286.0 mg.

Chef Bob Smith
Akron, Ohio

HANK'S FISH BATTER FOR-A-GANG

1 medium package
  buttermilk baking mix
1 cup cornmeal
6 eggs
3 tablespoons seafood
  seasoning
1 tablespoon pepper
Milk

Combine baking mix, cornmeal, eggs, seasonings and enough milk to make of pancake consistency in bowl; mix well. Use to coat perch-sized fish fillets for frying.

Nutritional information for this recipe is not available.

Captain Hank Stanic
Henderson Harbor, New York

SAUCE FOR FISH

1/4 cup butter
1 1/2 cups flour
2 cups fish stock
1 cup heavy cream
1 1/2 cups half and half
1 1/4 cups shredded sharp
  Cheddar cheese
1/8 teaspoon Old Bay
  seasoning
1 cup (heaping) chopped
  parsley

Melt butter in large skillet. Add flour and stock alternately a small amount at a time, stirring constantly with wire whisk. Add mixture of cream and half and half. Cook until thickened, stirring constantly. Add cheese gradually, cooking until cheese melts after each addition and stirring constantly. Blend in seasoning. Stir in parsley. Serve immediately over fish. As usual, the exact measurements are only for cooks who demand such deliberate and finite measure. My own measurements tend to be a "handful" of chopped parsley, "however much" fish stock I happen to have on hand, and "whatever" pieces of cheese I wish to "use up" or experiment with. Please experiment and make the recipe your own. Be careful, however, with the Old Bay—a little goes a long way. Try American blue cheese for something really unique. Yield: 8 cups.

Approx Per Cup: Cal 375; Prot 9.7 g; Carbo 21.4 g; T Fat 28.3 g;
Chol 91.8 mg; Potas 195.5 mg; Sod 386.4 mg.

D. Paige Gorham
Elbridge, New York

REGAL SPLENDOR

Main Dishes

Regal Splendor

The Chinook "King" Salmon, here being held by my son, Captain Bill Saiff III, is the heavyweight champion of fresh water fishing. Born first in the ocean, this Pacific salmon adapted well to many large fresh-water lakes and provides spectacular fishing during the months of July, August and September. The Chinook, nicknamed "the King," earned his reputation for the long sustained battles he provides the angler lucky enough to make contact with him.

Henderson Harbor Holiday Feast

Shrimp Louis
page 40

Grape Ring with Creamy Dressing
page 37

Baked Ham with Stuffing Supreme
page 99

Cheesy Asparagus and Sweet Potato Bake
pages 133 and 139

Easy Cranberry Relish
page 141

Christmas Muffins
page 161

Pumpkin Cheesecake
page 172

PEPPERED BEEF BRISKET

1/4 cup coarsely ground
  pepper
1 5-pound beef brisket
2/3 cup soy sauce
1/2 cup vinegar
1 tablespoon tomato paste
1 teaspoon paprika
1 clove of garlic, crushed

Press pepper firmly over all surfaces of brisket. Place brisket in shallow dish. Combine soy sauce, vinegar, tomato paste, paprika and garlic in small bowl; mix well. Pour over brisket. Chill for several hours to overnight, turning occasionally. Drain brisket well. Place in center of large piece of heavy foil; fold foil over brisket and seal tightly. Place in shallow baking pan. Bake at 200 degrees for 6 hours to overnight. Let stand for 30 minutes before slicing thinly. Serve hot or cold. Yield: 20 servings.

Approx Per Serving: Cal 143; Prot 15.9 g; Carbo 1.4 g; T Fat 8.0 g; Chol 41.4 mg; Potas 237.0 mg; Sod 577.0 mg.

FRUITED BEEF ROAST

1 envelope dry onion
  soup mix
1 2-pound beef brisket
1 8-ounce package dried
  apricots, chopped
1 cup chopped prunes
1 teaspoon cinnamon
2 tablespoons light brown
  sugar
1 teaspoon pepper
3/4 teaspoon ginger
1 tablespoon grated
  lemon rind
1/4 cup honey
2 tablespoons orange
  marmalade
1 tablespoon Brandy
1 teaspoon
  Worcestershire sauce
1 12-ounce can beer

Sprinkle half the dry soup mix over large piece of heavy foil. Place brisket on foil; sprinkle remaining dry soup mix over top. Seal foil tightly. Place in baking dish. Bake at 350 degrees for 3 hours. Combine apricots, prunes, cinnamon, brown sugar, pepper, ginger, lemon rind, honey, orange marmalade, Brandy, Worcestershire sauce and beer in bowl; mix well. Open foil on brisket carefully. Pour fruit mixture over and around brisket; reseal foil. Bake for 1 hour longer or until brisket is tender. Slice thinly. Serve over hot cooked noodles. Yield: 6 servings.

Approx Per Serving: Cal 434; Prot 22.7 g; Carbo 60.4 g; T Fat 11.0 g; Chol 55.1 mg; Potas 1001.0 mg; Sod 176.0 mg.

COMPANY ROAST BEEF

1   3-pound sirloin tip
    roast
1¹/₂ teaspoons garlic
    pepper
³/₄ cup catsup
³/₄ cup Amaretto
¹/₃ cup currant jelly
¹/₄ teaspoon Tabasco sauce

Rub all surfaces of roast with garlic pepper. Preheat large cast-iron skillet until drop of water dances on surface. Sear roast on all sides in skillet. Bake at 350 degrees for 1 hour or to 150 degrees on meat thermometer for medium-rare. Combine catsup, Amaretto, jelly and Tabasco sauce in saucepan. Bring just to the boiling point, stirring until jelly melts. Pour over roast. Turn off oven. Let stand in closed oven for 10 minutes. Place roast on serving platter. Heat sauce in small skillet over medium heat, stirring to deglaze skillet. Serve sauce with roast.
Yield: 6 servings.

Approx Per Serving: Cal 619; Prot 39.6 g; Carbo 36.1 g; T Fat 28.7 g; Chol 119.0 mg; Potas 680.0 mg; Sod 460.0 mg.

POT ROAST WITH COFFEE GRAVY

1   4-pound pot roast
2 tablespoons oil
6 cloves of garlic
2 cups strong coffee
¹/₄ cup vinegar

Brown roast on all sides in hot oil in 5-quart Dutch oven. Cut 6 slits in each side of roast. Cut garlic cloves into halves; insert in slits. Sprinkle with salt and pepper to taste. Pour coffee and vinegar over and around roast. Cook, covered, over low heat for 3 hours or until tender, adding a small amount of water if necessary. The coffee and vinegar help to tenderize the roast and makes delicious gravy. Yield: 6 servings.

Approx Per Serving: Cal 593; Prot 61.6 g; Carbo 1.9 g; T Fat 36.6 g; Chol 165.0 mg; Potas 887.0 mg; Sod 136.0 mg.

*Phyllis Wendt
Constableville, New York*

GRILLED STEAK WITH WINE SAUCE

1 2-pound boneless
   sirloin steak,
   1¹/2 inches thick
2 tablespoons oil
6 tablespoons finely
   chopped shallots
1¹/2 cups Burgundy
³/4 cup butter

Brush steak on both sides with oil; sprinkle with salt and pepper to taste. Place on rack in broiler pan. Broil 4 inches from heat source for 3 to 5 minutes on each side or to desired degree of doneness. Place on heated serving platter; cover loosely with foil. Let stand for 5 minutes. Slice diagonally cross grain. Bring shallots and wine to a boil in saucepan. Cook until liquid is reduced to ¹/3 cup. Add butter; heat until melted. Add salt and freshly ground pepper to taste. Serve steak with hot wine sauce. Yield: 4 servings.

Approx Per Serving: Cal 869; Prot 41.0 g; Carbo 2.1 g; T Fat 70.7 g; Chol 217.0 mg; Potas 684.0 mg; Sod 395.0 mg.

RICE-STUFFED FLANK STEAK

¹/2 cup chopped onion
¹/4 cup butter
1¹/2 cups cooked rice
¹/2 cup chopped parsley
¹/2 cup Parmesan cheese
¹/2 teaspoon salt
¹/4 teaspoon pepper
1 2-pound flank steak
1 beef bouillon cube
1 cup boiling water
2 tablespoons minced
   parsley
1 tablespoon sugar
¹/2 teaspoon dried thyme

Sauté onion in butter in small skillet until golden. Add rice, ¹/2 cup parsley, cheese, salt and pepper; mix well. Cut pocket in steak. Spoon rice mixture into pocket; secure with toothpicks. Place in baking pan. Dissolve bouillon cube in water. Add minced parsley, sugar and thyme. Pour over steak. Bake, covered, at 350 degrees for 1¹/2 hours or until tender. Yield: 5 servings.

Approx Per Serving: Cal 549; Prot 37.3 g; Carbo 19.2 g; T Fat 34.8 g; Chol 137.0 mg; Potas 528.0 mg; Sod 722.0 mg.

BRAISED SIRLOIN TIPS

2 pounds lean sirloin tips
1/2 cup butter
5 large onions, chopped
1/4 cup butter
3 tablespoons brown
   sugar
1 12-ounce can dark beer

Sprinkle sirloin tips with salt and pepper to taste. Brown lightly in 1/2 cup butter in large skillet. Place in Crock•Pot. Sauté onions in 1/4 cup butter in skillet. Layer onions and brown sugar over sirloin tips. Pour beer over all. Cook on Low for 3 to 5 hours or until tender. Serve over hot cooked noodles or rice. Yield: 6 servings.

Approx Per Serving: Cal 589; Prot 28.9 g; Carbo 18.5 g; T Fat 43.0 g; Chol 144.5 mg; Potas 619.0 mg; Sod 268.5 mg.

BEEF CATALAN

2 pounds lean beef cubes
1/4 cup flour
1 teaspoon salt
1/8 teaspoon pepper
3 medium onions, sliced
1 cup Catalina salad
   dressing
1 16-ounce can baby
   carrots, drained
1 cup water
2 cups fresh whole
   mushrooms

Coat beef cubes with mixture of flour, salt and pepper. Sauté beef cubes and onions in about 1/3 of the salad dressing in large skillet until brown. Add remaining salad dressing, carrots and water. Simmer, covered, for 45 minutes. Add mushrooms. Simmer for 10 minutes longer or until beef and mushrooms are tender. Serve over hot cooked rice. Yield: 6 servings.

Approx Per Serving: Cal 542; Prot 29.7 g; Carbo 19.2 g; T Fat 38.8 g; Chol 111.7 mg; Potas 792.5 mg; Sod 931.0 mg.

SAUERBRATEN AND NOODLES

3 lemons
3 pounds beef chuck
    cubes
2 cups cider vinegar
2 cups sugar
2 tablespoons pickling
    spice
2 large onions, chopped
2 quarts water
1 tablespoon salt
2 teaspoons pepper
1/4 cup flour
10 gingersnaps, crushed
1 tablespoon cornstarch
1/2 cup water
1   8-ounce package
    noodles

Cut lemons into wedges; discard seed. Combine lemons, beef cubes, vinegar, sugar, pickling spice, onions, 2 quarts water, salt and pepper in large saucepan. Marinate overnight. Bring to a boil; reduce heat. Simmer for 1 1/2 hours or until beef is very tender. Cook flour in skillet over medium heat until brown, stirring constantly. Combine gingersnaps, browned flour, cornstarch and water in small bowl; mix until smooth. Bring beef mixture to a boil. Stir in gingersnap mixture gradually. Cook for 5 minutes, stirring constantly. Let stand for several minutes. Cook noodles using package directions. Serve Sauerbraten over hot noodles. Yield: 8 servings.

Approx Per Serving: Cal 869; Prot 35.6 g; Carbo 91.6 g; T Fat 41.2 g; Chol 129.0 mg; Potas 430.0 mg; Sod 962.0 mg.

FRENCH STEW

2 pounds stew beef
1 cup Burgundy
1 can cream of mushroom
    soup
1 envelope dry onion
    soup mix
1 cup cooked small onions
1 cup cooked baby carrots
1 cup green olives

Cut beef into small chunks; place in large casserole. Add wine, soup and soup mix; mix well. Bake, covered, at 250 degrees for 4 1/2 hours. Add onions, carrots and olives; mix well. Bake for 30 minutes longer. Serve with salad and French or Italian bread. Yield: 6 servings.

Approx Per Serving: Cal 543; Prot 28.5 g; Carbo 9.4 g; T Fat 41.6 g; Chol 107.0 mg; Potas 440.0 mg; Sod 1497.0 mg.

GREEK BEEF AND ONION STEW

1 pound flank steak
Juice of 1 lemon
1/4 cup olive oil
3 pounds yellow onions
6 cloves of garlic, minced
1 6-ounce can tomato
    paste
1/2 cup red wine

Trim steak; slice into strips. Coat strips with lemon juice. Heat olive oil in heavy 4-quart stew pot. Add steak strips. Cook until lightly browned on all sides. Add onions, garlic, tomato paste and wine; mix well. Reduce heat as low as possible. Cook, covered, for 3 hours. Stir gently. Cook, covered, for 2 hours longer or until onions are reddish golden. Serve with bread. Yield: 4 servings.

Approx Per Serving: Cal 512; Prot 30.3 g; Carbo 35.6 g; T Fat 26.8 g; Chol 82.8 mg; Potas 1190.0 mg; Sod 92.2 mg.

Phyllis Wendt
Constableville, New York

REUBEN CASSEROLE

10 slices rye bread
1 1/2 pounds corned beef,
    shredded
16 ounces sauerkraut
2 1/2 cups shredded Swiss
    cheese
6 eggs, beaten
2 1/2 cups milk

Cut bread into 3/4-inch cubes. Layer bread, corned beef, sauerkraut and cheese in 9x13-inch baking dish. Beat eggs with milk and pepper to taste. Pour over layers. Chill, covered with foil, for 1 hour to overnight. Bake, covered, at 350 degrees for 45 minutes. Bake, uncovered, for 15 minutes longer or until puffed and golden.
Yield: 8 servings.

Approx Per Serving: Cal 435; Prot 35.4 g; Carbo 22.6 g; T Fat 22.0 g; Chol 275.0 mg; Potas 406.0 mg; Sod 1430.0 mg.

VEAL MEDALLIONS

16 ounces veal cutlets
2 tablespoons butter
1 cup whipping cream
2 teaspoons freshly grated
    horseradish
1 tomato, peeled, seeded,
    chopped
2 teaspoons minced fresh
    parsley
2 teaspoons minced fresh
    chives

Pound veal to 1/2-inch thickness. Cook in butter in skillet until lightly browned on both sides, turning once. Remove to warm platter; keep warm. Add cream and horseradish to skillet; stir to deglaze. Cook over medium heat for 5 minutes or until reduced by half, stirring occasionally. Add tomato, parsley and chives. Cook for 2 minutes, stirring constantly. Season with salt and pepper to taste. Spoon over veal. Yield: 4 servings.

Approx Per Serving: Cal 384; Prot 23.8 g; Carbo 3.0 g; T Fat 30.8 g; Chol 189.0 mg; Potas 406.0 mg; Sod 130.0 mg.

VEAL CUTLETS WITH MUSTARD SAUCE

16 ounces veal cutlets
1/3 cup flour
2 eggs, slightly beaten
3/4 cup fine dry bread
  crumbs
2 tablespoons butter
2 tablespoons corn oil
1 small onion, sliced
1/3 cup beef broth
1 tablespoon flour
1 tablespoon Dijon
  mustard
1/2 teaspoon sugar
1/2 teaspoon salt
Freshly ground pepper to
  taste
1 cup light cream

Flatten cutlets to 1/4-inch thickness between waxed paper. Coat lightly with 1/3 cup flour; dip into eggs and coat with crumbs. Brown on both sides in mixture of butter and corn oil in skillet. Remove to warm platter; keep warm. Sauté onion in pan drippings in skillet until tender. Blend broth, 1 tablespoon flour, mustard, sugar, salt and pepper in small bowl. Stir into skillet. Cook until thickened, stirring constantly. Add cream. Cook for 1 minute, stirring constantly; do not boil. Spoon over cutlets. Yield: 4 servings.

Approx Per Serving: Cal 598; Prot 31.7 g; Carbo 31.7 g; T Fat 38.3 g; Chol 312.0 mg; Potas 568.0 mg; Sod 680.0 mg.

CRANBERRY MEATBALLS

2 pounds ground beef
1 cup cornflake crumbs
1/3 cup parsley flakes
2 eggs
2 tablespoons soy sauce
1/2 teaspoon pepper
1/2 teaspoon garlic powder
2 tablespoons instant
  minced onion
1   16-ounce can jellied
  cranberry sauce
1   12-ounce bottle of chili
  sauce
1/3 cup catsup
2 tablespoons brown sugar
1 tablespoon lemon juice

Combine ground beef, cornflake crumbs, parsley flakes, eggs, soy sauce, pepper, garlic powder and onion in bowl; mix well. Shape into meatballs; place in 9x13-inch baking dish. Combine cranberry sauce, chili sauce, catsup, brown sugar and lemon juice in sauce-pan. Heat until blended, stirring constantly. Pour over meatballs. Bake at 350 degrees for 30 minutes or until meatballs are cooked through. Yield: 6 servings.

Approx Per Serving: Cal 599; Prot 30.9 g; Carbo 63.5 g; T Fat 25.1 g; Chol 189.0 mg; Potas 684.0 mg; Sod 1535.0 mg.

MEATBALLS AND YORKSHIRE PUDDING

1¹/₂ pounds ground beef
1 envelope dry onion
  soup mix
2 tablespoons chopped
  parsley
¹/₄ teaspoon poultry
  seasoning
¹/₄ cup chili sauce
1 egg, beaten
1 tablespoon water
1¹/₂ cups sifted flour
1¹/₂ teaspoons baking
  powder
1 teaspoon salt
4 eggs, beaten
1¹/₂ cups milk
3 tablespoons melted
  butter

Combine ground beef, soup mix, parsley, poultry seasoning, chili sauce, 1 egg and water in bowl; mix well. Shape into meatballs; place in greased 9x13-inch baking dish. Sift flour, baking powder and salt into bowl. Beat 4 eggs with milk and butter in small bowl. Add to flour mixture; beat until smooth. Pour evenly over meatballs. Bake at 350 degrees for 50 minutes or until golden. Yield: 8 servings.

Approx Per Serving: Cal 390; Prot 22.6 g; Carbo 23.2 g; T Fat 22.5 g; Chol 244.0 mg; Potas 348.0 mg; Sod 670.0 mg.

GROUND BEEF PATTIES CORDON BLEU

3 pounds lean ground beef
1 teaspoon salt
4 ounces Swiss cheese,
  sliced
8 slices Canadian bacon
2 eggs
¹/₄ cup water
1 cup bread crumbs
¹/₃ cup butter
1 can golden mushroom
  soup
1 can cream of mushroom
  soup
1 cup milk

Divide ground beef into 8 portions; pat each into rectangle. Sprinkle with salt; layer cheese and bacon on each. Roll as for jelly roll, sealing edges and ends. Beat eggs with water in shallow dish. Dip ground beef rolls into egg mixture; coat with crumbs. Brown on all sides in butter in skillet. Cook for 25 minutes, turning frequently. Remove to warm platter; keep warm. Add soups and milk to pan drippings; deglaze skillet. Cook over low heat for several minutes, stirring constantly. Spoon over ground beef rolls. Serve over hot cooked rice or noodles. Yield: 8 servings.

Approx Per Serving: Cal 642; Prot 40.9 g; Carbo 17.1 g; T Fat 44.9 g; Chol 220.0 mg; Potas 577.0 mg; Sod 1584.0 mg.

DELUXE GROUND BEEF ROLL

2 pounds lean ground beef
1 onion, chopped
2 eggs, beaten
3 slices bread, crumbled
1/2 cup tomato sauce
Oregano to taste
1/4 teaspoon salt
4 ounces baked ham,
   thinly sliced
1 1/2 cups shredded
   mozzarella cheese
3 ounces Swiss cheese,
   sliced

Combine ground beef, onion, eggs, bread, tomato sauce, oregano, salt and pepper to taste in bowl; mix well. Pat into rectangle on foil or waxed paper. Layer ham and mozzarella cheese on rectangle; roll as for jelly roll, sealing edge and ends. Place seam side down in foil-lined baking dish. Bake at 350 degrees for 1 1/2 hours. Cut Swiss cheese into triangles; arrange overlapping triangles on top of roll. Bake for 5 minutes longer or until cheese melts. Remove roll to serving platter. Let stand for 10 minutes before slicing. Yield: 8 servings.

Approx Per Serving: Cal 506; Prot 33.8 g; Carbo 8.7 g; T Fat 36.4 g; Chol 187.0 mg; Potas 365.0 mg; Sod 557.0 mg.

MEAT LOAF SURPRISE

3/4 cup chopped onion
1 tablespoon butter
1 1/2 cups shredded carrots
1/4 teaspoon salt
1 1/2 pounds lean ground
   beef
1 1/2 cups soft bread
   crumbs
1 egg, beaten
2 tablespoons milk
3/4 teaspoon salt
3/4 teaspoon thyme
1/8 teaspoon garlic powder
1 16-ounce jar spiced
   crab apples
1/3 cup pineapple
   preserves
1 teaspoon prepared
   mustard

Sauté onion in butter in skillet until tender. Cook carrots in a small amount of boiling water in saucepan for 5 minutes; drain. Mix carrots with half the sautéed onion and 1/4 teaspoon salt; set aside. Combine ground beef, bread crumbs, remaining sautéed onion, egg, milk, 3/4 teaspoon salt, thyme, garlic powder and pepper to taste in bowl; mix well. Pat into rectangle on waxed paper. Spread with carrot mixture to within 1/2 inch of edge; roll as for jelly roll, sealing edge and ends. Place meat loaf seam side down in 9x13-inch baking dish. Bake at 350 degrees for 1 hour; drain. Drain crab apples, reserving 1 cup liquid. Blend reserved liquid with preserves and mustard in saucepan. Simmer for 15 minutes. Spoon over meat loaf. Bake for 15 minutes longer. Remove to serving platter. Let stand for 10 minutes before slicing. Arrange crab apples around loaf. Yield: 8 servings.

Approx Per Serving: Cal 308; Prot 18.0 g; Carbo 26.4 g; T Fat 15.0 g; Chol 94.2 mg; Potas 357.0 mg; Sod 400.0 mg.

MEAT LOAF ITALIANO

1¹/2 pounds lean ground
    beef
¹/2 cup bread crumbs
¹/4 cup Parmesan cheese
³/4 cup chopped onion
¹/4 cup finely chopped
    fresh parsley
¹/2 teaspoon garlic powder
1 teaspoon salt
¹/2 teaspoon pepper
1 teaspoon basil
3 eggs
¹/4 cup (about) milk

Combine ground beef, crumbs, cheese, onion, parsley, garlic powder, salt, pepper, basil and eggs in bowl; mix well. Add enough milk gradually to make of consistency to shape into loaf. Place in baking dish. Bake at 350 degrees for 1 hour. Remove to serving plate. Serve with favorite pizza sauce if desired. Yield: 6 servings.

Approx Per Serving: Cal 348; Prot 26.2 g; Carbo 8.9 g; T Fat 22.4 g;
    Chol 217.0 mg; Potas 352.0 mg; Sod 589.0 mg.

MINIATURE MEXICALI MEAT LOAVES

1 pound lean ground beef
¹/2 cup oats
1 egg
1 8-ounce can tomato
    sauce
1 4-ounce can chopped
    green chilies
1 tablespoon instant
    minced onion
1 teaspoon chili powder
¹/2 teaspoon salt
¹/8 teaspoon garlic powder
¹/2 cup shredded Cheddar
    cheese

Combine ground beef, oats, egg, ¹/4 cup tomato sauce, half the green chilies, onion, chili powder and salt in bowl; mix well. Shape into 4 small loaves; place in glass baking dish. Microwave on High for 6 minutes; drain. Combine remaining tomato sauce, green chilies and garlic powder in small glass bowl; mix well. Microwave on High for 1 minute. Spoon over loaves. Microwave for 1 minute longer. Sprinkle cheese on top. Let stand until melted. Yield: 4 servings.

Approx Per Serving: Cal 369; Prot 26.1 g; Carbo 13.5 g; T Fat 23.4 g;
    Chol 153.0 mg; Potas 561.0 mg; Sod 1194.0 mg.

GROUND BEEF WELLINGTON

1 9-ounce package
   frozen chopped broccoli,
   thawed
1 pound ground beef
1 cup shredded
   mozzarella cheese
1/2 cup chopped onion
1/2 cup sour cream
1/4 teaspoon salt
1/4 teaspoon pepper
2 8-count packaged
   refrigerator crescent
   rolls
1 egg, beaten
2 teaspoons poppy seed

Drain broccoli; squeeze dry. Brown ground beef in skillet, stirring until crumbly; drain. Add broccoli, cheese, onion, sour cream, salt and pepper. Cook over low heat for 10 minutes, stirring frequently. Separate roll dough into 4 rectangles. Place 2 rectangles on ungreased baking sheet overlapping long sides about 1/2 inch; press into 7x13-inch rectangle, sealing overlap and perforations. Spoon half the ground beef mixture in 3-inch strip down center of rectangle. Fold sides to center to enclose filling; seal edge and ends. Repeat with remaining roll dough and ground beef mixture. Brush with beaten egg; sprinkle with poppy seed. Bake at 375 degrees for 18 minutes or until brown. Serve immediately. Yield: 6 servings.

Approx Per Serving: Cal 390; Prot 21.2 g; Carbo 16.6 g; T Fat 26.3 g; Chol 117.0 mg; Potas 376.0 mg; Sod 488.0 mg.

CORNISH PASTIES WITH MUSHROOM SAUCE

1 cup flour
1/4 teaspoon salt
1/3 cup shortening
2 tablespoons cold water
1/2 pound ground beef
2 tablespoons chopped
   onion
1 cup chopped cooked
   potato
1 tablespoon tomato paste
1 tablespoon chili sauce
1 3-ounce can sliced
   mushrooms
2 tablespoons melted
   margarine
2 tablespoons flour
1 teaspoon instant beef
   bouillon

Combine 1 cup flour and salt in bowl. Cut in shortening until crumbly. Add water; mix until mixture forms ball. Chill for several minutes. Brown ground beef with onion in skillet, stirring until crumbly; drain. Add potato, tomato paste and chili sauce; mix well. Roll dough on floured surface; cut into 4 rectangles. Spoon ground beef mixture onto rectangles. Fold over to make triangles; seal edges. Place on baking sheet. Bake at 400 degrees for 10 minutes or until brown. Drain mushrooms, reserving liquid. Add enough water to reserved liquid to measure 1 cup. Blend margarine, 2 tablespoons flour and bouillon in saucepan. Stir in mushroom liquid gradually. Cook until thickened, stirring constantly. Add mushrooms. Heat to serving temperature. Serve mushroom sauce over pasties. Yield: 4 servings.

Approx Per Serving: Cal 512; Prot 15.6 g; Carbo 44.2 g; T Fat 30.6 g; Chol 34.2 mg; Potas 477.0 mg; Sod 697.0 mg.

GROUND BEEF AND BROCCOLI PIE

1 pound ground beef
1/4 cup chopped onion
2 tablespoons flour
3/4 teaspoon salt
1/4 teaspoon garlic salt
11/4 cups milk
3 ounces cream cheese,
  softened
1 egg, beaten
1 9-ounce package
  frozen chopped broccoli
1 recipe 2-crust pie pastry
1 cup shredded Monterey
  Jack cheese
1 tablespoon milk

Brown ground beef with onion in skillet, stirring until crumbly; drain. Mix in flour, salt and garlic salt. Add 11/4 cups milk and cream cheese. Cook until bubbly, stirring constantly. Stir a small amount of ground beef mixture into egg; stir egg mixture into ground beef mixture. Remove from heat. Cook broccoli using package directions for 6 minutes; drain well. Mix into ground beef mixture. Spoon into pastry-lined pie plate; sprinkle with shredded cheese. Top with remaining pastry, sealing edge and cutting vents. Brush with 1 tablespoon milk. Bake at 350 degrees for 45 minutes or until golden brown. Let stand for 10 minutes before cutting. Yield: 6 servings.

Approx Per Serving: Cal 682; Prot 26.4 g; Carbo 31.6 g; T Fat 42.7 g; Chol 134.0 mg; Potas 406.0 mg; Sod 956.0 mg.

ALL-IN-ONE GROUND BEEF CASSEROLE

1 cup instant rice
3 tablespoons flour
1 teaspoon chili powder
11/2 teaspoons salt
1/4 teaspoon pepper
1/2 tablespoon butter
1 pound ground beef
2 tablespoons chopped
  onion
1/2 tablespoon butter
1 20-ounce can tomatoes
1/2 tablespoon butter
1 12-ounce can
  cream-style corn
1/2 tablespoon butter

Spread rice evenly in greased 2-quart casserole. Combine flour, chili powder, salt and pepper in small bowl. Sprinkle 1/3 of the mixture over rice; dot with 1/2 tablespoon butter. Mix ground beef with onion; crumble over rice layer. Sprinkle with half the remaining flour mixture; dot with 1/2 tablespoon butter. Add layers of undrained tomatoes, remaining flour mixture and 1/2 tablespoon butter. Top with corn; dot with remaining 1/2 tablespoon butter. Bake, covered, at 350 degrees for 45 to 50 minutes. Yield: 6 servings.

Approx Per Serving: Cal 325; Prot 16.4 g; Carbo 30.6 g; T Fat 15.8 g; Chol 59.0 mg; Potas 482.0 mg; Sod 926.0 mg.

Toni Stanton
Carthage, New York

LEBANESE LUBI (Bean Supper)

2 pounds fresh green or
   yellow string beans
1 pound ground beef
1 very small onion,
   chopped
1 46-ounce can tomato
   juice
3/4 cup orzo
1 tablespoon margarine
3/4 cup uncooked rice
1 can chicken vegetable
   soup

Wash and snap ends from beans; place in Dutch oven. Brown ground beef with onion in skillet, stirring until crumbly; drain. Spoon over beans. Add enough tomato juice to cover beans, adding water if necessary. Cook, covered, over low heat until beans are tender. Sauté orzo in margarine in skillet until golden brown. Add rice and soup. Add enough water to cover rice with 1/2-inch liquid. Bring to a boil; reduce heat. Cook, covered, until rice is tender. Serve bean mixture over rice mixture. Yield: 6 servings.

Approx Per Serving: Cal 369; Prot 21.8 g; Carbo 40.5 g; T Fat 14.8 g;
Chol 52.2 mg; Potas 1054.0 mg; Sod 1082.0 mg.

Joy M.J. Karam
Ottawa, Ontario, Canada

BAKED SPANISH STEW

3/4 cup pearl barley
1 1/2 cups water
1 pound lean ground beef
1/2 cup chopped onion
1/2 cup chopped celery
1/2 cup chopped green bell
   pepper
2 tablespoons olive oil
1 28-ounce can tomatoes
1/2 cup chili sauce
1 teaspoon
   Worcestershire sauce
1 teaspoon sugar
1/2 teaspoon marjoram
1/2 cup shredded Cheddar
   cheese
1/2 cup sliced black olives
1 7-ounce package
   tortilla chips

Cook barley in water in covered saucepan for 30 minutes or until tender. Brown ground beef with onion, celery and green pepper in olive oil in skillet, stirring frequently. Add barley, tomatoes, chili sauce, Worcestershire sauce, sugar, marjoram and salt and pepper to taste. Simmer for 10 minutes. Pour into 3-quart baking dish. Sprinkle cheese and olives over top. Arrange tortilla chips around edge. Bake at 350 degrees for 20 minutes. Yield: 6 servings.

Approx Per Serving: Cal 555; Prot 22.6 g; Carbo 53.7 g; T Fat 29.9 g;
Chol 57.3 mg; Potas 699.0 mg; Sod 890.0 mg.

FAVORITE TAGLIARINI

1 pound ground round
1 cup chopped onion
1 clove of garlic, minced
1 green bell pepper,
   chopped
2 tablespoons olive oil
1 can tomato soup
2 soup cans water
2 4-ounce cans chopped
   mushrooms
1 cup Parmesan cheese
1 20-ounce can
   cream-style corn
1/2 cup chopped black
   olives
1/4 cup parsley flakes
1 teaspoon basil
1 teaspoon oregano
1 5-ounce package
   noodles
2 cups shredded Cheddar
   cheese

Brown ground round in skillet, stirring until crumbly; drain and place in large bowl. Sauté onion, garlic and green pepper in olive oil in skillet until brown. Combine with ground round, soup, water, mushrooms, Parmesan cheese, corn, olives, parsley, basil and oregano; mix well. Stir in uncooked noodles. Spoon into greased 4-quart baking dish. Bake, covered, at 350 degrees for 30 minutes. Top with Cheddar cheese. Bake, uncovered, for 10 minutes longer or until noodles are tender. Yield: 8 servings.

Approx Per Serving: Cal 475; Prot 26.6 g; Carbo 35.0 g; T Fat 26.9 g; Chol 70.4 mg; Potas 463.0 mg; Sod 1046.0 mg.

SAUCY ROAST PORK

1 4-pound boned rolled
   pork loin roast
1/2 teaspoon salt
1/2 teaspoon chili powder
1 cup apple jelly
1 cup catsup
2 tablespoons vinegar
2 teaspoons chili powder

Rub all surfaces of roast with mixture of salt and 1/2 teaspoon chili powder. Place fat side up on rack in shallow roasting pan. Roast, uncovered, at 325 degrees for 2 hours. Blend jelly, catsup, vinegar and 2 teaspoons chili powder in small saucepan. Bring to a boil; reduce heat. Simmer for 1 minute. Brush over roast. Roast to 170 degrees on meat thermometer. Place on warm serving platter. Let stand for 10 minutes before slicing. Blend about 1/2 cup skimmed pan drippings with remaining jelly mixture. Serve with roast. Yield: 12 servings.

Approx Per Serving: Cal 496; Prot 30.4 g; Carbo 22.8 g; T Fat 30.9 g; Chol 113.0 mg; Potas 487.0 mg; Sod 403.0 mg.

GRILLED PORK CHOPS ORIENTAL

1/2 cup teriyaki sauce
1/4 cup minced green
  onions
1/4 cup lemon juice
2 tablespoons peanut oil
4 cloves of garlic, minced
2 teaspoons crushed red
  pepper
4 3/4-inch pork chops

Combine teriyaki sauce, green onions, lemon juice, peanut oil, garlic and red pepper in small bowl; mix well. Place pork chops in shallow dish. Pour marinade over pork chops. Chill for 4 hours to overnight, turning pork chops occasionally. Drain, reserving marinade. Place 6 to 8 inches above hot coals. Grill for 30 to 45 minutes or until cooked through, turning and basting frequently with reserved marinade.
Yield: 4 servings.

Approx Per Serving: Cal 333; Prot 30.5 g; Carbo 8.7 g; T Fat 19.4 g; Chol 89.7 mg; Potas 488.0 mg; Sod 1444.0 mg.

PIZZA-STYLE PORK CHOPS

8 3/4-inch pork chops
8 ounces mozzarella
  cheese
Seasoned salt to taste
2 tablespoons oil
2 envelopes spaghetti
  sauce mix
1   16-ounce can stewed
  tomatoes
1   6-ounce can tomato
  paste
1 medium onion, chopped
2 cups shredded Cheddar
  cheese

Cut pockets in pork chops. Cut mozzarella cheese into 8 pieces; insert into pockets and fasten with toothpicks. Sprinkle chops with seasoned salt and pepper to taste. Brown on both sides in oil in skillet; place in baking pan. Combine sauce mix, tomatoes, tomato paste and onion in saucepan. Bring to a boil; spoon over chops. Bake at 350 degrees for 30 minutes. Sprinkle Cheddar cheese over top. Bake for 30 minutes longer.
Yield: 8 servings.

Approx Per Serving: Cal 528; Prot 37.0 g; Carbo 10.5 g; T Fat 37.2 g; Chol 132.0 mg; Potas 719.0 mg; Sod 658.0 mg.

PORK CHOPS AND SAUERKRAUT

1 16-ounce can
   sauerkraut, drained
2 pounds center cut pork
   chops
1/2 cup flour
1/4 cup olive oil
3 tomatoes, skinned,
   chopped
10 green onions, chopped
1 8-ounce can tomato
   sauce
1 cup sliced fresh
   mushrooms
2 stalks celery, chopped
1 cup water
1 tablespoon Italian
   seasoning
1 teaspoon garlic powder
1 teaspoon salt
1 teaspoon pepper

Spread sauerkraut in 8x12-inch baking dish. Coat chops with flour. Brown on both sides in olive oil in skillet; arrange over sauerkraut. Add tomatoes, green onions, tomato sauce, mushrooms, celery, water, Italian seasoning, garlic powder, salt and pepper to pan drippings. Simmer for 15 to 20 minutes or to desired consistency. Spoon over chops. Bake at 325 degrees for 30 minutes or until chops are tender. Garnish with additional chopped tomatoes and green onions. Yield: 8 servings.

Approx Per Serving: Cal 428; Prot 25.1 g; Carbo 13.9 g; T Fat 30.2 g; Chol 85.1 mg; Potas 683.0 mg; Sod 880.0 mg.

CROCK•POT RIBS

3 pounds country-style
   pork ribs
1 bottle of barbecue sauce
3 cups (about) water

Place ribs in Crock•Pot. Add barbecue sauce and enough water to cover ribs. Cook on Low for 9 to 10 hours. This is a great recipe to use when fishing or camping.

Nutritional information for this recipe is not available.

Mrs. Ken (Sly Fox) Hollister
Owego, New York

CANADIAN BACON AND EGG BAKE

1/4 **cup melted butter**
1/4 **cup flour**
1/2 **teaspoon salt**
1/8 **teaspoon pepper**
2 **cups milk**
1 **cup sour cream**
2 **tablespoons minced**
   parsley
8 **eggs, beaten**
1/2 **cup shredded sharp**
   Cheddar cheese
8 **ounces frozen hashed**
   brown potatoes, thawed
1 **pound Canadian bacon**

Blend butter, flour, salt and pepper in large saucepan. Stir in milk. Cook until thickened, stirring constantly. Remove from heat. Add sour cream, parsley, eggs, cheese and potatoes; mix well. Spoon mixture into greased 9x13-inch baking dish. Arrange overlapping slices of Canadian bacon on top. Bake at 350 degrees for 45 minutes or until set. Yield: 8 servings.

Approx Per Serving: Cal 422; Prot 23.8 g; Carbo 16.8 g; T Fat 29.0 g; Chol 346.0 mg; Potas 523.0 mg; Sod 1140.0 mg.

HOT SAUSAGE STEW

2 **pounds hot sausage**
6 **potatoes, peeled**
8 **carrots**
6 **small onions**
2 **green bell peppers,**
   cut up
2 **8-ounce cans tomato**
   sauce
1/2 **cup water**
1/2 **teaspoon salt**

Brown sausage in skillet, stirring until crumbly; drain. Cut potatoes into quarters and carrots into 2-inch pieces. Layer sausage and vegetables in shallow 8x12-inch baking dish. Pour mixture of tomato sauce and water over top. Sprinkle with salt. Bake, covered, at 350 degrees for 1 hour. Yield: 6 servings.

Approx Per Serving: Cal 653; Prot 17.3 g; Carbo 78.5 g; T Fat 31.5 g; Chol 51.7 mg; Potas 1861.0 mg; Sod 1192.0 mg.

Phyllis Wendt
Constableville, New York

MEDITERRANEAN IRISH STEW

2 pounds sweet Italian
   sausage
2 green bell peppers
2 onions
1 medium zucchini
1 medium yellow squash
12 ounces fresh
   mushrooms
8 ounces fresh green beans
8 medium potatoes, peeled
2 tablespoons olive oil
1   20-ounce can whole
   Italian plum tomatoes
1   6-ounce can tomato
   paste
1 tomato paste can water
Garlic, basil and oregano
   to taste

Cut sausage, green peppers, onions, zucchini, squash, mushrooms, green beans and potatoes into bite-sized pieces. Brown sausage in olive oil in 8-quart saucepan. Add tomatoes, tomato paste and water; mix well. Add vegetables. Season with garlic, basil, oregano and salt and pepper to taste. Simmer, covered, until potatoes are tender. Yield: 8 servings.

Approx Per Serving: Cal 509; Prot 19.9 g; Carbo 68.3 g; T Fat 19.1 g; Chol 44.0 mg; Potas 1771.0 mg; Sod 674.0 mg.

Beverly Carbone
Watertown, New York

SAUSAGE-STUFFED FRENCH TOAST

8 ounces hot sausage
1/2 cup chopped onion
4 ounces cream cheese,
   softened
1/4 teaspoon salt
1/2 teaspoon pepper
4 ounces bacon,
   crisp-fried, crumbled
1   16-ounce loaf unsliced
   bread
6 eggs, beaten
1/2 cup milk
2 tablespoons butter

Cook sausage with onion in skillet until brown and crumbly; drain. Combine with cream cheese, salt, pepper and bacon in bowl; mix well. Cut bread into 6 thick slices; cut pocket in each. Spoon sausage mixture into pockets. Beat eggs with milk. Dip filled bread slices into egg mixture. Brown on both sides in butter in skillet. Serve with warm maple syrup. Yield: 6 servings.

Approx Per Serving: Cal 558; Prot 21.7 g; Carbo 35.3 g; T Fat 36.2 g; Chol 337.0 mg; Potas 340.0 mg; Sod 1018.0 mg.

HORSERADISH-GLAZED HAM

1 6-pound boned ham
1 cup packed light brown
  sugar
1/3 cup horseradish
1/4 cup lemon juice
Ground cloves to taste

Have butcher cut ham into 1/4 inch thick slices, reassemble and tie. Place ham on rack in shallow roasting pan. Bake at 325 degrees for 1 1/2 hours. Combine brown sugar, horseradish, lemon juice and cloves in small saucepan. Bring to a boil, stirring constantly. Increase oven temperature to 400 degrees. Bake ham for 15 minutes longer, basting occasionally with horseradish mixture. Yield: 10 servings.

Approx Per Serving: Cal 746; Prot 58.7 g; Carbo 21.7 g; T Fat 45.7 g; Chol 167.0 mg; Potas 861.0 mg; Sod 3239.0 mg.

BAKED HAM WITH STUFFING SUPREME

1 5-pound boned ham
3/4 cup chopped onion
3/4 cup chopped celery
6 tablespoons butter
6 slices bread, cubed
1 1/2 cups chopped peeled
  apples
1/3 cup raisins
1 cup chicken broth
1/2 teaspoon cinnamon
1 10-ounce jar pineapple
  preserves

Cut ham into 1/4 inch slices; reassemble in shallow baking pan. Sauté onion and celery in butter in skillet until tender but not brown. Combine with bread, apples, raisins, broth and cinnamon in bowl; mix well. Spoon stuffing between ham slices, leaving 2 ham slices between stuffing layers. Tie ham securely. Bake, loosely covered with foil, at 350 degrees for 1 hour. Melt preserves in small saucepan over low heat. Bake ham, uncovered, for 1 hour longer, basting occasionally with preserves. Yield: 12 servings.

Approx Per Serving: Cal 498; Prot 41.7 g; Carbo 31.0 g; T Fat 22.5 g; Chol 92.6 mg; Potas 805.0 mg; Sod 2213.0 mg.

GLAZED HAM LOAF

1 pound lean ground ham
1 pound lean ground pork
3/4 cup cracker crumbs
3 tablespoons chopped
  onion
3/4 teaspoon salt
2 eggs, beaten
1 cup milk
1/2 cup packed brown
  sugar
1/4 cup cider vinegar
3/4 teaspoon dry mustard
1/4 cup mayonnaise
1/4 cup sour cream
1 tablespoon horseradish
1/4 cup sugar
1 tablespoon lemon juice

Combine ham, pork, crumbs, onion, salt, eggs and milk in bowl; mix well. Shape into loaf in greased loaf pan. Bake at 350 degrees for 30 minutes. Combine brown sugar, vinegar and dry mustard in saucepan. Bring to a boil. Cook for 1 minute, stirring constantly. Pour over ham loaf. Bake for 1 hour longer. Blend mayonnaise, sour cream, horseradish, sugar and lemon juice in small bowl. Serve with ham loaf.
Yield: 6 servings.

Approx Per Serving: Cal 522; Prot 36.2 g; Carbo 37.6 g; T Fat 24.6 g; Chol 199.0 mg; Potas 598.0 mg; Sod 1281.0 mg.

HAM AND BROCCOLI STRATA

1   20-ounce package
  frozen chopped broccoli
12 slices bread, crusts
  trimmed
3 cups shredded Cheddar
  cheese
3 cups chopped cooked
  ham
6 eggs, beaten
31/2 cups milk
1/2 teaspoon salt
1/4 teaspoon dry mustard
Chopped onion to taste

Cook broccoli using package directions; drain. Alternate layers of bread, cheese, broccoli and ham in greased 9x13-inch baking dish, ending with cheese. Beat eggs with milk, salt and dry mustard. Pour over layers. Sprinkle with onion. Chill, covered, for several hours to overnight. Let stand at room temperature for 1 hour before baking. Bake at 325 degrees for 1 hour or until set. Let stand for 10 minutes before serving.
Yield: 10 servings.

Approx Per Serving: Cal 445; Prot 28.5 g; Carbo 24.2 g; T Fat 25.9 g; Chol 237.0 mg; Potas 446.0 mg; Sod 1079.0 mg.

HAM AND CHEESE OMELET ROLL

1/2 cup mayonnaise
2 tablespoons flour
1 cup milk
12 egg yolks, beaten
12 egg whites, stiffly
  beaten
1/2 teaspoon salt
1/8 teaspoon pepper
11/2 cups chopped ham
1 cup shredded Swiss
  cheese
1 cup mayonnaise
2 tablespoons prepared
  mustard
2 tablespoons chopped
  green onion

Line 10x15-inch jelly roll pan with waxed paper; grease with a small amount of mayonnaise. Blend 1/2 cup mayonnaise and flour in large saucepan. Stir in milk and egg yolks gradually. Cook over low heat until thickened, stirring constantly. Let stand for 20 minutes, stirring occasionally. Fold in stiffly beaten egg whites, salt and pepper gently. Spread in prepared pan. Bake at 425 degrees for 20 minutes. Invert onto towel; peel off waxed paper. Sprinkle with ham and cheese; roll as for jelly roll. Place on serving plate. Blend 1 cup mayonnaise and mustard in small bowl. Stir in green onion. Serve with omelet roll. May heat sauce if desired; do not boil. Yield: 6 servings.

Approx Per Serving: Cal 748; Prot 27.5 g; Carbo 7.7 g; T Fat 67.6 g; Chol 625.0 mg; Potas 339.0 mg; Sod 1175.0 mg.

HAM AND RICE QUICHE OLÉ

1 6-ounce package
  Spanish rice mix
8 ounces cooked ham,
  cubed
11/2 cups shredded Swiss
  cheese
1/3 cup chopped onion
1/3 cup chopped green bell
  pepper
2 tablespoons chopped
  pimento
4 eggs, beaten
11/4 cups milk
1/4 teaspoon salt
1/4 teaspoon hot pepper
  sauce

Prepare rice mix using package directions. Cool. Press over bottom and side of buttered 10-inch pie plate, shaping rim. Layer ham, cheese, onion, green pepper and pimento in prepared pie plate. Beat eggs with milk, salt and hot pepper sauce. Pour over layers. Bake at 350 degrees for 50 minutes or until set. Yield: 6 servings.

Approx Per Serving: Cal 290; Prot 22.1 g; Carbo 5.2 g; T Fat 19.6 g; Chol 239.0 mg; Potas 275.0 mg; Sod 681.0 mg.

BROILED CHICKEN AND RICE

2 2¹/₂-pound chickens,
  cut up
³/₄ cup flour
Cinnamon to taste
³/₄ cup orzo
1 tablespoon margarine
³/₄ cup uncooked rice
1 can chicken vegetable
  soup

Rinse chicken pieces. Shake chicken with flour in plastic bag to coat. Arrange in foil-lined baking pan. Sprinkle generously with cinnamon. Place on lowest oven rack. Broil for 15 minutes. Turn chicken over; sprinkle with cinnamon. Broil for 15 minutes longer or until chicken is tender. Sauté orzo in margarine in large skillet until golden brown, stirring constantly. Add rice, soup and enough water to cover with ¹/₂-inch liquid. Bring to a boil; reduce heat. Simmer, covered, until rice is tender. Serve with chicken. Yield: 6 servings.

Approx Per Serving: Cal 645; Prot 71.2 g; Carbo 39.4 g; T Fat 20.3 g; Chol 206.0 mg; Potas 667.0 mg; Sod 610.0 mg.

Joy M.J. Karam
Ottawa, Ontario, Canada

CHERRY CHICKEN

2¹/₂ pounds chicken pieces
¹/₂ teaspoon salt
¹/₄ teaspoon pepper
3 tablespoons oil
1 21-ounce can cherry
  pie filling
¹/₂ cup dry white wine
¹/₂ cup orange juice
¹/₄ cup packed light
  brown sugar
¹/₂ teaspoon salt
¹/₄ teaspoon allspice
¹/₄ teaspoon nutmeg
¹/₄ teaspoon cloves

Rinse chicken; pat dry. Season with salt and pepper. Brown in oil in skillet for 10 minutes on each side; drain. Combine pie filling, wine, orange juice, brown sugar, salt, allspice, nutmeg and cloves in bowl; mix well. Spoon over chicken. Cook, covered, over low heat for 20 minutes or until chicken is tender. Serve with hot cooked rice. Yield: 4 servings.

Approx Per Serving: Cal 562; Prot 44.5 g; Carbo 54.1 g; T Fat 16.6 g; Chol 119.0 mg; Potas 597.0 mg; Sod 695.0 mg.

FRIED CHICKEN ITALIANO

3 cups self-rising flour
2 1-serving envelopes
   instant tomato soup mix
2 envelopes dry Italian
   salad dressing mix
1 teaspoon salt
5 pounds chicken pieces
1/2 cup melted butter

Combine flour, soup mix, salad dressing mix and salt in large bowl; mix well. Rinse chicken pieces. Coat with flour mixture; place on baking sheet. Brush chicken with butter. Bake at 350 degrees for 1 hour or until tender. For extra-crispy chicken, coat pieces 2 times and baste with mixture of 1 table-spoon oil and 1 tablespoon water every 15 minutes. Yield: 12 servings.

Approx Per Serving: Cal 412; Prot 31.9 g; Carbo 33.5 g; T Fat 16.2 g; Chol 106.0 mg; Potas 409.0 mg; Sod 794.0 mg.
Nutritional information does not include salad dressing mix.

GOLDEN GLAZED CHICKEN

2 2-pound chickens,
   quartered
3 tablespoons butter
3/4 cup maple syrup
1/4 cup vinegar
3 tablespoons soy sauce
1 bay leaf
1/4 teaspoon salt
Cayenne pepper to taste
3 cups sliced peeled
   nectarines

Rinse chicken; pat dry. Season lightly with salt to taste. Brown in butter in skillet; place in shallow 10x12-inch baking dish. Combine maple syrup, vinegar, soy sauce, bay leaf, salt and cayenne pepper in saucepan; mix well. Brush over chicken. Bake at 375 degrees for 45 minutes, brushing every 15 minutes with syrup mixture. Pour pan drippings into syrup mixture. Bring to a boil. Cook until sauce is reduced to 3/4 cup. Remove bay leaf. Add nectarines. Bring to a boil; spoon over chicken. Bake for 15 minutes. Serve chicken with sauce. Yield: 8 servings.

Approx Per Serving: Cal 375; Prot 34.0 g; Carbo 30.2 g; T Fat 13.1 g; Chol 113.0 mg; Potas 515.0 mg; Sod 591.0 mg.

Margaret E. Gardner
Ottawa, Ontario, Canada

GARLIC BAKED CHICKEN

1/2 **cup lemon juice**
1/4 **cup oil**
1 tablespoon soy sauce
1 clove of garlic, crushed
1/2 **teaspoon salt**
1/4 **teaspoon pepper**
2   2 1/2-pound chickens,
  split
1/2 **cup flour**
2 teaspoons paprika
1 teaspoon salt
1/2 **teaspoon pepper**
1/2 **cup melted butter**

Combine lemon juice, oil, soy sauce, garlic, 1/2 teaspoon salt and 1/4 teaspoon pepper in bowl. Chill for 1 hour. Rinse chicken. Coat with mixture of flour, paprika, 1 teaspoon salt and 1/2 teaspoon pepper. Arrange in 9x13-inch baking dish; brush with butter. Bake at 400 degrees for 30 minutes. Turn chicken over. Pour lemon mixture over chicken. Bake for 30 minutes. Yield: 4 servings.

   Approx Per Serving: Cal 828; Prot 84.2 g; Carbo 15.2 g; T Fat 46.4 g; Chol 284.0 mg; Potas 756.0 mg; Sod 1397.0 mg.

CHICKEN CACCIATORE

6 chicken breasts
1 small onion, chopped
1 green bell pepper,
  chopped
1/2 **cup sugar**
1   46-ounce can tomato
  juice
1   15-ounce can Italian
  tomato sauce
1   6-ounce can Italian
  tomato paste
3/4 **cup water**
1 tablespoon garlic
  powder

Rinse chicken. Cook in water to cover in saucepan for 30 minutes or until tender. Bone and cut into bite-sized pieces. Combine onion, green pepper, sugar, tomato juice, tomato sauce, tomato paste, water and garlic powder in saucepan. Cook over medium heat for 45 minutes or to desired consistency. Add chicken. Cook for 10 minutes longer. Serve over hot cooked noodles. Yield: 6 servings.

   Approx Per Serving: Cal 353; Prot 39.1 g; Carbo 38.5 g; T Fat 5.7 g; Chol 95.6 mg; Potas 1349.0 mg; Sod 1321.0 mg.

CHICKEN JUNK

1 pound chicken breast
    filets
4 ounces Swiss cheese,
    sliced
2 cans cream of
    mushroom soup
3/4 cup white wine
2 cups dry herb-seasoned
    stuffing mix

Rinse chicken; pat dry. Cut into bite-sized pieces. Layer chicken and cheese in 9x12-inch baking dish. Blend soup and wine in bowl. Spoon over cheese. Sprinkle stuffing mix over top. Bake, covered, at 350 degrees for 30 minutes. Bake, uncovered, for 15 to 20 minutes longer. Yield: 4 servings.

Approx Per Serving: Cal 735; Prot 50.1 g; Carbo 37.2 g; T Fat 39.4 g; Chol 123.0 mg; Potas 508.0 mg; Sod 1996.0 mg.

Bonnie Corbin
Sackets Harbor, New York

CHICKEN DIJON

4 chicken breast filets
3 tablespoons butter
3 tablespoons flour
1 cup chicken broth
1 cup half and half
2 tablespoons Dijon
    mustard

Rinse chicken; pat dry. Cut into strips. Cook in butter in skillet until tender. Remove to warm serving platter. Blend flour into pan drippings. Stir in broth and half and half gradually. Cook until thickened, stirring constantly. Blend in mustard. Add chicken. Cook, covered, over low heat for 10 minutes. Serve with hot cooked rice. Yield: 4 servings.

Approx Per Serving: Cal 388; Prot 39.2 g; Carbo 7.8 g; T Fat 21.4 g; Chol 141.0 mg; Potas 429.0 mg; Sod 476.0 mg.

MEXICAN CHICKEN KIEV

8 chicken breast filets
1   7-ounce can chopped
    green chilies
4 ounces Monterey Jack
    cheese, cut into strips
1/2 cup bread crumbs
1/4 cup Parmesan cheese
1 tablespoon chili powder
1/2 teaspoon salt
1/4 teaspoon cumin
1/4 teaspoon pepper
3/4 cup melted butter

Rinse chicken; pat dry. Pound filets to 1/4-inch thickness. Place green chilies and Monterey Jack cheese strip on each; roll to enclose filling and tuck ends under. Combine crumbs, Parmesan cheese and seasonings in bowl. Dip chicken rolls into butter; coat with crumb mixture. Place in baking dish. Drizzle any remaining butter over rolls. Chill, covered, for 4 hours or longer. Bake at 400 degrees for 25 minutes or until tender. Serve with salsa. Yield: 8 servings.

Approx Per Serving: Cal 447; Prot 41.1 g; Carbo 7.1 g; T Fat 27.8 g; Chol 157.0 mg; Potas 393.0 mg; Sod 1203.0 mg.

CHICKEN BREASTS SUPREME

8 chicken breast filets
4 slices bacon
1 can cream of mushroom
  soup
1 cup sour cream
1 tablespoon Dijon
  mustard
1 tablespoon
  Worcestershire sauce

Rinse chicken; pat dry. Pound to 1/4-inch thickness. Cut bacon slices into halves; place on chicken. Roll up from narrow end; secure with toothpicks. Place in large baking dish. Combine soup, sour cream, mustard and Worcestershire sauce in bowl; mix well. Pour over chicken. Bake at 400 degrees for 10 minutes. Reduce oven temperature to 250 degrees. Bake for 2 1/2 hours longer. Serve over hot cooked rice. Yield: 8 servings.

Approx Per Serving: Cal 315; Prot 37.6 g; Carbo 4.3 g; T Fat 15.5 g; Chol 111.0 mg; Potas 377.0 mg; Sod 483.0 mg.

TIPSY CHICKEN

8 chicken breast filets
1 cup flour
1/2 cup margarine
5 green onions, chopped
3 stalks celery, chopped
1/2 cup chopped parsley
2 chicken bouillon cubes
1 4-ounce jar sliced
  mushrooms
1 cup white wine
1 tablespoon
  Worcestershire sauce

Rinse chicken; pat dry. Sprinkle chicken with salt and pepper to taste; coat with flour. Arrange in 9x13-inch baking dish. Combine margarine, green onions, celery, parsley, bouillon cubes, undrained mushrooms, wine and Worcestershire sauce in small saucepan. Cook over medium heat for 10 minutes or until celery is tender. Cool. Pour over chicken. Chill, tightly covered, for several hours to overnight. Bake, uncovered, at 325 degrees for 40 minutes or until tender. Yield: 8 servings.

Approx Per Serving: Cal 390; Prot 37.8 g; Carbo 15.1 g; T Fat 16.9 g; Chol 95.7 mg; Potas 459.0 mg; Sod 572.0 mg.

CHICKEN SPAGHETTI FOR-A-CROWD

1 10-ounce can Ro-Tel tomatoes
1 4-ounce jar pimentos
2 medium onions, chopped
2 large green bell peppers, chopped
3/4 cup margarine
5 cups chopped cooked chicken
2 pounds Velveeta cheese, chopped
1 16-ounce can peas, drained
1 8-ounce can sliced mushrooms, drained
20 black olives, sliced
20 ounces spaghetti

Process tomatoes and pimentos in blender container until smooth; set aside. Sauté onions and green peppers in margarine in skillet until tender. Add tomatoes, chicken, cheese, peas, mushrooms and olives. Cook over low heat until cheese is melted, stirring occasionally. Cook spaghetti using package directions. Place spaghetti in 3 greased 9x13-inch baking pans. Add sauce; mix lightly. Bake, covered, at 350 degrees for 30 minutes or until bubbly. Yield: 25 servings.

Approx Per Serving: Cal 390; Prot 21.0 g; Carbo 24.3 g; T Fat 24.4 g; Chol 59.5 mg; Potas 304.0 mg; Sod 896.0 mg.

CHICKEN SUPREME

3 slices bread, cubed
2 cups chopped cooked chicken
1/2 cup chopped celery
1/2 cup chopped onion
1/2 cup mayonnaise
1/4 teaspoon pepper
4 slices bread, cubed
2 eggs, beaten
1 1/2 cups milk
1 can cream of mushroom soup
1/2 cup shredded Cheddar cheese

Place 3 slices bread cubes in greased 2 1/2-quart casserole. Combine chicken, celery, onion, mayonnaise and pepper in bowl; mix lightly. Spoon into prepared casserole. Top with remaining bread cubes. Beat eggs with milk; pour over layers. Chill, covered, for 6 hours to overnight. Spread soup over top; sprinkle with cheese. Bake at 350 degrees for 1 1/2 hours. Yield: 10 servings.

Approx Per Serving: Cal 280; Prot 14.3 g; Carbo 14.9 g; T Fat 18.1 g; Chol 97.6 mg; Potas 211.0 mg; Sod 504.0 mg.

Phyllis Wendt
Constableville, New York

INDIVIDUAL TURKEY LOAVES

1 pound fresh ground
  turkey
4 egg yolks
3/4 cup whole wheat bread
  crumbs
1/4 cup sliced green onion
1/4 cup water
2 tablespoons minced
  parsley
1/2 teaspoon salt
1/4 teaspoon sage
1/2 cup cranberry-orange
  relish

Combine turkey, egg yolks, bread crumbs, green onion, water, parsley, salt and sage in bowl; mix well. Shape into 4 small loaves; place in shallow baking dish. Bake at 350 degrees for 30 minutes; drain. Spoon relish over loaves. Bake for 3 minutes longer. Yield: 4 servings.

Approx Per Serving: Cal 360; Prot 26.9 g; Carbo 24.2 g; T Fat 17.5 g; Chol 343.0 mg; Potas 276.0 mg; Sod 494.0 mg.

DEEP-DISH TURKEY PIE

6 medium potatoes
6 medium carrots
1 small onion
1/4 cup chopped green bell
  pepper
2 tablespoons butter
1 can cream of chicken
  soup
3 cups chopped cooked
  turkey
1 1/2 cups flour
2 teaspoons baking
  powder
1/2 teaspoon salt
1/4 cup butter
1/2 cup milk

Peel potatoes and carrots; cut into pieces. Cook in boiling salted water to cover in saucepan for 15 to 20 minutes or until tender. Drain, reserving 1 cup liquid. Sauté onion and green pepper in 2 tablespoons butter in skillet until tender. Blend soup and reserved liquid in bowl. Place vegetables and turkey in 2-quart casserole. Pour soup mixture over top. Bake at 425 degrees for 15 minutes. Combine flour, baking powder and salt in bowl. Cut in 1/4 cup butter until crumbly. Add milk; mix well. Knead lightly on floured surface. Roll and cut with floured 2-inch biscuit cutter. Arrange over turkey mixture. Brush biscuits with additional milk. Bake for 15 minutes longer. Yield: 6 servings.

Approx Per Serving: Cal 625; Prot 31.6 g; Carbo 88.8 g; T Fat 16.0 g; Chol 82.3 mg; Potas 1422.0 mg; Sod 855.0 mg.

BLACK BEANS AND RICE

1 clove of garlic, minced
1 teaspoon red pepper
  flakes
1 bay leaf
1/4 cup oil
1 onion, chopped
1 stalk celery, chopped
1/2 green bell pepper,
  chopped
2 cups cooked black beans
2 cups cooked brown rice

Sauté garlic, pepper flakes and bay leaf in oil in skillet for several minutes. Discard bay leaf. Add onion, celery and green pepper. Sauté until tender. Add beans. Cook until heated through, stirring constantly. Spoon bean mixture over hot cooked rice. Garnish with tomato wedges, minced green onions and shredded sharp Cheddar cheese. Yield: 2 servings.

Approx Per Serving: Cal 405; Prot 13.2 g; Carbo 56.0 g; T Fat 15.0 g; Chol 0.0 mg; Potas 590.0 mg; Sod 10.8 mg.

EGGS FLORENTINE

2   10-ounce packages
    frozen chopped spinach
6 eggs
1 can cream of celery soup
1 1/2 cups shredded
    Cheddar cheese

Cook spinach using package directions; drain well. Place in 8x10-inch baking dish; spread in dish, shaping 6 slight depressions. Break egg into each depression. Heat soup with 1 cup cheese in saucepan over low heat until cheese melts, stirring constantly. Spoon around eggs. Sprinkle remaining cheese over top. Bake at 350 degrees for 30 minutes. Yield: 6 servings.

Approx Per Serving: Cal 253; Prot 16.7 g; Carbo 9.4 g; T Fat 17.3 g; Chol 309.0 mg; Potas 421.0 mg; Sod 683.0 mg.

EGGPLANT PARMESAN

1 onion, chopped
1 green bell pepper,
  chopped
3 large cloves of garlic,
  minced
2 tablespoons olive oil
4 cups chopped, seeded,
  peeled tomatoes
1   12-can tomato paste
1 teaspoon basil
1 teaspoon oregano
1/8 teaspoon cinnamon
1 large eggplant
1/2 cup whole wheat flour
6 tablespoons olive oil
1 pound mozzarella
  cheese, shredded
1 cup whole wheat bread
  crumbs
1 cup Parmesan cheese

Sauté onion, green pepper and half the garlic in 2 tablespoons olive oil in large skillet until tender. Add tomatoes, tomato paste, remaining garlic and salt and pepper to taste. Simmer, covered, for 30 minutes. Add basil, oregano and cinnamon. Simmer, uncovered, for 30 minutes, stirring occasionally. Cut eggplant lengthwise into halves. Place cut side down in greased baking pan. Cut lengthwise slits in each half and pierce several times with fork. Bake at 350 degrees for 10 minutes. Cool. Slice crosswise 1/4 inch thick. Coat each slice with flour. Cook in 6 tablespoons olive oil in skillet until crisp; drain on paper towels. Cool. Alternate layers of sauce, eggplant, mozzarella cheese, crumbs and Parmesan cheese in 3-quart baking dish. Bake at 350 degrees for 30 minutes. Yield: 6 servings.

Approx Per Serving: Cal 628; Prot 28.5 g; Carbo 43.4 g; T Fat 39.6 g; Chol 69.0 mg; Potas 1150.0 mg; Sod 733.0 mg.

VEGETARIAN CHILI

2/3 cup chopped onion
1 green bell pepper,
  chopped
1 clove of garlic, minced
1 tablespoon oil
1 cup beef stock
1   28-ounce can tomatoes
1   10-ounce can corn
1   8-ounce can tomato
  sauce
1   16-ounce can kidney
  beans
1 tablespoon chili powder
1/2 teaspoon cumin

Sauté onion, green pepper and garlic in oil in large saucepan. Add stock, tomatoes, corn, tomato sauce, kidney beans, chili powder, cumin and salt and pepper to taste. Simmer, covered, for 1 hour. Simmer, uncovered, until of desired consistency, stirring occasionally. Ladle into soup bowls or serve over hot cooked pasta or rice. Yield: 6 servings.

Approx Per Serving: Cal 170; Prot 7.7 g; Carbo 30.8 g; T Fat 3.6 g; Chol 0.1 mg; Potas 782.0 mg; Sod 947.0 mg.

FETTUCINI ALFREDO VERDE

1 pound fettucini
1 onion, chopped
1 pound mushrooms,
  sliced
1/2 cup butter
1 10-ounce package
  frozen chopped spinach,
  thawed
Garlic salt to taste
2 cups sour cream
1 cup shredded Romano
  cheese
1/4 cup milk

Cook fettucini using package directions. Sauté onion and mushrooms in butter in large skillet until tender. Add spinach, garlic salt and pepper to taste. Add sour cream. Cook over low heat until heated through; do not boil. Remove from heat. Add cheese; stir until cheese melts. Add enough milk to make of desired consistency. Place fettucini on serving plate; spoon sauce over top. Yield: 8 servings.

Approx Per Serving: Cal 514; Prot 15.5 g; Carbo 51.9 g; T Fat 27.9 g; Chol 69.0 mg; Potas 579.0 mg; Sod 306.0 mg.

VEGETABLE SPAGHETTI

1 pound spaghetti
1 cup sliced fresh
  mushrooms
1 cup chopped onion
1/2 cup thinly sliced
  carrots
1 cup chopped fresh
  broccoli
2 tablespoons oil
1/2 cup butter
1/3 cup Parmesan cheese

Cook spaghetti using package directions. Stir-fry mushrooms, chopped onion, carrots and broccoli in oil in skillet until tender-crisp. Add butter and spaghetti; toss until butter is melted. Top with Parmesan cheese. Serve with additional Parmesan cheese. Yield: 6 servings.

Approx Per Serving: Cal 495; Prot 12.6 g; Carbo 61.2 g; T Fat 22.3 g; Chol 44.9 mg; Potas 338.0 mg; Sod 222.0 mg.

RICE AND ZUCCHINI

2 pounds zucchini, sliced
2¹/2 cups water
1 cup uncooked rice
¹/2 cup thinly sliced green
  onions
¹/3 cup chopped fresh
  parsley
1 cup shredded sharp
  Cheddar cheese
¹/3 cup olive oil
3 eggs, slightly beaten
Rosemary to taste
Garlic powder to taste

Cook zucchini in water in saucepan for 7 minutes; drain, reserving liquid. Cook rice in reserved liquid until tender. Combine rice, zucchini, green onions, parsley, cheese, olive oil and eggs in large bowl. Add rosemary, garlic powder and salt and pepper to taste; mix well. Spoon into baking dish. Bake at 350 degrees for 45 minutes.
Yield: 6 servings.

    Approx Per Serving: Cal 357; Prot 11.7 g; Carbo 30.5 g; T Fat 21.3 g; Chol 157.0 mg; Potas 493.0 mg; Sod 158.0 mg.

ZUCCHINI SPAGHETTI

1¹/2 cups sliced onions
³/4 cup chopped green bell
  pepper
1¹/2 cups thinly sliced
  celery
¹/2 cup oil
8 cups thinly sliced
  zucchini
1   16-ounce can tomatoes
1   16-ounce can tomato
  sauce
1 teaspoon minced garlic
³/4 teaspoon salt
¹/4 teaspoon cayenne
  pepper
1 bay leaf
8 ounces spaghetti

Sauté onions, green pepper and celery in oil in skillet until tender. Add zucchini, tomatoes, tomato sauce, garlic, salt, cayenne pepper and bay leaf. Simmer, covered, for 30 minutes. Simmer, uncovered, until of desired consistency, stirring occasionally. Discard bay leaf. Cook spaghetti using package directions. Ladle sauce over spaghetti in bowl; toss lightly. Serve with Parmesan cheese. Yield: 6 servings.

    Approx Per Serving: Cal 384; Prot 9.2 g; Carbo 46.8 g; T Fat 19.4 g; Chol 0.0 mg; Potas 1131.0 mg; Sod 879.0 mg.

THE CONTEST
Game

The Contest

This yellow fin tuna, proudly displayed by my son, Darin, often shows fearsome strength and stamina in its contest with the angler. Yellow fin and albacore tuna, top game fish in our oceans, are fine table fare.

Adirondack Potluck Game Supper

Old-Fashioned Tomato Soup
page 34

Summer Salad
page 44

Venison Stew with Dumplings or
page 119

Duck with Apple Dressing
page 122

Seven-Bean Casserole
page 134

Baked Onions
page 137

Herbed Cheese Rolls
page 166

Nobby Apple Cake
page 177

BEAR ROAST

4 pounds bear meat
Celery salt to taste
2 cloves of garlic
1 8-ounce piece salt pork
1 cup black coffee
Sliced onions

Season bear meat with celery salt and pepper to taste. Place in stockpot. Add garlic, salt pork, coffee and enough water to cover. Cook until bear meat is tender. Drain, reserving pan juices. Place bear meat in roasting pan. Season with additional salt and pepper. Top with sliced onions. Roast at 350 degrees until brown, basting with reserved juices. Thicken remaining juices for gravy. Serve with bear meat. To eliminate the "wild taste" of bear meat, parboil in mixture of 1 tablespoon soda and 2 quarts water for 10 minutes before cooking as above. Yield: 12 servings.

Nutritional information for this recipe is not available.

New York State Department of Environmental Conservation
Albany, New York

BIG BOB'S SHOULDER OF VENISON

1 5-pound shoulder of
   venison
1 teaspoon pepper
1 teaspoon allspice
1/4 cup butter, softened
1 large onion, chopped
1 12-ounce can beer
1 cup sour cream
1 can cream of mushroom
   soup

Season venison with pepper and allspice; rub in lightly. Spread butter over roast, covering completely. Place roast in 8x13-inch roasting pan. Sprinkle onion on top. Combine beer, sour cream and soup in mixer bowl; whisk until blended. Pour over roast. Bake at 300 degrees for 1 1/2 hours or until roast is fork-tender, adding a small amount of water if necessary. Thicken pan juices for gravy if desired. Serve with noodles or potatoes. This recipe makes a tough cut very tasty. Leftovers make great sandwiches. Yield: 6 servings.

Approx Per Serving: Cal 656; Prot 86.5 g; Carbo 11.3 g; T Fat 25.8 g; Chol 223.0 mg; Potas 1140.0 mg; Sod 689.0 mg.

Robert D. Robert
Canton, New York

VENISON CHILI

1 pound ground venison
1/2 cup chopped onion
1/2 teaspoon salt
1/4 teaspoon pepper
4 cups canned tomatoes
3/4 cup catsup
1   151/2-ounce can kidney
   beans

Brown ground venison with onion, salt and pepper in large skillet, stirring until crumbly; drain. Add tomatoes, catsup and kidney beans. Simmer for 45 minutes or until of desired consistency, stirring occasionally. Yield: 4 servings.

Approx Per Serving: Cal 322; Prot 34.2 g; Carbo 41.0 g; T Fat 3.06 g; Chol 55.3 mg; Potas 1314.0 mg; Sod 1631.0 mg.

Cyndie Steria
Carthage, New York

MARINATED VENISON

2 carrots, sliced
2 large onions, sliced
2 stalks celery, finely
   chopped
1/2 cup olive oil
2 cloves of garlic
2 teaspoons salt
1 teaspoon freshly ground
   pepper
1/2 cup sugar
1/2 teaspoon cloves
1/2 teaspoon allspice
1/2 teaspoon basil
2 bay leaves
1 tablespoon chopped
   parsley
4 cups vinegar
4 cups water
2 cups beer
4 pounds venison
   shoulder, cubed

Sauté carrots, onions and celery in 1 tablespoon olive oil in skillet over low heat for 15 minutes, stirring frequently. Add remaining olive oil, garlic, salt, pepper, sugar, cloves, allspice, basil, bay leaves, parsley, vinegar, water and beer; mix well. Pour into nonreactive bowl. Add venison. Marinate in refrigerator for 24 to 48 hours, stirring occasionally. Place venison with marinade in stockpot. Bring to a boil over medium-low heat. Simmer, covered, over low heat for 2 hours. Discard bay leaves. Thicken pan juices for gravy if desired. Yield: 12 servings.

Approx Per Serving: Cal 319; Prot 34.1 g; Carbo 18.1 g; T Fat 11.6 g; Chol 73.7 mg; Potas 574.0 mg; Sod 448.0 mg.

New York State Department of Environmental Conservation
Albany, New York

VENISON MEATBALLS

2 pounds coarsely ground
  venison
2¹/₂ cups grated potato
¹/₂ cup grated Bermuda
  onion
2 eggs, beaten
2 tablespoons lemon juice
¹/₂ teaspoon pepper
2 tablespoons flour
4 cups beef bouillon
¹/₂ cup shortening
³/₄ cup flour
Celery salt to taste

Combine venison, potato, onion, eggs, lemon juice and pepper in bowl; mix well. Shape into balls. Coat with 2 tablespoons flour. Bring bouillon to a boil in saucepan; reduce heat. Add meatballs to simmering bouillon. Poach for 30 minutes. Remove meatballs with slotted spoon. Melt shortening in saucepan. Blend in remaining ³/₄ cup flour. Stir in hot cooking liquid gradually. Cook until thickened, stirring constantly. Season well with celery salt or salt and pepper to taste. Add meatballs. Cook until heated through. Serve with buttered wide noodles. Yield: 8 servings.

Approx Per Serving: Cal 388; Prot 31.0 g; Carbo 27.6 g; T Fat 16.6 g; Chol 124.0 mg; Potas 664.0 mg; Sod 473.0 mg.

New York State Department of Environmental Conservation
Albany, New York

ROAST VENISON

1 5-pound venison roast
Milk
8 slices bacon

Place roast in nonreactive bowl. Add enough milk to cover. Let stand in refrigerator overnight. Drain and pat dry. Place in roasting pan. Arrange bacon slices on top. Season with salt and pepper to taste. Bake at 350 degrees for about 2 hours or to 140 degrees on meat thermometer. Serve with baked potatoes and vegetable. Yield: 6 servings.

Approx Per Serving: Cal 462; Prot 86.2 g; Carbo 0.0 g; T Fat 10.4 g; Chol 191.0 mg; Potas 993.0 mg; Sod 333.0 mg.

Ruth M. Morse
Henderson, New York

VENISON SAUSAGE

8¹/₄ pounds ground
  venison
3¹/₄ pounds bacon, ground
1¹/₂ tablespoons salt
1¹/₂ tablespoons pepper
1¹/₂ tablespoons poultry
  seasoning
¹/₂ teaspoon allspice
¹/₂ teaspoon sage
¹/₂ teaspoon nutmeg
1 cup water

Combine venison, bacon, salt, pepper, poultry seasoning, allspice, sage, nutmeg and water in large bowl; mix well. Shape into patties. Fry in skillet until brown on both sides. Sausage will be pink in center. May also be stuffed into casings and boiled. Yield: 12 pounds.

Approx Per Pound: Cal 701; Prot 88.2 g; Carbo 0.7 g; T Fat 35.9 g; Chol 205.0 mg; Potas 1093.0 mg; Sod 1958.0 mg.

Randy L. Riley
Carthage, New York

PAPRIKA VENISON SCHNITZEL

2 pounds venison top
  round, cut into ¹/₂-inch
  cubes
1 cup beef broth
8 slices crisp-fried bacon,
  crumbled
³/₄ cup chopped onion
2 cloves of garlic, chopped
2 teaspoons salt
2¹/₂ teaspoons paprika
1 cup tomato sauce
2 cups sour cream
¹/₂ cup chopped parsley

Combine venison and broth in large skillet. Cook, tightly covered, over medium-low heat for 1 hour or until venison is tender. Add bacon, onion, garlic, salt, paprika, tomato sauce and sour cream. Cook, uncovered, over low heat until thickened, stirring constantly. Pour into serving dish. Top with parsley. Yield: 6 servings.

Approx Per Serving: Cal 403; Prot 39.9 g; Carbo 8.4 g; T Fat 22.9 g; Chol 115.0 mg; Potas 767.0 mg; Sod 1345.0 mg.

New York State Department of Environmental Conservation
Albany, New York

VENISON STEW

1 pound cubed venison
  stew meat
2 tablespoons oil
6 cups water
1 cup chopped onion
1 cup peas
1 cup beans
4 large potatoes, peeled,
  chopped
1¹/₂ cups sliced carrots
1 cup corn
1 teaspoon salt
¹/₄ teaspoon pepper
2 bay leaves
3 tablespoons (about)
  cornstarch
1 cup cold water

Brown venison in oil in stockpot; drain. Add 6 cups water, onion, peas, beans, potatoes, carrots, corn, salt, pepper and bay leaves. Cook over medium heat for 45 minutes to 1 hour or until venison and vegetables are tender. Combine cornstarch and remaining 1 cup water in small bowl. Stir into stew gradually. Cook until thickened, stirring constantly. Discard bay leaves.
Yield: 6 servings.

Approx Per Serving: Cal 339; Prot 23.8 g; Carbo 47.4 g; T Fat 6.6 g; Chol 36.9 mg; Potas 965.0 mg; Sod 564.0 mg.

Cyndie Steria
Carthage, New York

VENISON STEW WITH DUMPLINGS

1 slice bacon
1 pound cubed venison
  stew meat
2 cups water
1 carrot, peeled, sliced
1 stalk celery, sliced
¹/₂ teaspoon oregano
1 teaspoon salt
Cooked stew vegetables
  and liquid to taste
1 recipe biscuit mix
  dumplings

Brown bacon in pressure cooker; remove bacon. Brown venison in bacon drippings. Add water, carrot, celery, oregano and salt. Cook, covered, according to manufacturer's instructions for 20 minutes. Cool. Remove lid. Add vegetables and enough vegetable liquid to almost cover stew. Spoon dumpling batter over stew. Cook, covered with no pressure, for 15 to 20 minutes or until dumplings are cooked through. Serve with tossed or gelatin salad and Italian bread or rolls.
Yield: 4 servings.

Approx Per Serving: Cal 500; Prot 34.6 g; Carbo 60.4 g; T Fat 13.0 g; Chol 60.7 mg; Potas 704.0 mg; Sod 1479.0 mg.

Matte Bicknell
Watertown, New York

VENISON STROGANOFF

1 pound venison steak,
  1/4 inch thick, trimmed
2 tablespoons flour
1 tablespoon salt
1/4 teaspoon pepper
1/2 cup minced onion
1/4 cup butter
1 cup condensed chicken
  broth
1 pound mushrooms,
  sliced
1 cup sour cream

Coat steak with mixture of flour, salt and pepper. Pound into steak. Cut into 1x1 1/2-inch strips. Brown onion lightly in butter in skillet. Add venison strips. Cook until brown on both sides. Simmer, covered, for 15 minutes. Add broth and mushrooms. Cook, covered, until mushrooms are tender. Cook, uncovered, over low heat until venison is tender and mixture is thickened. Stir in sour cream just before serving. Serve with rice. Yield: 4 servings.

Approx Per Serving: Cal 418; Prot 32.8 g; Carbo 12.6 g; T Fat 26.6 g; Chol 113.0 mg; Potas 935.0 mg; Sod 2184.0 mg.

James Trainham
Watertown, New York

VENISON SUPREME

2 cups flour
2 eggs, beaten
1/2 teaspoon salt
1/2 cup water
8 ounces thickly sliced
  bacon
2 pounds venison round
  steak
1/2 teaspoon garlic salt

Combine flour, eggs, salt and water in bowl; mix well. Let stand in cool place for 1 hour. Roll out thinly on floured surface. Arrange bacon slices on top. Pound venison with meat mallet. Rub with garlic salt. Place on bacon. Fold dough to enclose venison. Dampen edges; seal. Wrap in buttered foil. Bake at 375 degrees for about 1 1/2 hours or until venison is tender. Open foil; baste with pan juices. Bake at 400 degrees for 15 minutes or until pastry is golden brown. Serve with black current jelly. Yield: 6 servings.

Approx Per Serving: Cal 452; Prot 45.6 g; Carbo 32.0 g; T Fat 14.1 g; Chol 181.0 mg; Potas 534.0 mg; Sod 760.0 mg.

New York State Department of Environmental Conservation
Albany, New York

PORCUPINE STEW

1 butchered porcupine
  carcass
1/2 cup vinegar
8 cups water
1 beef bouillon cube
2 teaspoons salt
1 large carrot, chopped
2 small onions, sliced
1/2 green bell pepper,
  chopped
3 tablespoons flour
1/4 cup water
1 8-ounce can corn,
  drained
4 cups cooked rice

Soak porcupine in mixture of water to cover and vinegar in large bowl for 1 hour; drain. Place in stockpot. Add 4 cups water. Cook for 5 to 6 hours or until meat falls off bones, adding additional water as needed. Cool and debone. Combine 4 cups water, bouillon cube, salt, pepper to taste, carrot, onions and green pepper in large saucepan. Cook for 15 minutes. Add porcupine meat. Cook for 10 minutes. Blend flour with remaining 1/4 cup water. Stir into stew. Add corn. Simmer for 5 minutes, stirring constantly. Serve over hot rice with hot rolls or French bread and grated cheese. Yield: 8 to 12 cups.

Nutritional information for this recipe is not available.

Paula Anne Jay
Star Lake, New York

DOVE MONTEREY-STYLE

10 dove breasts
2 12-ounce bottles of
  ginger ale
1/2 teaspoon rosemary
1/2 teaspoon parsley flakes
1/2 teaspoon sage
1/2 teaspoon thyme
1 teaspoon seasoned salt
1 teaspoon pepper
1/4 cup margarine
11/2 cups corn syrup
2 fresh limes
2 large fresh oranges

Wash dove breasts and pat dry. Marinate in ginger ale in bowl in refrigerator overnight; drain. Place in baking dish. Sprinkle with mixture of rosemary, parsley flakes, sage, thyme, seasoned salt and pepper. Melt margarine in double broiler. Stir in corn syrup and juice of limes and oranges. Grate lime rind and cut orange rind into fine strips. Add to double boiler. Cook until heated through. Pour over dove breasts. Bake at 350 degrees for 40 minutes. Yield: 5 servings.

Approx Per Serving: Cal 511; Prot 14.0 g; Carbo 92.3 g; T Fat 10.2 g; Chol 54.4 mg; Potas 124.0 mg; Sod 588.0 mg.

DUCK WITH APPLE DRESSING

1 3¹/₂ to 4-pound duck
4 slices toasted bread
  crumbs
4 tablespoons melted
  butter
¹/₄ cup water
3 apples, peeled, sliced
2 tablespoons sugar
¹/₄ teaspoon nutmeg
¹/₂ cup raisins
¹/₂ cup cashews
1 slice bacon, cut into
  halves

Rinse duck; pat dry inside and out. Combine bread crumbs, butter, water, apples, sugar, nutmeg, raisins and cashews in bowl; mix well. Spoon into duck cavities. Place in baking pan. Place bacon strips over top. Bake, covered, at 350 degrees until duck is tender. Serve with wild rice and favorite vegetable. Yield: 4 servings.

Approx Per Serving: Cal 608; Prot 21.3 g; Carbo 57.0 g; T Fat 34.5 g; Chol 100.5 mg; Potas 614.5 mg; Sod 417.0 mg.

Matte Bicknell
Watertown, New York

BARBECUED DUCK

2 large mallards
¹/₂ cup melted butter
2 tablespoons orange juice
1 tablespoon lemon juice
¹/₄ cup chopped onion
Texas Pete sauce to taste
2 tablespoons
  Worcestershire sauce
¹/₂ teaspoon garlic salt
1 onion, cut into quarters
1 potato, cut into quarters

Rinse ducks. Parboil in large saucepan if desired; drain. Sprinkle with salt to taste. Combine melted butter with orange juice, lemon juice, chopped onion, Texas Pete sauce, Worcestershire sauce, garlic salt and pepper to taste; mix well. Fill duck cavities with quartered onion and potato. Make slit in each side of breast. Place on rack in roasting pan. Brush with butter sauce. Cover loosely with foil. Bake at 375 degrees for 1¹/₂ hours or until tender, basting with sauce every 15 minutes. Remove foil. Bake for 20 minutes longer or until brown. Yield: 4 servings.

Approx Per Serving: Cal 645; Prot 31.8 g; Carbo 18.9 g; T Fat 49.0 g; Chol 198.0 mg; Potas 799.0 mg; Sod 634.0 mg.

CHARCOAL-BROILED DUCK BREASTS

4 duck breast filets
4 slices bacon
2 beef bouillon cubes
1 cup water
1 tablespoon red currant
  jelly
1/2 teaspoon dry mustard
1 tablespoon Sherry
1 tablespoon Brandy
1/8 teaspoon marjoram
1/8 teaspoon oregano
Grated rind of 1 orange

Rinse duck breasts; pat dry. Wrap each duck breast filet with bacon as for filet mignon. Season with salt and pepper to taste. Grill over hot coals for exactly 2 minutes per side. Dissolve bouillon cubes in water in chafing dish or electric skillet. Stir in jelly, dry mustard, Sherry, Brandy, marjoram and oregano. Simmer until slightly thickened; stir in orange rind. Add grilled filets. Cook for 5 minutes or until medium-rare, basting constantly. Yield: 4 servings.

Approx Per Serving: Cal 213; Prot 25.0 g; Carbo 6.2 g; T Fat 8.4 g; Chol 87.8 mg; Potas 360.0 mg; Sod 724.0 mg.

CROCK•POT CASSOULET

1 cup chopped carrots
1/2 cup chopped onion
1/3 cup water
1 8-ounce can tomato
  sauce
1/2 cup dry red wine
1 teaspoon garlic powder
1/2 teaspoon thyme
1/8 teaspoon ground cloves
2 bay leaves
1 15-ounce can navy
  beans, drained
4 duck breast filets
8 ounces Polish sausage,
  sliced

Bring carrots, onion and water to a boil in saucepan; reduce heat. Simmer, covered, for 5 minutes. Place in 3 1/2 to 4-quart Crock•Pot. Stir in tomato sauce, wine, seasonings and beans. Place duck breasts and sausage on top of bean mixture. Cook on Low for 9 to 10 hours or on High for 5 1/2 to 6 hours or until duck breasts are tender. Remove bay leaves. Yield: 4 servings.

Approx Per Serving: Cal 563; Prot 38.5 g; Carbo 38.9 g; T Fat 26.6 g; Chol 116.0 mg; Potas 1102.0 mg; Sod 906.0 mg.

DUCK GUMBO

2 ducks
1¹/₂ cups margarine
1 cup flour
1 bunch celery, chopped
3 cloves of garlic, chopped
4 medium onions, chopped
1 bunch green onions,
  chopped
1 large green bell pepper,
  chopped
4 cups sliced okra
2 20-ounce cans tomatoes
1 15-ounce can tomato
  paste
2 teaspoons MSG
1 teaspoon oregano
2 tablespoons salt
2 tablespoons parsley
  flakes
1 teaspoon thyme
1 tablespoon black pepper
¹/₄ teaspoon red pepper

Rinse ducks; pat dry inside and out. Cook in water to cover in large saucepan until tender. Drain, reserving 2 quarts broth. Bone ducks. Melt margarine in skillet. Add flour. Cook until dark brown, stirring constantly. Stir into reserved broth in large saucepan. Cook until thickened, stirring constantly. Add duck, celery, garlic, onions, green pepper, okra, tomatoes, tomato paste and seasonings. Cook over low heat for 2 hours or until of desired consistency, stirring frequently. Serve over hot cooked rice.
Yield: 10 servings.

> **Approx Per Serving:** Cal 551; Prot 19.0 g; Carbo 35.7 g; T Fat 38.9 g;
> Chol 54.4 mg; Potas 1234.0 mg; Sod 2732.0 mg.

ORIENTAL DUCK WITH SNOW PEAS

12 duck breast filets
¹/₂ cup soy sauce
¹/₂ cup oil
¹/₂ cup white wine
2 cloves of garlic, minced
¹/₂ teaspoon ground ginger
1 to 2 tablespoons oil
1 large onion, sliced
6 to 8 fresh mushrooms,
  sliced
1 10-ounce package
  frozen pea pods

Rinse duck breasts; pat dry. Slice thinly. Mix soy sauce, oil, wine, garlic and ginger in bowl. Add duck. Marinate in refrigerator for 4 hours or longer. Drain, reserving ¹/₄ cup marinade. Heat 1 to 2 tablespoons oil in wok. Add duck. Stir-fry until cooked through; remove from wok. Add onion and mushrooms. Stir-fry until tender-crisp. Add duck, pea pods and reserved marinade. Heat to serving temperature. May thicken sauce with a small amount of cornstarch dissolved in a small amount of water if desired. Serve with steamed rice. Yield: 8 servings.

> **Approx Per Serving:** Cal 402; Prot 36.1 g; Carbo 6.1 g; T Fat 24.5 g;
> Chol 123.0 mg; Potas 615.0 mg; Sod 1128.0 mg.

BAKED WILD DUCKS IN SWEET AND SOUR SAUCE

2 wild ducks
1 orange, sliced
1 apple, sliced
2 tablespoons oil
2 tablespoons brown sugar
1/4 cup Worcestershire
   sauce
3/4 cup catsup
2 tablespoons lemon juice
1/2 cup grated onion
1/2 teaspoon paprika
1/4 cup white vinegar

Rinse ducks; pat dry inside and out. Stuff duck cavities with sliced fruit. Rub ducks with oil. Place in baking dish. Combine brown sugar, Worcestershire sauce, catsup, lemon juice, onion, paprika, vinegar and salt and pepper to taste in bowl; mix well. Spoon sauce over ducks. Bake, tightly covered with foil, at 325 degrees for 2 hours or until tender. Bake, uncovered, until brown. Yield: 4 servings.

Approx Per Serving: Cal 527; Prot 31.2 g; Carbo 26.4 g; T Fat 32.9 g; Chol 136.0 mg; Potas 821.0 mg; Sod 780.0 mg.

ORIENTAL GOOSE STIR-FRY

Fileted breast of 1 wild
   goose
3 medium onions,
   chopped
2 8-ounce cans sliced
   mushrooms, drained
1 2½-ounce package
   slivered almonds
Seasoned salt to taste
2 packages oriental
   Rice-A-Roni
3 large stalks celery, cut
   into 1½-inch pieces
2 green or red bell
   peppers, cut into strips

Rinse goose breast; pat dry. Cut into 1-inch thick slices. Parboil for 20 minutes. Drain, reserving broth. Cool and cut into 1-inch cubes. Sauté goose, onions, mushrooms and almonds in skillet for 15 minutes. Add salt, pepper and seasoned salt to taste. Prepare Rice-A-Roni according to package directions using reserved broth and adding celery and bell peppers halfway through cooking time. Combine goose mixture and rice mixture. Simmer for 15 minutes. Yield: 6 servings.

Approx Per Serving: Cal 160; Prot 11.6 g; Carbo 14.5 g; T Fat 7.8 g; Chol 40.3 mg; Potas 431.0 mg; Sod 343.0 mg.
Nutritional information does not include Rice-A-Roni.

SAVORY WILD GOOSE STEW

3 geese, boned, cubed
$^1/_2$ cup (about) flour
$^1/_2$ cup oil
2 envelopes dry onion
   soup mix
5 carrots, cut into
   quarters
4 stalks celery, chopped
8 small onions
2 cups frozen green beans
8 ounces fresh
   mushrooms, sliced
1 teaspoon sweet basil
1 teaspoon tarragon
2 cloves of garlic, crushed
2 bay leaves
Cavendars Greek
   seasoning to taste
6 potatoes, peeled, cut
   into halves

Rinse goose meat; pat dry. Coat with mixture of flour and salt and pepper to taste. Brown in oil in skillet. Place in large roaster. Add soup mix, carrots, celery, onions, green beans, mushrooms, seasonings and water to cover. Bake at 325 degrees for 2 hours. Reduce temperature to 275 degrees. Add potatoes. Bake for 1 hour longer. Thicken if desired. Bake until goose is tender. Remove bay leaves. Yield: 10 servings.

Approx Per Serving: Cal 502; Prot 42.9 g; Carbo 46.8 g; T Fat 17.4 g; Chol 233.0 mg; Potas 875.0 mg; Sod 167.0 mg.

GROUSE AND WILD RICE

$^2/_3$ cup wild rice
2 cups chicken broth
$^1/_4$ cup butter
8 grouse breast filets
3 eggs, beaten
$^1/_2$ cup flour
Garlic salt, oregano and
   basil to taste
2 tablespoons butter
$^1/_2$ cup chicken broth
4 ounces mozzarella
   cheese, sliced

Combine wild rice with 2 cups broth and $^1/_4$ cup butter in saucepan. Cook, covered, until tender; keep warm. Rinse grouse filets; pat dry. Pound filets between waxed paper with meat mallet until tender. Combine with eggs in bowl. Let stand for 1 hour. Combine flour, garlic salt, oregano, basil and pepper to taste in bowl. Roll filets in flour mixture, coating well. Brown on both sides in 2 tablespoons butter in skillet. Add enough remaining broth to cover bottom of skillet. Simmer, covered, for 10 minutes. Place $^1/_2$ slice cheese on each filet. Cook just until cheese is melted. Serve with rice. Yield: 4 servings.

Approx Per Serving: Cal 978; Prot 102.0 g; Carbo 38.8 g; T Fat 29.7 g; Chol 632.0 mg; Potas 256.0 mg; Sod 833.0 mg.

PARTRIDGE CORDON BLEU

1 egg
1/2 cup milk
1 cup cornflake crumbs
1 teaspoon parsley flakes
1/2 teaspoon paprika
1/2 teaspoon salt
1/2 teaspoon pepper
8 grouse breast filets
4 slices ham
4 slices Swiss cheese
Oil for frying

Beat egg and milk in small bowl. Combine cornflake crumbs, parsley flakes, paprika, salt and pepper in bowl. Rinse grouse filets; pat dry. Pound thin with meat mallet. Place ham slices and cheese slices on 4 filets. Top with remaining filets, pressing edges to seal. Dip in egg mixture. Coat well with crumb mixture. Place on plate. Chill for 1 hour or longer. Fry in 1/2-inch oil in skillet over medium heat for 2 minutes on each side. Serve with baked potato and favorite vegetable. Yield: 4 servings.

Approx Per Serving: Cal 415; Prot 47.3 g; Carbo 17.6 g; T Fat 10.4 g; Chol 253.0 mg; Potas 184.0 mg; Sod 917.0 mg.
Nutritional information does not include oil for frying.

CHILI PHEASANT

8 pheasant breasts, boned
1 1/2 7-ounce cans
   chopped green chilies
8 ounces Monterey Jack
   cheese, cut into 8 strips
1/4 cup bread crumbs
1/4 cup Parmesan cheese
1 tablespoon chili powder
1/2 teaspoon salt
1/4 teaspoon pepper
1/4 teaspoon cumin
10 tablespoons melted
   butter
1   15-ounce can tomato
   sauce
1/2 teaspoon cumin
1/3 cup sliced green onion
Hot pepper sauce to taste

Flatten pheasant breasts with meat mallet to 1/4-inch thickness. Place 1 tablespoon green chiles and 1 strip Monterey Jack cheese on each breast. Roll to enclose filling; secure with toothpicks. Combine bread crumbs, Parmesan cheese, chili powder, 1/2 teaspoon salt and 1/4 teaspoon each pepper and cumin; mix well. Dip breast rolls in butter; coat with crumb mixture. Place in baking dish. Chill for 4 hours or longer. Drizzle with remaining butter. Bake at 400 degrees for 20 to 30 minutes or until brown. Combine tomato sauce, 1/2 teaspoon cumin, onion and remaining chilies with hot pepper sauce, salt and pepper to taste in saucepan. Cook until heated through. Spoon over rolls.
Yield: 10 servings.

Approx Per Serving: Cal 334; Prot 20.8 g; Carbo 8.2 g; T Fat 24.5 g; Chol 96.0 mg; Potas 434.0 mg; Sod 600.0 mg.

PHEASANT CASSEROLE

2 pheasant breasts, cooked
1   10-ounce package
    frozen French-style
    green beans
1/2 cup melted butter
1 package Pepperidge
    Farm stuffing mix
1/4 cup chicken broth
1 can cream of mushroom
    soup
1/2 cup chicken broth
1/4 cup sour cream

Bone pheasant breasts; tear meat into large pieces. Cook green beans using package directions; drain. Combine butter, stuffing mix and 1/4 cup broth in large bowl; mix well. Spoon half the stuffing into 2-quart casserole. Arrange pheasant over top. Season with salt and pepper to taste. Mix soup with remaining 1/2 cup broth and sour cream in small bowl. Pour over pheasant. Sprinkle remaining stuffing on top. Bake at 350 degrees for 30 minutes. Yield: 4 servings.

Approx Per Serving: Cal 441; Prot 13.7 g; Carbo 22.9 g; T Fat 33.7 g;
    Chol 89.8 mg; Potas 266.0 mg; Sod 1071.0 mg.

ROAST PHEASANT IN APPLEJACK AND CREAM SAUCE

2 pheasant
1/4 cup finely chopped
    onion
2 pheasant livers,
    coarsely chopped
2 tablespoons butter
11/2 cups cubed day-old
    bread
2 tablespoons butter
1/2 cup chopped peeled
    apple
1 tablespoon parsley
2 tablespoons butter,
    softened
4 slices bacon, cut into
    halves
1/4 cup applejack
1/2 cup chicken stock
1/4 cup applejack
1/4 cup heavy cream

Rinse pheasant; pat dry inside and out. Sauté onion and livers in 2 tablespoons butter in skillet for 2 to 3 minutes, stirring frequently. Pour into bowl. Sauté bread in mixture of pan drippings and 2 tablespoons butter for 3 to 4 minutes. Add to liver mixture. Add apple, parsley and salt and pepper to taste; mix well. Rub pheasant with 2 tablespoons butter. Spoon stuffing into cavities. Truss as for chicken. Arrange bacon over breasts and legs. Place, breast side up, on rack in roasting pan. Roast at 375 degrees for 30 minutes. Sprinkle with salt and pepper to taste. Heat 1/4 cup applejack in small saucepan. Ignite; pour over pheasant. Baste with pan juices. Bake for 10 minutes longer or until brown, crisp and tender. Place pheasant on heated platter. Add chicken stock and remaining 1/4 cup applejack to pan juices. Boil for 2 to 3 minutes, stirring frequently. Add cream. Bring to a boil; adjust seasoning. Serve over pheasant.
Yield: 4 servings.

Approx Per Serving: Cal 577; Prot 30.0 g; Carbo 30.7 g; T Fat 37.0 g;
    Chol 149.0 mg; Potas 377.0 mg; Sod 568.0 mg.
    Nutritional information does not include applejack.

QUAIL WITH WHITE GRAPES

4 quail
1 tablespoon lemon juice
1/2 teaspoon seasoned salt
White pepper to taste
1/2 cup flour
1/3 cup butter
1/3 cup dry white wine
1/3 cup chicken broth
1 tablespoon lemon juice
1/4 cup seedless white
   grapes
2 tablespoons sliced
   toasted almonds

Rinse quail; pat dry inside and out. Drizzle with 1 tablespoon lemon juice. Sprinkle with seasonings. Let stand for 1 hour. Coat with flour. Sauté in butter in saucepan until golden. Add wine, broth and 1 tablespoon lemon juice. Simmer, covered, for 20 minutes. Add grapes and almonds. Cook for 5 minutes or until quail are tender. Yield: 2 servings.

Approx Per Serving: Cal 1138; Prot 73.1 g; Carbo 30.8 g; T Fat 76.4 g; Chol 82.2 mg; Potas 949.0 mg; Sod 1101.0 mg.

CROCK•POT QUAIL

8 quail, cut up
1 cup flour
1/2 cup peanut oil
2 cans cream of chicken
   soup
2 cans cream of celery
   soup
2 cans chicken broth
1/2 cup dry white wine
2 white onions, thinly
   sliced
2 bay leaves
1/3 cup grated Parmesan
   cheese

Rinse quail; pat dry inside and out. Season quail with salt and pepper to taste; coat with flour. Brown in hot peanut oil in skillet. Combine quail with soups, broth, wine, onions and bay leaves in Crock•Pot. Cook on High for 4 hours or on Low for 7 to 8 hours or until quail are tender. Remove bay leaves; add cheese. Cook for 30 minutes longer. Serve over rice or noodles. Yield: 8 servings.

Approx Per Serving: Cal 579; Prot 45.0 g; Carbo 26.3 g; T Fat 30.8 g; Chol 17.5 mg; Potas 683.5 mg; Sod 1551.1 mg.

QUAIL BAKED IN MUSHROOM SAUCE

4 quail, split
1/4 cup flour
3 tablespoons oil
1 3-ounce can sliced
  mushrooms, drained
1 can cream of mushroom
  soup
1/2 soup can white wine
1 cup sour cream

Rinse quail; pat dry inside and out. Season with salt and pepper to taste; coat with flour. Brown on both sides in oil in skillet. Arrange in shallow baking dish. Combine mushrooms, soup, wine and sour cream in bowl; mix well. Pour over quail. Bake at 350 degrees for 1 hour. Yield: 4 servings.

Approx Per Serving: Cal 681; Prot 37.9 g; Carbo 16.5 g; T Fat 48.5 g; Chol 26.4 mg; Potas 567.0 mg; Sod 830.5 mg.

STUFFED WILD TURKEY

1 10-pound wild turkey,
  dressed
8 slices bacon
1 cup chopped onion
1/4 cup chopped celery
1/2 cup water
1 package herb-seasoned
  corn bread stuffing mix
1 chicken bouillon cube
1/2 cup hot water
1/2 cup Burgundy
6 slices bacon
1/2 cup Burgundy

Rinse turkey; pat dry inside and out. Brown 8 slices bacon in skillet until crisp; drain, reserving drippings. Sauté onion and celery in reserved bacon drippings in skillet until brown. Add 1/2 cup water. Simmer for 5 minutes. Combine stuffing mix, bouillon cube dissolved in 1/2 cup hot water, 1/2 cup Burgundy, onion mixture and crumbled bacon in bowl; mix well. Stuff and truss turkey. Place turkey in roaster. Arrange 4 slices bacon across breast; wrap 1 bacon slice around each leg. Cover tightly with foil. Place lid on roaster. Bake at 300 degrees for 4 1/2 hours. Pour remaining 1/2 cup Burgundy over turkey. Bake, uncovered, for 40 minutes longer, basting every 10 minutes. Let stand for 10 minutes before slicing. Yield: 6 servings.

Approx Per Serving: Cal 995; Prot 131.0 g; Carbo 37.3 g; T Fat 29.6 g; Chol 325.0 mg; Potas 1474.0 mg; Sod 1346.0 mg.
Nutritional information does not include bacon drippings.

LAKER DELIGHT
Vegetables and Side Dishes

Laker Delight

Lake trout, once the most bountiful fish in Lake Ontario, was all but wiped out by the parasitic lamprey eel. In 1973, a Federal and State restoration program, together with sea lamprey control, brought this fish back to large and stable numbers in many of the Great Lakes.

1,000 Islands' Dressings

Cold Carrot Soup
page 29

Garden Salad Loaf
page 41

Vegetarian Chili or
page 110

Noodles Neapolitan
page 145

Buffet Vegetable Bake
page 140

Refrigerator Oatmeal Bread
page 159

Surprise Bread Pudding
page 170

ASPARAGUS DELUXE

2 pounds fresh asparagus
1/4 cup butter
6 tablespoons bread
  crumbs
1/2 teaspoon salt
1/8 teaspoon pepper
1/3 cup pancake mix
1/4 cup shredded Cheddar
  cheese
1/4 cup Parmesan cheese
3 egg whites, stiffly
  beaten

Parboil asparagus until tender-crisp; drain. Melt butter in shallow baking dish. Stir in bread crumbs. Mix salt and pepper in small bowl. Add 1/4 teaspoon salt mixture to bread crumbs; mix well. Arrange asparagus spears over bread crumbs. Prepare pancake mix using package directions. Add remaining salt mixture, Cheddar cheese and Parmesan cheese; mix well. Fold in egg whites gently. Spread over asparagus. Bake at 400 degrees for 15 minutes or until brown. Yield: 8 servings.

Approx Per Serving: Cal 126; Prot 7.3 g; Carbo 7.9 g; T Fat 8.2 g; Chol 21.4 mg; Potas 374.0 mg; Sod 306.0 mg.
Nutritional information does not include pancake mix.

MICROWAVE CHEESY ASPARAGUS

2 pounds fresh asparagus
1/2 cup evaporated milk
3 ounces cream cheese,
  softened
1 tablespoon Parmesan
  cheese
1/2 cup shredded sharp
  Cheddar cheese

Place asparagus in 2-quart glass baking dish. Sprinkle with water. Microwave, covered, on High for 4 to 4 1/2 minutes or until tender-crisp; drain. Process evaporated milk and cream cheese in blender container until smooth. Pour into 2-cup glass measure. Microwave on High for 2 minutes, stirring twice. Stir in Parmesan cheese and salt to taste. Pour over hot asparagus. Sprinkle with Cheddar cheese. Yield: 4 servings.

Approx Per Serving: Cal 230; Prot 14.7 g; Carbo 12.3 g; T Fat 15.4 g; Chol 48.3 mg; Potas 820.0 mg; Sod 211.0 mg.

NIPPY GREEN BEAN CASSEROLE

1/4 **cup melted butter**
1/4 **cup flour**
1/2 **teaspoon pepper**
1/2 **teaspoon paprika**
1 **teaspoon salt**
2 **cups milk**
1/2 **cup prepared**
  horseradish
2 **16-ounce cans**
  French-style green
  beans, drained

Blend butter, flour, pepper, paprika and salt in saucepan. Cook for several minutes. Stir in milk. Cook until thickened, stirring constantly. Add horseradish and beans. Pour bean mixture into greased 2-quart baking dish. Bake at 350 degrees for 20 minutes or until bubbly. Yield: 8 servings.

Approx Per Serving: Cal 130; Prot 4.0 g; Carbo 12.3 g; T Fat 8.0 g; Chol 23.8 mg; Potas 255.0 mg; Sod 639.0 mg.

SEVEN-BEAN CASSEROLE

1 **pound sausage**
1/2 **cup chopped onion**
1/2 **cup chopped celery**
2 **cans tomato soup**
1 **6-ounce can tomato**
  paste
2 **tablespoons brown**
  sugar
1 **16-ounce can butter**
  beans, drained
1 **16-ounce can kidney**
  beans
1 **16-ounce can green**
  beans, drained
1 **16-ounce can wax**
  beans, drained
1 **28-ounce can pork and**
  beans
1 **16-ounce can pinto**
  beans, drained
1 **16-ounce can hot chili**
  beans

Brown sausage in skillet, stirring until crumbly. Remove sausage to large bowl with slotted spoon. Drain all but 2 tablespoons drippings. Sauté onion and celery in drippings. Add to sausage. Add soup, tomato paste, brown sugar and beans; mix well. Spoon into large baking pan. Bake at 350 degrees for 1 hour. Yield: 12 servings.

Approx Per Serving: Cal 436; Prot 22.4 g; Carbo 57.8 g; T Fat 14.3 g; Chol 35.2 mg; Potas 1120.0 mg; Sod 1621.0 mg.

Ginny Sramek
Alexandria Bay, New York

GREATEST BAKED BEANS

2 pounds dried navy or
  pea beans
12 cups water
1 teaspoon soda
1 pound salt pork, cut
  into 1/2-inch pieces
1 large onion, chopped
1 cup molasses
1/2 cup sugar
1 tablespoon dry mustard
1 teaspoon pepper

Combine beans with water in large bowl. Let soak overnight. Place in large saucepan. Add soda. Bring to a boil; reduce heat. Cook for 10 minutes. Drain into large bowl, reserving liquid. Combine salt pork, onion and beans in 5-quart baking dish. Mix 2 cups reserved liquid with remaining ingredients in bowl. Pour over beans; mix well. Add just enough reserved liquid to cover beans. Bake, covered, at 300 degrees for 2 hours. Add 2 cups reserved liquid; mix well. Bake for 2 hours longer or until beans are tender and liquid is absorbed. May uncover during last 30 minutes of baking time if preferred. Yield: 20 servings.

Approx Per Serving: Cal 248; Prot 10.7 g; Carbo 26.2 g; T Fat 11.4 g; Chol 19.1 mg; Potas 803.0 mg; Sod 419.0 mg.

Dr. Harold J. Lyness
Baldwinsville, New York

BROCCOLI AND NOODLES

2 6-ounce packages
  small noodles, cooked
1/4 cup butter
2 bunches green onions,
  finely chopped
1/4 cup butter
2 10-ounce packages
  frozen chopped
  broccoli, cooked
1 can cheese soup
1/2 teaspoon rosemary
1 teaspoon
  Worcestershire sauce
Tabasco sauce to taste
1 cup shredded Cheddar
  cheese

Mix noodles and 1/4 cup butter in large bowl. Sauté green onions in 1/4 cup butter in skillet. Add sautéed green onions, broccoli, soup, rosemary, Worcestershire sauce and Tabasco sauce to noodles; mix well. Spoon into greased baking dish. Top with cheese. Bake at 350 degrees for 50 minutes. Yield: 10 servings.

Approx Per Serving: Cal 309; Prot 10.4 g; Carbo 32.1 g; T Fat 15.9g; Chol 43.7 mg; Potas 268.0 mg; Sod 389.0 mg.

CARROT AND APPLE CASSEROLE

1 cup sliced peeled carrots
2 cups cooked sliced
   apples
1 tablespoon lemon juice
1/2 cup sugar
1 tablespoon cornstarch
1 tablespoon margarine

Cook carrots in a small amount of water in saucepan until tender-crisp; drain. Combine with apples in greased 1-quart baking dish. Sprinkle with lemon juice. Stir in mixture of sugar and cornstarch. Dot with margarine. Bake at 350 degrees for 30 minutes. Yield: 6 servings.

Approx Per Serving: Cal 116; Prot 0.3 g; Carbo 25.5 g; T Fat 2.1 g; Chol 0.0 mg; Potas 106.0 mg; Sod 29.1 mg.

CARROT AND RICE BAKE

3 cups shredded carrots
1 1/2 cups water
2/3 cup uncooked rice
1/2 teaspoon salt
1 1/2 cups shredded
   Cheddar cheese
1 cup milk
2 eggs, beaten
2 tablespoons onion flakes
1/4 teaspoon pepper
1/2 cup shredded
   Cheddar cheese

Combine carrots, water, rice and salt in saucepan. Bring to a boil; reduce heat. Simmer, covered, for 15 minutes or until rice is tender. Stir in 1 1/2 cups cheese, milk, eggs, onion flakes and pepper. Spoon into 6x10-inch baking dish. Bake at 350 degrees for 20 to 25 minutes or until set. Top with 1/2 cup cheese. Bake for 2 minutes longer or until cheese is melted. Yield: 6 servings.

Approx Per Serving: Cal 304; Prot 14.8 g; Carbo 25.5 g; T Fat 15.9 g; Chol 136.0 mg; Potas 329.0 mg; Sod 472.0 mg.

SCALLOPED CORN

1 16-ounce can
   cream-style corn
1 cup milk
1 egg, beaten
1/4 cup chopped onion
1/4 cup chopped pimento
3/4 teaspoon salt
1 1/2 cups cracker crumbs
1 tablespoon melted
   butter

Combine corn, milk, egg, onion, pimento and salt in bowl; mix well. Stir in 3/4 cup cracker crumbs. Spoon into buttered 1 1/2-quart baking dish. Top with mixture of remaining 3/4 cup cracker crumbs and butter. Bake at 350 degrees for 30 to 45 minutes or until knife inserted in center comes out clean. Yield: 4 servings.

Approx Per Serving: Cal 303; Prot 6.8 g; Carbo 48.2 g; T Fat 9.8 g; Chol 95.0 mg; Potas 311.0 mg; Sod 1197.0 mg.

BAKED ONIONS

8 medium onions
3 ounces cream cheese,
    softened
1 can cream of mushroom
    soup
2 6-ounce cans tomato
    paste
1 4-ounce can chopped
    pimento, drained
1 tablespoon
    Worcestershire sauce
2 hard-boiled eggs,
    chopped
4 slices bread, toasted,
    crumbled

Cook whole onions in water to cover in saucepan just until tender; drain. Slice onions. Combine cream cheese, soup, tomato paste, pimento and Worcestershire sauce in bowl; mix well. Mix in eggs. Reserve 1/3 of the crumbs. Layer onions, remaining crumbs and soup mixture 1/2 at a time in greased baking dish. Top with reserved crumbs. Bake at 350 degrees until bubbly.
Yield: 8 servings.

Approx Per Serving: Cal 230; Prot 7.8 g; Carbo 31.2 g; T Fat 9.4 g; Chol 80.6 mg; Potas 729.0 mg; Sod 477.0 mg.

COLCANNON

2 pounds potatoes, peeled,
    cut into quarters
5 tablespoons margarine
2 cups shredded cabbage
6 scallions, chopped
1/2 cup hot milk
1 teaspoon salt   ·
1/4 teaspoon pepper
3 tablespoons margarine

Cook potatoes in water to cover in saucepan until tender. Melt 5 tablespoons margarine in saucepan over low heat. Add cabbage and scallions. Cook, tightly covered, over low heat for 5 minutes or until tender. Drain potatoes. Add hot milk gradually, beating until fluffy. Beat in salt and pepper. Add cabbage; mix well. Spoon into serving dish. Dot with 3 tablespoons margarine. Serve with seafood. Yield: 6 servings.

Approx Per Serving: Cal 321; Prot 4.7 g; Carbo 41.0 g; T Fat 16.0 g; Chol 2.8 mg; Potas 746.0 mg; Sod 558.0 mg.

Ginny Sramek
Alexandria Bay, New York

POTATO CASSEROLE

2 pounds frozen hashed
  brown potatoes, thawed
1/2 cup melted margarine
1 can cream of mushroom
  soup
1/2 cup chopped onion
2 cups sour cream
2 cups shredded Cheddar
  cheese
1 teaspoon salt
1/4 teaspoon pepper
1 cup bread crumbs

Combine potatoes, margarine, soup, onion, sour cream, cheese, salt and pepper in bowl; mix well. Spoon into 9x13-inch baking dish. Top with bread crumbs. Bake at 350 degrees for 1 hour. Yield: 6 servings.

Approx Per Serving: Cal 903; Prot 19.9 g; Carbo 63.5 g; T Fat 65.9 g; Chol 75.1 mg; Potas 894.0 mg; Sod 1394.0 mg.

RATATOUILLE

2 medium onions, thinly
  sliced
1 clove of garlic, crushed
1/3 cup olive oil
3 small zucchini, sliced
1 medium eggplant, cubed
3 tomatoes, coarsely
  chopped
1 large green bell pepper,
  cut into strips
1/2 teaspoon oregano
1 teaspoon salt
1/4 teaspoon pepper

Sauté onions and garlic in olive oil in large skillet. Layer zucchini, eggplant, tomatoes and green pepper over onions, sprinkling each layer with seasonings. Simmer for 20 to 25 minutes or until vegetables are tender. Serve hot or cold. Yield: 6 servings.

Approx Per Serving: Cal 160; Prot 2.6 g; Carbo 12.1 g; T Fat 12.4 g; Chol 0.0 mg; Potas 496.0 mg; Sod 365.0 mg.

STIR-FRIED SQUASH

1/4 cup oil
4 yellow squash, cut into
   1-inch strips
1 large onion, sliced
1 large green bell pepper,
   cut into strips
1/4 cup soy sauce
Garlic powder to taste

Heat oil in skillet until very hot. Add squash, onion, green pepper and soy sauce. Stir-fry until vegetables are tender. Sprinkle with garlic powder, salt and pepper to taste. Yield: 6 servings.

Approx Per Serving: Cal 112; Prot 1.8 g; Carbo 6.7 g; T Fat 9.4 g; Chol 0.0 mg; Potas 222.0 mg; Sod 689.0 mg.

SWEET POTATO BAKE

4 large sweet potatoes,
   cooked
1/4 cup warm milk
1 tablespoon butter
1 teaspoon salt
3/4 cup drained crushed
   pineapple
3 bananas
2 tablespoons butter
1/4 cup packed brown
   sugar
1/2 teaspoon cinnamon

Peel and mash sweet potatoes in bowl. Add milk, 1 tablespoon butter and salt; beat until light and fluffy. Spoon into 1-quart baking dish. Spoon half the pineapple over sweet potatoes. Slice bananas 1/2 inch thick over pineapple. Dot with 2 tablespoons butter. Spoon remaining pineapple over top. Sprinkle with brown sugar and cinnamon. Bake at 350 degrees for 30 minutes. Yield: 8 servings.

Approx Per Serving: Cal 179; Prot 1.8 g; Carbo 34.0 g; T Fat 4.9 g; Chol 12.7 mg; Potas 428.0 mg; Sod 316.0 mg.

FRIED GREEN TOMATOES

2/3 cup cornmeal
1 teaspoon salt
1/8 teaspoon pepper
4 firm green tomatoes
5 tablespoons bacon
   drippings

Mix cornmeal, salt and pepper in shallow bowl. Slice tomatoes 1/4 inch thick. Dip slices into cornmeal, coating well. Fry in bacon drippings in skillet until tender and brown. Yield: 6 servings.

Approx Per Serving: Cal 176; Prot 1.9 g; Carbo 15.4 g; T Fat 12.0 g; Chol 70.0 mg; Potas 188.0 mg; Sod 479.0 mg.

GREEN AND GOLD CASSEROLE

1 pound zucchini, sliced
1¹/₂ cups small-curd
  cottage cheese
2 tablespoons sour cream
2 tablespoons flour
1 tablespoon lemon juice
2 eggs
¹/₄ teaspoon Tabasco sauce
¹/₄ teaspoon pepper
1 16-ounce can corn,
  drained
2 tablespoons chopped
  green chilies
¹/₂ cup shredded Cheddar
  cheese
¹/₂ cup bread crumbs

Cook zucchini in a small amount of water in saucepan until tender-crisp; drain. Combine cottage cheese, sour cream, flour, lemon juice, eggs, Tabasco sauce and pepper in blender container. Process until smooth. Combine with zucchini, corn and green chilies in bowl; mix well. Spoon into 1¹/₂-quart baking dish. Top with Cheddar cheese and bread crumbs. Bake at 350 degrees for 45 minutes. Yield: 6 servings.

Approx Per Serving: Cal 244; Prot 15.4 g; Carbo 26.7 g; T Fat 9.5 g; Chol 112.0 mg; Potas 415.0 mg; Sod 538.0 mg.

BUFFET VEGETABLE BAKE

2 10-ounce packages
  frozen mixed peas and
  carrots
1 10-ounce package
  frozen green beans
1 5-ounce can sliced
  water chestnuts,
  drained
1 3-ounce can broiled in
  butter sliced
  mushrooms
1 can cream of mushroom
  soup
3 tablespoons Sherry
1 teaspoon
  Worcestershire sauce
Dash of hot pepper sauce
2 cups shredded sharp
  Cheddar cheese
¹/₄ cup butter cracker
  crumbs

Cook frozen vegetables using package directions until tender-crisp; drain. Combine with water chestnuts and mushrooms in bowl; mix well. Combine soup, Sherry, Worcestershire sauce, pepper sauce and cheese in bowl. Add to vegetables; mix well. Spoon into greased 2-quart baking dish. Bake at 350 degrees until bubbly, stirring occasionally. Sprinkle with crumbs. Bake for 5 minutes longer. Yield: 10 servings.

Approx Per Serving: Cal 192; Prot 8.9 g; Carbo 15.9 g; T Fat 10.8 g; Chol 24.2 mg; Potas 285.0 mg; Sod 499.0 mg.

PINEAPPLE BAKE

4 20-ounce cans
    juice-pack pineapple
    chunks, drained
2 cups sugar
²/₃ cup flour
3 cups shredded Cheddar
    cheese
2 cups butter cracker
    crumbs
1 cup melted butter

Place pineapple in greased baking dish. Sprinkle with mixture of sugar and flour. Top with Cheddar cheese and cracker crumbs. Drizzle with butter. Bake at 350 degrees for 30 minutes. Serve with entrées or as dessert. Yield: 10 servings.

Approx Per Serving: Cal 601; Prot 10.9 g; Carbo 67.4 g; T Fat 35.2 g; Chol 85.4 mg; Potas 140.0 mg; Sod 535.0 mg.

EASY CRANBERRY RELISH

1 3-ounce package
    orange gelatin
1 cup hot water
1 pound cranberries,
    ground
1 cup sugar
1 20-ounce can crushed
    pineapple

Dissolve gelatin in hot water in medium bowl. Stir in cranberries, sugar and pineapple. Chill until serving time. Yield: 8 servings.

Approx Per Serving: Cal 218; Prot 1.5 g; Carbo 55.7 g; T Fat 0.2 g; Chol 0.0 mg; Potas 115.0 mg; Sod 35.8 mg.

Phyllis Wendt
Constableville, New York

CURRIED FRUIT

1 16-ounce can peach
    halves
1 16-ounce can pear
    halves
1 16-ounce can
    pineapple chunks
¹/₃ cup margarine
1 cup packed brown sugar
¹/₂ teaspoon curry powder

Drain peaches, pears and pineapple. Place fruit in large baking dish. Melt margarine and brown sugar in saucepan. Stir in curry powder. Drizzle over fruit. Bake at 325 degrees for 45 minutes or until bubbly. Yield: 10 servings.

Approx Per Serving: Cal 238; Prot 0.5 g; Carbo 48.2 g; T Fat 6.2 g; Chol 0.0 mg; Potas 197.0 mg; Sod 86.0 mg.

BEST BREAD AND BUTTER PICKLES

2¹/4 cups cider vinegar
³/4 cup water
3 cups sugar
4 teaspoons mustard seed
¹/2 teaspoon alum
2 teaspoons turmeric
1 teaspoon dry mustard
4 quarts sliced cucumbers
8 onions, sliced
2 green bell peppers,
  sliced
2 red bell peppers, sliced

Combine vinegar, water, sugar, mustard seed, alum, turmeric and dry mustard in large saucepan; mix well. Add cucumbers, onions, green peppers and red peppers. Bring to a boil. Spoon into 8 hot sterilized 1-pint jars, leaving ¹/2-inch head space; seal with 2-piece lids. Yield: 64 servings.

Approx Per Servings: Cal 49; Prot 0.4 g; Carbo 12.4 g; T Fat 0.1 g; Chol 0.0 mg; Potas 93.9 mg; Sod 1.5 mg.

Phyllis Wendt
Constableville, New York

OVERNIGHT PICKLED VEGETABLES

1 cup sugar
2 teaspoons pickling spice
1 cup water
²/3 cup vinegar
2 medium zucchini, sliced
  ¹/2 inch thick
3 medium carrots, cut
  into ¹/2x1¹/2-inch sticks
2 medium red bell
  peppers, cut into
  ¹/2x1¹/2-inch sticks
1 small yellow squash,
  sliced ¹/2 inch thick

Bring sugar, pickling spice and water to a boil in saucepan; reduce heat. Simmer for 5 minutes; do not stir. Cool. Stir in vinegar. Pack zucchini slices into 1-quart jar. Stand carrots and red pepper sticks on zucchini layer. Pack yellow squash slices on top. Pour vinegar mixture over vegetables; seal. Chill for 1 to 3 days. Serve with hamburgers, roast or on sandwiches. Yield: 24 servings.

Approx Per Serving: Cal 41; Prot 0.4 g; Carbo 10.6 g; T Fat 0.1 g; Chol 0.0 mg; Potas 89.7 mg; Sod 4.1 mg.

CANDIED DILLS

1¹/₂-quart jar sliced dill
   pickles, drained
2³/₄ cups sugar
2 cups cider vinegar
2 tablespoons pickling
   spices

Combine pickles with sugar and vinegar in bowl. Add pickling spices tied in cheesecloth bag. Let stand at room temperature for 4 hours, stirring occasionally to dissolve sugar well. Drain, reserving vinegar. Layer half the pickles, spice bag and remaining pickles in jar. Fill jar with vinegar; seal. Chill for 4 days or longer before serving. Remove spice bag after 7 days. Yield: 24 servings.

Approx Per Serving: Cal 94; Prot 0.3 g; Carbo 24.8 g; T Fat 0.1 g;
Chol 0.0 mg; Potas 96.4 mg; Sod 432.0 mg.

Phyllis Wendt
Constableville, New York

CROCK•POT DRESSING

2 cups chopped onion
2 cups chopped celery
1   4-ounce can chopped
   mushrooms, drained
1 cup butter
12 cups dry bread crumbs
2 eggs, beaten
1 teaspoon poultry
   seasoning
1¹/₂ teaspoons salt
1¹/₂ teaspoons sage
¹/₂ teaspoon pepper
1 teaspoon thyme
4¹/₂ cups (about) chicken
   broth

Sauté onion, celery and mushrooms in butter in skillet. Combine with bread crumbs in large bowl; mix well. Mix in eggs, poultry seasoning, salt, sage, pepper and thyme. Stir in enough broth to moisten. Spoon loosely into Crock•Pot. Cook on High for 45 to 60 minutes. Turn Crock•Pot temperature to Low. Cook for 4 to 8 hours, adding additional broth if necessary. Yield: 10 servings.

Approx Per Serving: Cal 681; Prot 20.0 g; Carbo 91.9 g; T Fat 26.3 g;
Chol 111.0 mg; Potas 428.0 mg; Sod 1791.0 mg.

POTATO DRESSING

3 pounds potatoes,
  cooked, mashed
6 slices bread, cubed
1 medium onion, chopped
2 cups chopped celery

Combine potatoes, bread, onion, celery and salt and pepper to taste in large bowl; mix well. Spoon into baking dish. Bake, covered, at 350 degrees for 1 hour. May use to stuff turkey or round steak if preferred.
Yield: 10 servings.

Approx Per Serving: Cal 202; Prot 4.9 g; Carbo 44.6 g; T Fat 0.9 g;
Chol 0.0 mg; Potas 680.0 mg; Sod 119.0 mg.

GRITS CASSEROLE

2 cups grits, cooked
1 6-ounce roll garlic
  cheese
2 tablespoons butter
1 cup light cream
4 eggs, beaten
1/2 teaspoon salt
1/8 teaspoon pepper
1/8 teaspoon Tabasco sauce
1 cup shredded Cheddar
  cheese

Combine grits, garlic cheese and butter in large bowl; mix well. Stir in cream, eggs, salt, pepper and Tabasco sauce. Spoon into greased 3-quart baking dish. Bake at 350 degrees for 45 minutes. Sprinkle with Cheddar cheese. Bake for 15 minutes longer.
Yield: 10 servings.

Approx Per Serving: Cal 352; Prot 12.8 g; Carbo 26.1 g; T Fat 21.7 g;
Chol 172.0 mg; Potas 120.0 mg; Sod 231.0 mg.

PARTY MACARONI

1 1/2 cups milk, scalded
1 cup soft bread cubes
1/4 cup chopped pimento
1/4 cup chopped green bell
  pepper
1 tablespoon minced
  onion
1/4 cup margarine
1 1/2 cups shredded
  Cheddar cheese
3 eggs, slightly beaten
1 cup macaroni, cooked

Pour milk over bread cubes; set aside. Sauté pimento, green pepper and onion in margarine in skillet until golden brown. Stir into bread mixture. Add cheese, eggs, macaroni and salt and pepper to taste; mix well. Spoon into greased 9x12-inch baking dish. Bake at 325 degrees for 50 minutes.
Yield: 4 servings.

Approx Per Serving: Cal 623; Prot 26.1 g; Carbo 53.0 g; T Fat 33.8 g;
Chol 263.0 mg; Potas 368.0 mg; Sod 527.0 mg.

PASTA WITH PESTO

3/4 cup olive oil
1 1/2 cups fresh basil leaves
2 cloves of garlic
1/2 cup pine nuts
1 cup fresh sprigs of
   parsley
3/4 cup grated Romano
   cheese
1 teaspoon salt
1   8-ounce package
   vermicelli, cooked,
   drained

Combine olive oil, basil, garlic, pine nuts, parsley and cheese in blender container; process until smooth. Add salt. Process to mix well. Combine with hot vermicelli in serving dish; mix well. Yield: 6 servings.

   Approx Per Serving: Cal 442; Prot 10.5 g; Carbo 15.5 g; T Fat 40.0 g;
      Chol 11.8 mg; Potas 209.0 mg; Sod 502.0 mg.

NOODLES NEAPOLITAN

1 large onion, chopped
2 cloves of garlic, minced
1 tablespoon oil
8 cups chopped tomatoes
1   6-ounce can tomato
   paste
1/8 teaspoon oregano
1/4 teaspoon basil
1 1/2 teaspoons salt
8 ounces wide egg
   noodles, cooked,
   drained
8 ounces Muenster
   cheese, sliced

Sauté onion and garlic in oil in large saucepan over low heat for 10 to 15 minutes or until tender. Add tomatoes, tomato paste, oregano, basil and salt; mix well. Bring mixture to a boil; reduce heat. Simmer, covered, for 1 1/2 hours or until of consistency of chili sauce. Alternate layers of noodles, sauce and cheese in greased 3-quart baking dish until all ingredients are used. Bake at 350 degrees for 30 minutes or until sauce is bubbly and cheese is melted. May be prepared the day ahead to improve flavor. Yield: 8 servings.

   Approx Per Serving: Cal 267; Prot 11.8 g; Carbo 31.3 g; T Fat 10.9 g;
      Chol 27.0 mg; Potas 519.0 mg; Sod 600.0 mg.

Toni Stanton
Carthage, New York

NOODLE PUDDING

1   16-ounce package
 wide noodles
3 eggs, beaten
1/4 cup sugar
16 ounces cottage cheese
1/4 cup margarine

Cook noodles using package directions; drain. Place in lightly greased baking dish. Combine eggs, sugar and cottage cheese in mixer bowl; mix well. Add to noodles; mix well. Dot with margarine. Bake at 350 degrees for 1 1/2 hours. Yield: 10 servings.

Approx Per Serving: Cal 298; Prot 13.2 g; Carbo 40.5 g; T Fat 8.7 g;
 Chol 88.9 mg; Potas 160.0 mg; Sod 259.0 mg.

Ruth Oot
Watertown, New York

BROWN RICE

2 teaspoons instant beef
 bouillon
3 tablespoons dry onion
 soup mix
3 cups boiling water
1/2 cup margarine
1 cup rice
1   4-ounce can
 mushrooms, drained

Dissolve bouillon and soup mix in boiling water in saucepan. Melt margarine in baking dish. Add rice, mushrooms and soup mixture; mix well. Bake at 350 degrees for 45 minutes or until rice is tender, stirring occasionally. Use only 1/2 cup margarine when doubling recipe. Yield: 6 servings.

Approx Per Serving: Cal 293; Prot 5.1 g; Carbo 29.2 g; T Fat 17.4 g;
 Chol 2.4 mg; Potas 114.0 mg; Sod 2999.0 mg.

RICE CASSEROLE

1   5-ounce package long
 grain and wild rice mix
1   12-ounce can
 Mexicorn, drained
1/2 cup margarine,
 softened
1 can cream of celery soup
1 cup shredded Cheddar
 cheese

Prepare rice using package directions. Add Mexicorn, margarine and soup; mix well. Spoon into 8x10-inch baking dish. Top with cheese. Bake at 350 degrees for 20 to 30 minutes or until golden brown.
Yield: 10 servings.

Approx Per Serving: Cal 231; Prot 5.6 g; Carbo 20.4 g; T Fat 14.5 g;
 Chol 15.1 mg; Potas 97.8 mg; Sod 721.0 mg.

GREEN RICE

1 onion, chopped
2 cups minute rice
3 tablespoons margarine
1/2 teaspoon salt
2 cups water
1   10-ounce package
    frozen chopped broccoli
1 can cream of mushroom
    soup
1   8-ounce jar Cheez
    Whiz
1/2   3-ounce can French-
    fried onions, crushed

Sauté chopped onion and rice in margarine in skillet until brown. Stir in salt and water. Bring to a boil; remove from heat. Let stand, covered, for 20 minutes. Cook broccoli in saucepan just until tender-crisp; drain. Heat soup and Cheez Whiz in saucepan until cheese is melted. Stir in broccoli and rice. Spoon into greased baking dish. Top with crushed onions. Bake at 350 degrees for 20 minutes or until heated through.
Yield: 6 servings.

Approx Per Serving: Cal 492; Prot 14.5 g; Carbo 63.0 g; T Fat 20.2 g; Chol 27.0 mg; Potas 323.0 mg; Sod 1102.0 mg.

HERBED RICE

1 cup rice
1 tablespoon each thyme
    summer savory, basil
    and tarragon
1 teaspoon rosemary
2 tablespoons parsley
3 tablespoons butter

Cook rice using package directions. Add thyme, summer savory, basil, tarragon, rosemary, parsley and butter; mix lightly to coat well. Serve hot. Yield: 4 servings.

Approx Per Serving: Cal 132; Prot 1.1 g; Carbo 12.4 g; T Fat 8.7 g; Chol 23.3 mg; Potas 17.1 mg; Sod 72.6 mg.

RICE PRIMAVERA

1 1/2 pounds zucchini,
3/4 cup chopped onion
3 tablespoons margarine
3 cups cooked rice
1   16-ounce can tomatoes
1   16-ounce can whole
    kernel corn, drained
1/2 teaspoon oregano
1 1/2 teaspoons salt
1/4 teaspoon pepper

Cut zucchini into thin slices. Sauté onion and zucchini in margarine in skillet until tender. Add rice, tomatoes, corn, oregano, salt and pepper; mix well. Simmer for 15 minutes. Yield: 8 servings.

Approx Per Serving: Cal 196; Prot 4.8 g; Carbo 35.2 g; T Fat 5.2 g; Chol 0.0 mg; Potas 470.0 mg; Sod 676.0 mg.

RICE PILAF

2 cups long grain rice
1/4 cup butter
1/4 teaspoon saffron
1 teaspoon salt
1/4 teaspoon freshly
  ground pepper
3 10-ounce cans
  consommé
1 cup raisins
2 medium onions, thinly
  sliced into rings
1/4 cup butter

Sauté rice in 1/4 cup butter in Dutch oven until golden brown. Stir in saffron, salt, pepper and consommé. Bake, covered, for 1 1/2 hours. Stir in raisins. Let stand for 5 minutes. Sauté onions in 1/4 cup butter in skillet. Spoon rice onto serving plate. Top with sautéed onions. Yield: 10 servings.

Approx Per Serving: Cal 281; Prot 4.5 g; Carbo 45.3 g; T Fat 9.7 g; Chol 25.1 mg; Potas 257.0 mg; Sod 572.0 mg.

CREAMY CHEESE SAUCE

1/4 cup sliced green onions
1 tablespoon butter
1 can cream of mushroom
  soup
1/2 cup sour cream
1 teaspoon lemon juice
1 cup shredded Cheddar
  cheese

Sauté green onions in butter in saucepan until tender. Stir in soup, sour cream and lemon juice. Heat until well blended. Add cheese. Cook until cheese is melted, stirring constantly. Serve over cooked vegetables or fish. Yield: 6 servings.

Approx Per Serving: Cal 148; Prot 6.5 g; Carbo 3.7 g; T Fat 12.4 g; Chol 33.5 mg; Potas 247.0 mg; Sod 145.0 mg.

HORSERADISH SAUCE

2/3 cup sour cream
1/4 cup drained prepared
  horseradish

Mix sour cream and horseradish in bowl. Add salt to taste. Chill until serving time. Serve with fish or pork. Yield: 10 servings.

Approx Per Serving: Cal 35.4; Prot 0.6 g; Carbo 1.2 g; T Fat 3.2 g; Chol 6.8 mg; Potas 40.0 mg; Sod 13.8 mg.

Yvonne Schriock
Carthage, New York

Breads

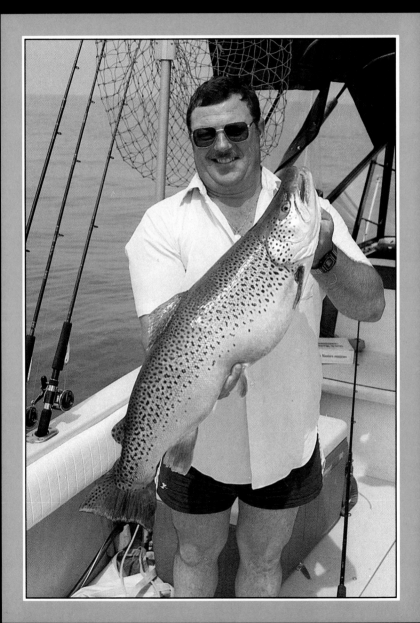

Bred to Fight

"Brute" brown trout, like the one displayed in our photo, are raised in large numbers in our State hatchery and have become the most sought-after fish by the angler when the spring ice goes out in Lake Ontario. Prized for their ability to strike and fight, and for the fine eating fish they are, brown trout are a welcome addition to any fresh water fisheries.

Golden Crescent Brunch Buffet

Sweet and Sour Sausage Bites
page 28

Eggs Florentine or
page 109

Canadian Bacon and Egg Bake
page 97

Curried Fruit
page 141

Sugary Apple Spiced Muffins
page 159

Yeast Bread Sweet Rolls
page 165

Cold Strawberry Soup
page 34

SAUSAGE AND SOUR CREAM BISCUITS

1 8-ounce package
  brown and serve
  sausage links
1 cup melted margarine
1 cup sour cream
2 cups self-rising flour

Cook sausage links for half the time given in package directions. Slice links 1/4 inch thick. Blend margarine and sour cream in large bowl. Add flour; mix well. Drop by teaspoonfuls into ungreased miniature muffin cups. Press sausage slices lightly into dough. Bake at 450 degrees for 15 minutes. Yield: 30 biscuits.

Approx Per Biscuit: Cal 129; Prot 2.3 g; Carbo 6.7 g; T Fat 10.7 g; Chol 8.6 mg; Potas 36.3 mg; Sod 226.0 mg.

SCONES WITH MOCK DEVONSHIRE CREAM

2 cups flour
1/2 teaspoon soda
1/2 teaspoon cream of
  tartar
1 1/2 tablespoons sugar
1/2 teaspoon salt
2 tablespoons unsalted
  butter
1 cup (or less) buttermilk
Mock Devonshire Cream

Sift flour, soda, cream of tartar, sugar and salt into large bowl. Cut in butter until crumbly. Stir in enough buttermilk to make a medium dough. Knead 2 or 3 times on floured surface. Roll 1/2 inch thick; cut with 2-inch cutter. Place on baking sheet. Bake at 475 degrees for 15 minutes or until golden brown. Split scones. Serve with strawberry jam and Mock Devonshire Cream. Yield: 10 servings.

Approx Per Serving: Cal 128; Prot 3.5 g; Carbo 22.1 g; T Fat 2.8 g; Chol 7.1 mg; Potas 61.7 mg; Sod 174.0 mg.

MOCK DEVONSHIRE CREAM

3 ounces cream cheese,
  softened
1/4 cup sour cream
2 1/2 tablespoons
  confectioners' sugar
1/4 cup whipping cream

Blend cream cheese and sour cream in mixer bowl until light and fluffy. Beat in confectioners' sugar and cream. Chill for 1 hour. Yield: 10 servings.

Approx Per Serving: Cal 159; Prot 0.9 g; Carbo 25.4 g; T Fat 6.4 g; Chol 20.0 mg; Potas 24.0 mg; Sod 31.0 mg.

OVERNIGHT COFFEE CAKE

1 cup packed light brown
  sugar
1/2 cup coconut
1 teaspoon cinnamon
1/2 cup chopped pecans
2 cups flour
1 cup sugar
2 teaspoons baking
  powder
1 teaspoon salt
2 4-ounce packages
  vanilla instant
  pudding mix
1 cup water
3/4 cup corn oil
1 teaspoon vanilla extract
4 eggs

Mix brown sugar, coconut, cinnamon and pecans in bowl; set aside. Combine flour, sugar, baking powder, salt and pudding mix in mixer bowl. Add water, oil, vanilla and eggs; mix well. Beat at low speed for 30 seconds. Beat at medium speed for 2 minutes. Layer batter and coconut mixture 1/2 at a time in greased and floured 9x13-inch baking pan. Chill overnight if desired. Bake at 325 degrees for 40 to 60 minutes or until coffee cake tests done. Yield: 15 servings.

Approx Per Serving: Cal 379; Prot 3.8 g; Carbo 56.5 g; T Fat 16.1 g; Chol 73.1 mg; Potas 110.0 mg; Sod 313.0 mg.

POPPY SEED COFFEE CAKE

1/4 cup poppy seed
1 cup buttermilk
1 teaspoon almond extract
1 cup margarine, softened
1 1/2 cups sugar
4 egg yolks
2 1/2 cups flour
1 teaspoon soda
1/8 teaspoon salt
4 egg whites, stiffly beaten
1/2 cup sugar
1 teaspoon cinnamon

Combine poppy seed, buttermilk and almond extract in bowl. Let stand for several minutes. Cream margarine, 1 1/2 cups sugar and egg yolks in mixer bowl. Add mixture of sifted flour, soda and salt alternately with poppy seed mixture, mixing well after each addition. Fold in stiffly beaten egg whites gently. Mix 1/2 cup sugar and cinnamon in small bowl. Layer batter and cinnamon-sugar 1/2 at a time in greased bundt pan. Cut through with knife to marbleize. Bake at 350 degrees for 1 hour or until coffee cake tests done. Cool in pan for 10 minutes. Invert onto serving plate; serve warm.
Yield: 16 servings.

Approx Per Serving: Cal 296; Prot 4.2 g; Carbo 40.8 g; T Fat 13.1 g; Chol 68.6 mg; Potas 64.4 mg; Sod 233.0 mg.

JALAPEÑO CORN BREAD

3 cups corn bread mix
2 large onions, grated
1 cup cream-style corn
1¹/₂ cups shredded
  longhorn cheese
2 tablespoons sugar
1 clove of garlic, minced
3 eggs, beaten
¹/₂ cup corn oil
2 cups milk
1 pound bacon,
  crisp-fried, crumbled
1 cup chopped jalapeño
  peppers

Combine corn bread mix, onions, corn, cheese, sugar and garlic in bowl. Add eggs, oil and milk; mix well. Stir in bacon and peppers. Pour into greased 9x13-inch baking pan. Bake at 400 degrees for 35 to 40 minutes or until golden brown. Yield: 12 servings.

Approx Per Serving: Cal 581; Prot 21.3 g; Carbo 37.6 g; T Fat 38.0 g; Chol 121.0 mg; Potas 394.0 mg; Sod 1325.0 mg.

APRICOT BREAD

1¹/₂ cups boiling water
1 cup chopped dried
  apricots
1¹/₂ cups sugar
1 egg, beaten
2¹/₂ cups sifted flour
¹/₂ teaspoon salt
¹/₂ teaspoon baking
  powder
2 teaspoons soda
1 cup chopped walnuts
1 tablespoon melted
  shortening
1 teaspoon vanilla extract

Pour boiling water over dried apricots in bowl. Let stand for 10 minutes. Beat sugar gradually into egg with spoon. Sift flour, salt, baking powder and soda into bowl. Mix in walnuts. Add to apricots alternately with egg mixture, mixing well after each addition. Stir in shortening and vanilla. Pour into greased loaf pan. Bake at 350 degrees for 1 hour or until bread tests done.
Yield: 10 servings.

Approx Per Serving: Cal 348; Prot 5.8 g; Carbo 62.0 g; T Fat 9.6 g; Chol 27.4 mg; Potas 274.0 mg; Sod 298.0 mg.

AVOCADO BREAD

2²/₃ cups sifted flour
³/₄ teaspoon cinnamon
³/₄ teaspoon allspice
³/₄ teaspoon salt
1¹/₂ teaspoons soda
1 teaspoon baking powder
¹/₂ cup butter, softened
3 eggs
1³/₄ cups plus 2
   tablespoons sugar
³/₄ cup buttermilk
1¹/₂ cups mashed avocados
³/₄ cup chopped pecans
¹/₂ cup raisins
¹/₃ cup sugar
1 teaspoon cinnamon

Sift flour, ³/₄ teaspoon cinnamon, allspice, salt, soda and baking powder together. Combine butter, eggs and 1³/₄ cups plus 2 tablespoons sugar in mixer bowl. Beat for 2 minutes. Add buttermilk and avocados; mix well. Add dry ingredients; beat for 2 minutes. Stir in pecans and raisins. Pour into 2 greased and floured loaf pans. Sprinkle with mixture of ¹/₃ cup sugar and 1 teaspoon cinnamon. Bake at 350 degrees for 1 hour or until bread tests done. Cool on wire rack.
Yield: 20 servings.

Approx Per Serving: Cal 267; Prot 3.7 g; Carbo 39.7 g; T Fat 11.4 g; Chol 53.9 mg; Potas 193.0 mg; Sod 220.0 mg.

LEMON BREAD

³/₄ cup margarine,
   softened
1¹/₄ cups sugar
3 eggs
2¹/₂ cups flour
2 teaspoons baking
   powder
1 teaspoon salt
¹/₂ cup milk
¹/₃ cup lemon juice
³/₄ cup chopped pecans
2 teaspoons grated lemon
   rind

Cream margarine and sugar in mixer bowl until light and fluffy. Blend in eggs. Add mixture of flour, baking powder and salt alternately with milk and lemon juice, mixing well after each addition. Stir in pecans and lemon rind. Pour into greased and floured loaf pan. Bake at 350 degrees for 1 hour and 10 minutes. Cool in pan for 5 minutes. Remove loaf to wire rack to cool completely. Yield: 12 servings.

Approx Per Serving: Cal 355; Prot 5.3 g; Carbo 43.5 g; T Fat 18.4 g; Chol 69.9 mg; Potas 100.0 mg; Sod 389.0 mg.

ORANGE AND PECAN HONEY BREAD

2 tablespoons shortening
1 cup honey
1 egg, beaten
1¹/₄ tablespoons grated
  orange rind
2¹/₄ cups sifted flour
2¹/₂ teaspoons baking
  powder
¹/₂ teaspoon salt
¹/₄ cup orange juice
¹/₂ cup chopped pecans

Cream shortening and honey in bowl. Add egg and orange rind; mix well. Add mixture of sifted flour, baking powder and salt alternately with orange juice, mixing well after each addition. Stir in pecans. Pour into greased and floured loaf pan. Bake at 325 degrees for 1 hour and 10 minutes. Cool on wire rack. Serve with cream cheese blended with honey if desired. Yield: 10 servings.

Approx Per Serving: Cal 281; Prot 4.1 g; Carbo 51.9 g; T Fat 7.4 g; Chol 27.4 mg; Potas 122.0 mg; Sod 198.0 mg.

PEAR BREAD

3 eggs
1 cup oil
1¹/₂ cups sugar
¹/₂ teaspoon grated lemon
  rind
1 teaspoon vanilla extract
5 fresh pears, grated
3 cups sifted flour
1 teaspoon salt
1 teaspoon soda
¹/₄ teaspoon baking
  powder
1¹/₂ teaspoons cinnamon
²/₃ cup chopped pecans
¹/₂ cup oats
¹/₄ cup flour
³/₄ cup packed light
  brown sugar
3 tablespoons melted
  margarine

Beat eggs in mixer bowl until light. Add oil, sugar, lemon rind, vanilla and pears; mix well. Sift 3 cups flour, salt, soda, baking powder and cinnamon together. Add to pear mixture; mix just until moistened. Stir in pecans. Pour into 3 greased and floured 4x7-inch loaf pans. Mix oats, ¹/₄ cup flour, brown sugar and melted margarine in bowl. Sprinkle over loaves. Bake at 325 degrees for 50 to 60 minutes or until bread tests done. Cool on wire rack. Yield: 30 servings.

Approx Per Serving: Cal 226; Prot 2.5 g; Carbo 30.4 g; T Fat 11.1 g; Chol 27.4 mg; Potas 88.2 mg; Sod 125.0 mg.

POPPY SEED BREAD

3 eggs
1¹/₂ cups oil
2¹/₂ cups sugar
3 cups flour
1¹/₂ teaspoons baking
  powder
1¹/₂ teaspoons salt
1¹/₂ cups milk
1¹/₂ teaspoons poppy seed
1¹/₂ teaspoons almond
  flavoring
1¹/₂ teaspoons butter
  flavoring
1¹/₂ teaspoons vanilla
  extract
¹/₄ cup orange juice
³/₄ cup sugar
¹/₂ teaspoon almond
  flavoring
¹/₂ teaspoon butter
  flavoring
¹/₂ teaspoon vanilla extract

Beat eggs, oil and 2¹/₂ cups sugar in mixer bowl until thick and lemon-colored. Sift flour, baking powder and salt together. Add to egg mixture alternately with milk, mixing well after each addition. Stir in poppy seed and 1¹/₂ teaspoons each flavoring. Pour into 2 lightly greased and floured loaf pans. Bake at 350 degrees for 1 hour. Cool on wire rack for 15 to 20 minutes. Combine orange juice, ³/₄ cup sugar and remaining flavorings in bowl; mix well. Spoon over loaves.
Yield: 20 servings.

Approx Per Serving: Cal 363; Prot 3.5 g; Carbo 48.0 g; T Fat 18.0 g; Chol 43.6 mg; Potas 59.9 mg; Sod 204.0 mg.

PUMPKIN AND RAISIN BREAD

²/₃ cup shortening
2²/₃ cups sugar
4 eggs
1 16-ounce can pumpkin
²/₃ cup water
3¹/₃ cups flour
2 teaspoons soda
1¹/₂ teaspoons baking
  powder
1¹/₂ teaspoons salt
1 teaspoon cinnamon
1 teaspoon cloves
²/₃ cup chopped walnuts
²/₃ cup raisins

Cream shortening and sugar in mixer bowl until light and fluffy. Blend in eggs, pumpkin and water. Add flour, soda, baking powder, salt and spices; mix well. Stir in walnuts and raisins. Spoon into 2 greased and floured 5x9-inch loaf pans. Bake at 350 degrees for 1 hour and 5 minutes or until bread tests done. Remove to wire rack to cool.
Yield: 20 servings.

Approx Per Serving: Cal 245; Prot 2.7 g; Carbo 37.1 g; T Fat 10.5 g; Chol 54.8 mg; Potas 126.0 mg; Sod 283.0 mg.

STRAWBERRY BREAD WITH CREAMY SPREAD

2 10-ounce packages
   frozen strawberries
3 cups flour
2 cups sugar
1 teaspoon soda
1 teaspoon cinnamon
1/2 teaspoon salt
1 cup oil
4 eggs
8 ounces cream cheese,
   softened
1/3 cup whipped butter
1/2 cup confectioners'
   sugar

Drain thawed strawberries, reserving 1/3 cup juice. Mix flour, sugar, soda, cinnamon and salt in bowl. Add oil, eggs and strawberries; mix well. Tint with red food coloring if desired. Spoon into 2 greased and floured 5x9-inch loaf pans. Bake at 325 degrees for 30 to 40 minutes or until bread tests done. Remove to wire rack to cool. Blend reserved strawberry juice, cream cheese, butter and confectioners' sugar in bowl until smooth. Spoon into serving dish. Serve with bread. Yield: 20 servings.

Approx Per Serving: Cal 343; Prot 4.2 g; Carbo 39.7 g; T Fat 19.2 g; Chol 75.4 mg; Potas 88.3 mg; Sod 168.8 mg.

HONEY YEAST BREAD

1 package dry yeast
1/4 cup warm (115-degree)
   water
1 egg
1/2 cup honey
1 tablespoon coriander
1/2 teaspoon cinnamon
1/4 teaspoon cloves
1 teaspoon salt
1 cup lukewarm milk
1/4 cup melted butter
4 to 5 cups flour

Dissolve yeast in warm water. Let stand in warm place for 5 minutes or until bubbly. Combine egg, honey, spices and salt in bowl; mix with wire whisk. Add yeast, milk and butter; beat until smooth. Stir in flour 1/2 cup at a time until dough forms a soft ball. Knead on lightly floured surface for 10 minutes or until smooth and elastic. Place in greased bowl, turning to grease surface. Let rise, covered, until doubled in bulk. Knead lightly for 2 minutes; shape into ball. Place in buttered 3-quart soufflé dish. Let rise, covered, for 2 1/2 hours or until doubled in bulk; dough will rise slowly. Bake at 300 degrees for 50 to 60 minutes or until top is crusty and golden brown. Yield: 12 servings.

Approx Per Serving: Cal 287; Prot 6.9 g; Carbo 52.5 g; T Fat 5.5 g; Chol 35.9 mg; Potas 102.0 mg; Sod 226.0 mg.

EGG BRAID

1 cup all-purpose flour
1 cup whole wheat flour
2 packages dry yeast
2 tablespoons sugar
2 teaspoons salt
1/2 cup water
1/2 cup milk
2 tablespoons shortening
3 eggs, beaten
2 to 21/2 cups all-purpose
  flour

Combine 1 cup all-purpose flour, whole wheat flour, yeast, sugar and salt in mixer bowl. Heat water, milk and shortening in small saucepan. Add to flour mixture; mix well. Reserve 1 tablespoon egg for glaze. Beat in remaining eggs at low speed until moistened. Beat at medium speed for 3 minutes. Stir in enough remaining flour gradually to make a firm dough. Knead on floured surface for 5 minutes or until smooth and elastic. Place in greased bowl, turning to grease surface. Let rise, covered, in warm place for 1 hour or until doubled in bulk. Divide into 3 portions. Roll into ropes on floured surface. Braid ropes on greased baking sheet; tuck under ends. Let rise, covered, for 30 minutes or until doubled in bulk. Brush with reserved egg. Bake at 400 degrees for 25 minutes or until golden brown. Yield: 12 servings.

Approx Per Serving: Cal 222; Prot 7.4 g; Carbo 38.0 g; T Fat 4.5 g; Chol 69.9 mg; Potas 125.0 mg; Sod 379.0 mg.

FOOD PROCESSOR FRENCH BREAD

11/2 packages dry yeast
2 teaspoons sugar
11/2 cups warm
  (115-degree) water
31/2 to 4 cups flour
1/3 cup chopped fresh
  herbs
2 teaspoons salt
1 egg, beaten

Dissolve yeast and sugar in warm water in bowl. Let stand for 5 minutes or until foamy. Combine 31/2 cups flour, herbs and salt in food processor container fitted with steel blade. Process for 5 seconds. Add yeast and remaining flour if necessary to form medium dough, processing constantly. Knead on floured surface until smooth and elastic. Shape into 2 long loaves on greased baking sheet. Cut slashes in tops. Let rise until doubled in bulk. Brush tops with egg. Bake at 350 degrees for 15 to 20 minutes or until golden brown. Cool on wire rack. Yield: 20 servings.

Approx Per Serving: Cal 98; Prot 3.1 g; Carbo 19.7 g; T Fat 0.5 g; Chol 13.7 mg; Potas 37.6 mg; Sod 217.0 mg.

REFRIGERATOR OATMEAL BREAD

2 packages dry yeast
1/4 cup sugar
1/2 cup warm (115-degree)
    water
3 tablespoons margarine
13/4 cups milk, scalded,
    cooled
2 tablespoons molasses
1/2 teaspoon salt
5 to 6 cups flour
1 cup quick-cooking oats
1 tablespoon oil

Dissolve yeast and 1 teaspoon sugar in warm water in mixer bowl. Let stand until bubbly. Add remaining sugar, margarine, milk, molasses, salt and 2 cups flour; beat at medium speed until smooth. Add 1 cup flour and oats. Beat until smooth. Mix in enough remaining flour to make a soft dough. Knead on floured surface for 10 minutes or until smooth and elastic. Cover with plastic wrap and towel. Let rest for 10 minutes. Shape into 2 loaves; place in loaf pans. Brush tops with oil; cover with plastic wrap. Chill for 2 to 24 hours. Let stand at room temperature for 10 minutes. Puncture any air bubbles with toothpick. Bake at 375 degrees for 30 to 40 minutes or until brown. Cover with foil if necessary to prevent overbrowning. Yield: 20 servings.

Approx Per Serving: Cal 202; Prot 5.6 g; Carbo 36.1 g; T Fat 3.7 g; Chol 2.9 mg; Potas 152.0 mg; Sod 85.5 mg.

SUGARY APPLE SPICED MUFFINS

11/2 cups sifted flour
1/2 cup sugar
2 teaspoons baking
    powder
1/2 teaspoon cinnamon
1/4 teaspoon nutmeg
1/2 teaspoon salt
1/2 cup milk
1 egg
1/4 cup oil
1 cup finely chopped
    apple
1/4 cup sugar
1/2 teaspoon cinnamon

Sift flour, 1/2 cup sugar, baking powder, 1/2 teaspoon cinnamon, nutmeg and salt into large bowl. Combine milk, egg, oil and apple in bowl; mix well. Add to dry ingredients; mix just until moistened. Fill greased muffin cups 2/3 full. Sprinkle with mixture of 1/4 cup sugar and 1/2 teaspoon cinnamon. Bake at 400 degrees for 20 to 25 minutes or until muffins test done. Yield: 12 muffins.

Approx Per Muffin: Cal 160; Prot 2.4 g; Carbo 25.5 g; T Fat 5.5 g; Chol 24.2 mg; Potas 44.5 mg; Sod 154.0 mg.

Toni Stanton
Carthage, New York

BANANA AND WALNUT MUFFINS

1/2 cup oil
11/2 cups honey
2 eggs
1/4 cup milk
1 cup mashed banana
1 teaspoon vanilla extract
2 cups flour
1/2 teaspoon soda
1/4 teaspoon salt
1 cup chopped walnuts
1/4 cup cinnamon-sugar

Combine oil, honey, eggs, milk, banana and vanilla in mixer bowl; beat until smooth. Add flour, soda and salt; mix well. Stir in walnuts. Fill greased muffin cups 3/4 full. Sprinkle with cinnamon-sugar. Bake at 350 degrees until toothpick inserted in center comes out clean. Serve warm or cold. May add raisins and dates if desired. May bake in cake layer pans or tube pan. Yield: 12 muffins.

Approx Per Muffin: Cal 399; Prot 5.1 g; Carbo 61.4 g; T Fat 16.7 g; Chol 46.4 mg; Potas 184.0 mg; Sod 96.1 mg.

Deloris "Lorie" Okusko
Gouverneur, New York

CHEDDAR BRAN MUFFINS

11/4 cups buttermilk
1 cup whole bran
1/4 cup shortening
1/3 cup sugar
1 egg
11/2 cups sifted flour
11/2 teaspoons baking
   powder
1/2 teaspoon salt
1/4 teaspoon soda
1 cup shredded sharp
   Cheddar cheese

Pour buttermilk over bran in small bowl. Let stand until bran is softened. Cream shortening and sugar in bowl until light and fluffy. Beat in egg. Sift flour, baking powder, salt and soda. Add to creamed mixture alternately with bran, mixing well after each addition. Stir in cheese. Fill greased muffin cups 2/3 full. Bake at 400 degrees for 30 minutes or until golden brown. Serve immediately. Yield: 12 muffins.

Approx Per Muffin: Cal 178; Prot 5.8 g; Carbo 20.7 g; T Fat 8.4 g; Chol 33.7 mg; Potas 103.0 mg; Sod 239.0 mg.

CHRISTMAS MUFFINS

3 cups flour
2 teaspoons baking
  powder
1 teaspoon soda
1 teaspoon cinnamon
1/2 teaspoon nutmeg
8 ounces candied citrus
  peel, ground
4 ounces candied red
  cherries, chopped
1/2 cup coconut
8 ounces pecans, ground
3 eggs
11/2 cups sugar
3/4 cup oil
1 cup milk
1 teaspoon vanilla extract

Mix flour, baking powder, soda and spices in bowl. Stir in candied fruit, coconut and pecans. Combine eggs, sugar, oil, milk and vanilla in mixer bowl; beat until smooth. Add to fruit mixture; mix well with spoon. Spoon into waxed paper-lined muffin cups. Bake at 400 degrees for 15 to 20 minutes or until brown. Cool on wire rack.
Yield: 36 muffins.

Approx Per Muffin: Cal 198; Prot 2.4 g; Carbo 25.9 g; T Fat 10.0 g; Chol 23.8 mg; Potas 53.0 mg; Sod 52.8 mg.

Joy M.J. Karam
Ottawa, Ontario, Canada

GINGERBREAD MUFFINS

1 cup margarine, softened
1 cup sugar
1 cup molasses
4 eggs
1/2 cup raisins
1/2 cup chopped pecans
4 cups flour
1/8 teaspoon salt
2 teaspoons ginger
1/2 teaspoon cinnamon
1/4 teaspoon allspice
2 teaspoons soda
1 cup sour milk

Cream margarine and sugar in mixer bowl until light and fluffy. Beat in molasses and eggs. Toss raisins and pecans with a small amount of flour in bowl, coating well. Sift remaining flour with salt and spices. Stir soda into sour milk. Add dry ingredients to muffin batter alternately with sour milk, mixing well after each addition. Stir in pecans and raisins. Store in refrigerator for up to 1 month. Spoon into greased muffin cups. Bake at 400 degrees for 15 to 18 minutes or until muffins test done. Cool on wire rack. Yield: 30 muffins.

Approx Per Muffin: Cal 200; Prot 3.1 g; Carbo 28.3 g; T Fat 8.6 g; Chol 37.6 mg; Potas 380.0 mg; Sod 159.0 mg.

APPLE PANCAKES

4 cups flour
1/4 cup sugar
2 tablespoons baking
  powder
2 teaspoons salt
4 eggs, beaten
2 cups cottage cheese
1/2 cup yogurt
1 cup milk
3 tablespoons melted
  margarine
2 cups finely chopped
  apples

Sift flour, sugar, baking powder and salt into bowl. Mix eggs with cottage cheese, yogurt and milk in bowl. Add to dry ingredients; mix well. Stir in margarine and apples. Ladle by 1/4 cupfuls onto hot greased griddle. Bake until brown on both sides, turning 1 time. Yield: 36 pancakes.

Approx Per Pancake: Cal 96; Prot 3.9 g; Carbo 13.9 g; T Fat 2.6 g; Chol 33.5 mg; Potas 52.7 mg; Sod 244.0 mg.

MULTI-GRAIN PANCAKES

2/3 cup whole wheat flour
1/3 cup all-purpose flour
1/4 cup oat flour
2 tablespoons wheat germ
2 teaspoons sugar
1 teaspoon baking powder
1/2 teaspoon soda
1/4 teaspoon salt
1 cup buttermilk
1/4 cup skim milk
1 egg
1 tablespoon oil
1/4 teaspoon vanilla extract
1 egg white, stiffly beaten

Combine whole wheat flour, all-purpose flour, oat flour, wheat germ, sugar, baking powder, soda and salt in bowl. Beat buttermilk, skim milk, whole egg, oil and vanilla in small bowl. Add to dry ingredients; mix just until moistened. Fold in stiffly beaten egg white gently. Let stand at room temperature for 10 minutes or in refrigerator for 1 hour. Bake on hot lightly greased griddle until light brown on both sides. Serve with applesauce or other fruit sauce. Yield: 6 servings.

Approx Per Serving: Cal 137; Prot 6.2 g; Carbo 19.5 g; T Fat 4.1 g; Chol 47.3 mg; Potas 166.0 mg; Sod 281.0 mg.
Nutritional information does not include oat flour.

BEST-EVER HENDERSON WAFFLES

4 eggs
1¹/₂ cups buttermilk
1³/₄ cups flour
2 teaspoons baking
powder
1 teaspoon soda
¹/₂ cup oil

Heat Belgian waffle iron to Medium. Beat eggs in bowl. Add buttermilk, flour, baking powder, soda and oil; beat until smooth. Bake using manufacturer's instructions. Yield: 6 waffles.

Approx Per Waffle: Cal 372; Prot 9.9 g; Carbo 31.4 g; T Fat 22.8 g;
Chol 185.0 mg; Potas 173.0 mg; Sod 357.0 mg.

Dr. Harold J. Lyness
Baldwinsville, New York

MEXICAN WAFFLES

2 cups buttermilk baking
mix
1 egg
2 tablespoons corn oil
1¹/₃ cups milk
1 cup Mexicorn
¹/₈ teaspoon red pepper
Special Sauce

Combine baking mix, egg, oil and milk in mixer bowl; beat until smooth. Stir in corn and red pepper. Bake in heated waffle iron, using manufacturer's instructions. Serve with Special Sauce. Yield: 4 waffles.

Approx Per Waffle: Cal 435; Prot 9.8 g; Carbo 53.5 g; T Fat 20.4 g;
Chol 79.5 mg; Potas 279.0 mg; Sod 940.0 mg.

SPECIAL SAUCE

1 cup packed light brown
sugar
1 cup dark corn syrup
1 cup sour cream

Combine all ingredients in saucepan. Bring to a boil, stirring constantly; reduce heat. Simmer for 5 minutes. Serve hot or cold on waffles, pancakes or ice cream. Store in refrigerator. Yield: 40 tablespoons.

Approx Per Tablespoon: Cal 56; Prot 0.2 g; Carbo 11.7 g; T Fat 1.2 g;
Chol 2.6 mg; Potas 27.5 mg; Sod 11.1 mg.

BUTTERHORNS

4 cups sifted flour
1/2 teaspoon salt
2 cakes yeast, crumbled
11/4 cups butter
4 egg yolks, beaten
1/2 cup sour cream
1 teaspoon vanilla extract
3 egg whites
1 cup sugar
1 pound pecans, chopped
1 teaspoon vanilla extract
1/4 cup confectioners'
  sugar

Combine flour, salt and yeast in bowl. Cut in butter until crumbly. Add egg yolks, sour cream and 1 teaspoon vanilla. Shape into roll. Chill wrapped in waxed paper. Beat egg whites in bowl until stiff peaks form. Add sugar gradually, beating until very stiff. Fold in pecans and 1 teaspoon vanilla. Divide dough into 8 portions. Roll each portion into 9-inch circle on surface sprinkled with confectioners' sugar. Cut each circle into 12 wedges. Spread 1 teaspoon pecan mixture on each wedge. Roll up from wide end. Place on baking sheet. Bake at 400 degrees for 15 to 18 minutes or until golden brown. Cool on wire rack. Yield: 96 butterhorns.

Approx Per Butterhorn: Cal 87; Prot 1.3 g; Carbo 7.3 g; T Fat 6.1 g; Chol 18.3 mg; Potas 31.0 mg; Sod 34.1 mg.

CREAM CHEESE ROLLS

2 packages dry yeast
1/2 cup warm (115-degree)
  water
1 cup sour cream
1/2 cup sugar
1 teaspoon salt
1/2 cup melted butter
2 eggs, beaten
4 cups flour
16 ounces cream cheese,
  softened
3/4 cup sugar
1 egg, beaten
1/8 teaspoon salt
2 teaspoons vanilla extract
2 cups confectioners'
  sugar
1/4 cup milk
2 teaspoons vanilla extract

Dissolve yeast in water. Heat sour cream in saucepan. Combine sour cream with 1/2 cup sugar, 1 teaspoon salt, butter, 2 eggs and flour in large bowl; mix well. Mix in yeast. Combine cream cheese, 3/4 cup sugar, 1 egg, 1/8 teaspoon salt and 2 teaspoons vanilla in mixer bowl; beat until light and fluffy. Divide dough into 4 portions. Roll each portion into 8x12-inch rectangle on floured surface. Spread cream cheese mixture down center of each rectangle. Roll as for jelly roll; seal edges. Cut into slices. Place on baking sheet. Let rise for 1 hour. Bake for 12 minutes or until golden brown. Mix confectioners' sugar, milk and 2 teaspoons vanilla in bowl. Drizzle over warm rolls. Yield: 48 rolls.

Approx Per Roll: Cal 141; Prot 2.5 g; Carbo 17.9 g; T Fat 6.7 g; Chol 34.9 mg; Potas 40.7 mg; Sod 102.0 mg.

MASHED POTATO ROLLS

1 package dry yeast
1/2 cup warm (115-degree)
  water
1 cup milk
2/3 cup shortening
2/3 cup sugar
1 teaspoon salt
1 cup mashed potatoes
2 eggs, beaten
4 to 5 cups flour

Dissolve yeast in warm water. Bring milk to a boil in large saucepan, stirring constantly. Add shortening, sugar and salt; stir to dissolve well. Cool to lukewarm. Combine with mashed potatoes, eggs, yeast and enough flour to make a stiff dough in bowl; mix well. Knead on floured surface until smooth and elastic. Place in greased bowl, turning to grease surface. Let rise until doubled in bulk. Shape into rolls; place in greased 9x13-inch baking pan. Let rise until doubled in bulk. Bake at 400 degrees for 10 minutes or until golden brown. May store dough in refrigerator for up to 2 weeks. Yield: 30 rolls.

Approx Per Roll: Cal 149; Prot 3.1 g; Carbo 22.0 g; T Fat 5.4 g; Chol 19.5 mg; Potas 60.8 mg; Sod 101.0 mg.

YEAST BREAD SWEET ROLLS

2 packages dry yeast
1 cup warm water
3 eggs
1/3 cup sugar
1 teaspoon salt
4 cups flour
1/2 cup melted margarine
1 to 1 1/2 cups packed
  brown sugar
1/8 teaspoon each nutmeg,
  cinnamon, allspice,
  cloves and mace

Dissolve yeast in water. Let stand for 5 minutes. Beat eggs, sugar and salt in bowl. Add yeast; mix well. Add 3 1/2 cups flour 1 cup at a time, mixing well after each addition. Let rise for 1 1/2 to 2 hours. Stir dough down with wooden spoon. Place on floured surface, working in remaining 1/2 cup flour if necessary for easy handling. Pat into 12x18-inch rectangle. Brush with margarine. Sprinkle with 1 to 1 1/2 cups brown sugar and spices. Roll as for jelly roll. Cut into 1 1/2-inch slices. Place in greased baking pan. Bake at 325 to 350 degrees for 30 to 35 minutes or until golden brown. May frost warm rolls with confectioners' sugar frosting if desired. Yield: 20 servings.

Approx Per Serving: Cal 216; Prot 3.5 g; Carbo 38.6 g; T Fat 5.4 g; Chol 27.4 mg; Potas 104.0 mg; Sod 175.0 mg.
Nutritional information does not include frosting.

Mrs. Lewis Card
Black River, New York

CHEESE-FILLED SQUARES

2   8-count packages
    refrigerator crescent
    rolls
16 ounces cream cheese,
    softened
3/4 cup sugar
1 teaspoon lemon juice
1/2 teaspoon vanilla extract
1 egg yolk, beaten
1 egg white, beaten
1/2 cup chopped walnuts

Separate 1 package crescent rolls into rectangles. Place in greased 9x13-inch baking pan, sealing edges and perforations. Blend cream cheese, sugar, lemon juice, vanilla and egg yolk in bowl. Spread over roll dough. Separate remaining package roll dough into rectangles. Place over cream cheese layer; seal edges and perforations. Brush with beaten egg white; sprinkle with walnuts. Bake at 325 degrees for 25 minutes or until golden brown. Cut into squares. Garnish with confectioners' sugar. Yield: 12 servings.

   Approx Per Serving: Cal 352; Prot 6.0 g; Carbo 29.1 g; T Fat 24.1 g;
      Chol 64.1 mg; Potas 160.0 mg; Sod 425.0 mg.

HERBED CHEESE ROLLS

12 sourdough rolls
1/2 cup butter, softened
1/2 teaspoon basil
1/2 teaspoon oregano
2 cloves of garlic, minced
1/2 to 1 teaspoon lemon
    pepper
8 ounces Cheddar cheese,
    sliced

Slice rolls horizontally to form pockets. Mix butter, basil, oregano, garlic and lemon pepper in bowl. Spread on cut sides of rolls. Place 1 slice cheese in each roll. Wrap rolls individually in foil. Bake at 350 degrees for 15 to 20 minutes or until cheese is melted. Yield: 12 servings.

   Approx Per Serving: Cal 274; Prot 9.3 g; Carbo 25.6 g; T Fat 15.0 g;
      Chol 40.6 mg; Potas 354.0 mg; Sod 436.0 mg.

MONKEY BREAD

3   10-count packages
    refrigerator buttermilk
    biscuits, cut into
    quarters
3/4 cup sugar
1 tablespoon cinnamon
1 cup packed brown sugar
1/2 cup margarine

Coat biscuits with mixture of sugar and cinnamon. Place biscuits and any remaining sugar mixture in greased bundt pan. Melt brown sugar and margarine in saucepan. Pour over biscuits. Place in cold oven. Bake at 350 degrees for 35 minutes or until brown. Invert onto serving plate. Let stand for 5 to 10 minutes; remove pan. Yield: 8 servings.

   Approx Per Serving: Cal 523; Prot 5.4 g; Carbo 82.4 g; T Fat 19.3 g;
      Chol 3.8 mg; Potas 173.0 mg; Sod 1080.0 mg.

RETURN TO PORT

Desserts

Return to Port

As the sun sets over Stoney Island each day, charter boats and sport fishing boats alike return to the safety of Henderson Harbor with the promise of a hot meal in one of the Harbor's quaint restaurants. It's a time to reflect on the day's fishing—the ones we caught and released, and, yes, the ones that got away.

Sunset Delights Dessert Party

Tropical Fruit Dip
page 25

Microwave White Chocolate Cheesecake
page 171

Death by Chocolate
page 172

Cream Cheese Pound Cake or
page 185

Greek Cake
page 182

Lacy See-Through Cookies
page 190

Galette
page 194

Lemon Tarts
page 196

HONEY-CRUNCH BAKED APPLES

6 large tart apples
1/3 cup granola
1/3 cup chopped dates
1/4 cup chopped walnuts
2 teaspoons lemon juice
1/2 teaspoon cinnamon
1/4 teaspoon nutmeg
1/3 cup honey
3 tablespoons melted
   butter
3/4 cup apple juice

Peel and core apples; place in 9-inch baking pan. Combine granola, dates, walnuts, lemon juice, cinnamon, nutmeg and half the honey in bowl; mix well. Press into centers of apples. Blend remaining honey, butter and apple juice in bowl. Pour over apples. Bake, covered, at 350 degrees for 30 minutes. Bake, uncovered, for 30 minutes, basting occasionally with pan juices. Serve warm with ice cream. Yield: 6 servings.

Approx Per Serving: Cal 334; Prot 2.1 g; Carbo 63.4 g; T Fat 10.8 g; Chol 15.5 mg; Potas 405.0 mg; Sod 65.3 mg.

BANANA PUDDING DELUXE

2 3-ounce packages
   banana instant
   pudding mix
3 cups cold milk
1 14-ounce can
   sweetened condensed
   milk
12 ounces whipped
   topping
2 10-ounce packages
   vanilla wafers
5 bananas, sliced

Prepare pudding with milk using package directions. Fold in condensed milk and 1 cup whipped topping. Alternate layers of vanilla wafers, bananas and pudding in 9x13-inch dish. Top with remaining whipped topping. Chill, covered with plastic wrap, until serving time. Yield: 16 servings.

Approx Per Serving: Cal 330; Prot 5.0 g; Carbo 51.7 g; T Fat 12.4 g; Chol 25.7 mg; Potas 321.0 mg; Sod 194.0 mg.

SURPRISE BREAD PUDDING

8 cups day-old bread
  cubes
4 cups milk
2 cups sugar
1/2 cup melted butter
2 tablespoons vanilla
  extract
3 eggs, slightly beaten
1 cup raisins
1 cup coconut
1 cup chopped pecans
1 teaspoon cinnamon
1 teaspoon nutmeg
1/2 cup melted butter
11/2 cups confectioners'
  sugar
2 egg yolks, beaten
1/2 cup Bourbon or rum

Combine bread cubes, milk, sugar, butter, vanilla, eggs, raisins, coconut, pecans, cinnamon and nutmeg in bowl. Let stand for 5 minutes. Pour into buttered 9x13-inch baking dish. Bake at 350 degrees for 1 hour or until golden brown. Blend butter and confectioners' sugar in bowl. Add egg yolks; blend well. Add Bourbon gradually, stirring constantly. Serve sauce over warm pudding. Yield: 16 servings.

Approx Per Serving: Cal 607; Prot 11.2 g; Carbo 85.4 g; T Fat 24.3 g; Chol 127.0 mg; Potas 298.0 mg; Sod 518.0 mg.

CHERRY DUMP DESSERT

1 21-ounce can cherry
   pie filling
1 8-ounce can crushed
   pineapple
1 2-layer package yellow
   cake mix
1/2 cup melted butter
1/2 cup coconut
1/2 cup chopped pecans

Layer pie filling, undrained pineapple and dry cake mix in 9x13-inch baking dish. Drizzle butter over layers. Sprinkle coconut and pecans over top. Bake at 325 degrees for 1 hour. Yield: 10 servings.

Approx Per Serving: Cal 359; Prot 2.4 g; Carbo 50.9 g; T Fat 17.2 g; Chol 24.8 mg; Potas 109.0 mg; Sod 315.0 mg.

FROZEN MOCHA CHEESECAKE

1¹/₄ cups chocolate wafer
  crumbs
¹/₄ cup sugar
¹/₄ cup melted margarine
8 ounces cream cheese,
  softened
1 14-ounce can
  sweetened condensed
  milk
²/₃ cup chocolate syrup
2 tablespoons instant
  coffee powder
1 teaspoon hot water
1 cup whipping cream,
  whipped

Combine crumbs, sugar and margarine in bowl; mix well. Press over bottom and side of buttered 9-inch springform pan. Chill until firm. Beat cream cheese in mixer bowl until fluffy. Add condensed milk and chocolate syrup; beat until well blended. Dissolve coffee in hot water; blend into cream cheese mixture. Fold in whipped cream gently. Pour into prepared pan. Freeze, covered, for 6 hours or until firm. Place on serving plate; remove side of pan. Garnish with chocolate curls or drizzle additional chocolate syrup over top in decorative pattern. Yield: 12 servings.

Approx Per Serving: Cal 430; Prot 6.0 g; Carbo 48.2 g; T Fat 25.0 g; Chol 59.0 mg; Potas 256.0 mg; Sod 262.0 mg.

MICROWAVE WHITE CHOCOLATE CHEESECAKE

10 tablespoons graham
  cracker crumbs
1 tablespoon sugar
2 tablespoons melted
  butter
4 ounces white chocolate,
  melted
8 ounces cream cheese,
  softened
¹/₃ cup sugar
1 egg
1 cup sour cream
1 teaspoon instant coffee
  powder
1 teaspoon hot water
2 ounces white chocolate
2 tablespoons butter
1 teaspoon corn syrup

Combine crumbs, 1 tablespoon sugar and 2 tablespoons butter in bowl; mix well. Pat into pie plate. Microwave on Medium-High for 1 minute. Combine 4 ounces melted chocolate, cream cheese, ¹/₃ cup sugar, egg, sour cream and coffee powder dissolved in hot water in mixer bowl; beat until smooth. Pour into prepared pie plate. Microwave on Medium for 9 to 12 minutes or until center appears slightly soft. Cool to room temperature. Combine 2 ounces chocolate, 2 tablespoons butter and corn syrup in small glass bowl. Microwave on Medium for 2 minutes or until melted; blend well. Spread over cheesecake. Chill until serving time. Yield: 6 servings.

Approx Per Serving: Cal 546; Prot 8.0 g; Carbo 42.3 g; T Fat 40.0 g; Chol 130.0 mg; Potas 249.0 mg; Sod 309.0 mg.

Joy M.J. Karam
Ottawa, Ontario, Canada

PUMPKIN CHEESECAKE

1¹/₃ cups graham cracker
  crumbs
¹/₄ cup packed brown
  sugar
¹/₄ cup melted butter
¹/₂ teaspoon cinnamon
24 ounces cream cheese
¹/₂ cup packed brown
  sugar
¹/₄ cup maple syrup
1¹/₂ teaspoons vanilla
  extract
1 cup canned pumpkin
2 tablespoons flour
¹/₂ teaspoon cinnamon
¹/₂ teaspoon nutmeg
¹/₄ teaspoon cloves
¹/₄ teaspoon allspice
¹/₈ teaspoon ginger
4 eggs
¹/₄ cup melted butter
1 cup whipping cream,
  whipped

Combine crumbs, ¹/₄ cup brown sugar, ¹/₄ cup melted butter and ¹/₂ teaspoon cinnamon in bowl; mix well. Press into 10-inch springform pan. Combine cream cheese, ¹/₂ cup brown sugar, maple syrup and vanilla in mixer bowl; beat until creamy. Add pumpkin, flour and spices; mix well. Add eggs 1 at a time, beating well after each addition. Add ¹/₄ cup melted butter; beat until fluffy. Pour into prepared pan. Bake at 325 degrees for 30 minutes. Turn off oven. Let stand in closed oven for 30 minutes. Cool. Chill until serving time. Place on serving plate; remove side of pan. Top with whipped cream. Garnish with sprinkle of cinnamon.
Yield: 12 servings.

Approx Per Serving: Cal 501; Prot 8.1 g; Carbo 33.5 g; T Fat 38.2 g; Chol 201.0 mg; Potas 243.0 mg; Sod 359.0 mg.

Mary Laidlow
Ottawa, Ontario, Canada

DEATH BY CHOCOLATE

1   2-layer package
  chocolate cake mix
1 cup Kahlua or rum
4   3¹/₂-ounce packages
  chocolate mousse mix
24 ounces whipped
  topping
6   1-ounce Heath candy
  bars, crushed

Prepare and bake cake mix according to package directions using 9x13-inch cake pan. Prick top of cake. Drizzle Kahlua over cake. Let stand for several hours to overnight. Prepare mousse mix using package directions. Crumble half the cake into large glass bowl. Add layers of half the mousse, whipped topping and candy. Repeat layers.
Yield: 18 servings.

Approx Per Serving: Cal 450; Prot 2.1 g; Carbo 64.5 g; T Fat 18.5 g; Chol 0.0 mg; Potas 29.3 mg; Sod 365.0 mg.

Bettye LaRobardiere
Daytona Beach, Florida

FROZEN BUTTER BRICKLE DESSERT

2 cups flour
$^1/_2$ cup oats
1 cup chopped pecans
$^1/_2$ cup packed brown
   sugar
$^1/_2$ cup melted margarine
1 cup caramel ice cream
   topping
1 pint vanilla ice cream,
   softened

Combine flour, oats, pecans, brown sugar and margarine in bowl; mix well. Pat onto baking sheet. Bake at 400 degrees for 15 minutes; stir until crumbly. Sprinkle half the crumbs over bottom of 9x13-inch dish. Drizzle half the caramel topping over crumbs. Spread ice cream over caramel topping layer. Add layers of remaining crumbs and caramel topping. Freeze until firm.
Yield: 12 servings.

Approx Per Serving: Cal 371; Prot 4.7 g; Carbo 51.5 g; T Fat 17.1 g; Chol 9.8 mg; Potas 164.0 mg; Sod 181.0 mg.

CHOCOLATE-CHERRY ICE CREAM

3 eggs, slightly beaten
1 cup sugar
4 cups milk
1 cup chocolate syrup
2 cups whipping cream
1 tablespoon vanilla
   extract
1   1-ounce jar
   maraschino cherries,
   drained
5 ounces milk chocolate

Combine eggs, sugar, milk, chocolate syrup, cream and vanilla in large bowl; mix well. Pour into 4-quart ice cream freezer. Chop cherries and milk chocolate. Add to freezer. Freeze according to manufacturer's instructions. Yield: 12 servings.

Approx Per Serving: Cal 379; Prot 6.5 g; Carbo 42.0 g; T Fat 22.3 g; Chol 136.0 mg; Potas 246.0 mg; Sod 95.3 mg.

CRISPY ICE CREAM ROLL

$^1/_4$ cup melted margarine
1   16-ounce can vanilla
   frosting
$^1/_4$ cup light corn syrup
5 cups crisp rice cereal
1 quart favorite ice
   cream, softened

Combine margarine, frosting and corn syrup in bowl; blend well. Add cereal; mix until well coated. Press into waxed paper-lined 10x15-inch pan. Chill for 30 minutes or until firm. Spread ice cream over cereal layer. Roll as for jelly roll; wrap in plastic wrap. Freeze until firm. Slice with sharp knife.
Yield: 10 servings.

Approx Per Serving: Cal 413; Prot 2.9 g; Carbo 59.2 g; T Fat 10.4 g; Chol 23.6 mg; Potas 122.0 mg; Sod 371.0 mg.

LEMON LUSH

1 cup flour
1/2 cup chopped pecans
1/2 cup margarine,
   softened
1 cup confectioners' sugar
8 ounces cream cheese,
   softened
8 ounces whipped topping
1 6-ounce package lemon
   instant pudding mix
2²/3 cups milk
1/2 cup pecans

Combine flour, 1/2 cup pecans and margarine in bowl; mix well. Press into 8x11-inch baking dish. Bake at 375 degrees for 15 minutes or until light brown. Cool. Beat confectioners' sugar and cream cheese in mixer bowl until light and fluffy. Fold in 1 cup whipped topping. Spread over cooled crust. Combine pudding mix and milk in bowl; beat until thickened. Spoon over cream cheese mixture. Spread remaining whipped topping over top. Sprinkle with 1/2 cup pecans. Chill until serving time. Yield: 6 servings.

Approx Per Serving: Cal 832; Prot 10.7 g; Carbo 77.6 g; T Fat 55.3 g; Chol 55.9 mg; Potas 305.0 mg; Sod 536.0 mg.

PEACH CRISP

2 cups sliced fresh peaches
1/4 cup margarine,
   softened
3/4 cup sugar
1 cup flour
1 teaspoon baking powder
1/2 teaspoon salt
1/2 cup milk
1 cup sugar
1 tablespoon cornstarch
1/4 teaspoon nutmeg
1 cup boiling water

Place peaches in 8x8-inch baking dish. Cream margarine and 3/4 cup sugar in bowl until light and fluffy. Combine flour, baking powder and salt. Add to creamed mixture alternately with milk, mixing well after each addition. Spoon over peaches. Mix 1 cup sugar with cornstarch and nutmeg. Sprinkle over batter. Drizzle boiling water over top. Bake at 350 degrees for 1 hour or until brown. Yield: 6 servings.

Approx Per Serving: Cal 411; Prot 3.3 g; Carbo 82.6 g; T Fat 8.5 g; Chol 2.8 mg; Potas 166.0 mg; Sod 332.0 mg.

FRUIT PIZZA

1 2-layer package yellow
   cake mix
1 cup quick-cooking oats
6 tablespoons margarine,
   softened
1 egg, beaten
2 tablespoons margarine,
   softened
1/4 cup quick-cooking oats
1/2 cup chopped pecans
1/4 cup packed light
   brown sugar
1/2 teaspoon cinnamon
1 21-ounce can favorite
   fruit pie filling

Combine cake mix, 1 cup oats and 6 tablespoons margarine in large mixer bowl. Beat at low speed until crumbly. Reserve 1 cup for topping. Add egg to remaining crumbs; mix well. Press into greased 12-inch pizza pan. Bake at 350 degrees for 12 minutes. Cool. Combine reserved crumbs, 2 tablespoons margarine, 1/4 cup oats, pecans, brown sugar and cinnamon; beat until well mixed. Spoon pie filling over cooled crust; sprinkle pecan mixture over top. Bake at 350 degrees for 15 minutes or until light brown. Cool. Yield: 12 servings.

Approx Per Serving: Cal 376; Prot 3.6 g; Carbo 57.6 g; T Fat 15.3 g; Chol 22.8 mg; Potas 97.5 mg; Sod 424.0 mg.

DELICIOUS PUMPKIN DESSERT

1 cup flour
1 cup chopped pecans
1/2 cup margarine,
   softened
1 14-ounce can
   sweetened
   condensed milk
1 cup canned pumpkin
1 6-ounce package
   vanilla instant
   pudding mix
1 1/2 teaspoons pumpkin
   pie spice
24 ounces whipped
   topping

Combine flour, pecans and margarine in bowl; mix well. Pat into 9x13-inch baking dish. Bake at 325 degrees for 20 minutes. Cool. Combine condensed milk, pumpkin, pudding mix, spice and half the whipped topping in bowl; mix well. Spoon over baked layer. Top with remaining whipped topping. Chill until serving time. Yield: 12 servings.

Approx Per Serving: Cal 518; Prot 5.5 g; Carbo 55.8 g; T Fat 31.8 g; Chol 11.2 mg; Potas 229.0 mg; Sod 242.0 mg.

POOR MAN'S PUDDING

6 cups 2% milk
1/2 cup uncooked rice
1/2 cup sugar
1/8 teaspoon salt
Nutmeg to taste
1/2 cup raisins

Combine first 5 ingredients in buttered baking dish. Let stand for 1 hour, stirring occasionally. Bake at 350 degrees for 1¼ hours, stirring occasionally. Add raisins. Bake for 45 minutes longer. Pudding should be creamy and will set while cooling. Yield: 10 servings.

Approx Per Serving: Cal 169; Prot 5.8 g; Carbo 31.0 g; T Fat 2.9 g; Chol 13.2 mg; Potas 297.0 mg; Sod 101.0 mg.

Mrs. B. Grass
Kingston, Ontario, Canada

RASPBERRY JUBILEE

2 cups crushed pretzels
1/4 cup sugar
3/4 cup butter, softened
8 ounces cream cheese,
softened
2 cups whipped topping
1 cup sugar
2 3-ounce packages
raspberry gelatin
2 cups boiling water
2 10-ounce packages
frozen raspberries

Combine first 3 ingredients in bowl; mix well. Press into 9x13-inch baking pan. Bake at 350 degrees for 10 minutes. Cool. Combine cream cheese, whipped topping and 1 cup sugar in bowl; mix well. Spread over baked layer. Dissolve gelatin in boiling water in bowl. Add raspberries; stir until raspberries are thawed. Pour over cream cheese layer. Chill until firm. This dessert is wonderful made with strawberries. Yield: 12 servings.

Approx Per Serving: Cal 395; Prot 3.5 g; Carbo 50.6 g; T Fat 21.4 g; Chol 51.7 mg; Potas 85.2 mg; Sod 234.0 mg.

OLD-FASHIONED APPLESAUCE CAKE

1/2 cup butter, softened
1 cup sugar
1 1/2 cups flour
1 cup chopped raisins
1 teaspoon cinnamon
1/2 teaspoon cloves
1 teaspoon salt
1 teaspoon soda
1 cup unsweetened
applesauce

Cream butter and sugar in mixer bowl until light and fluffy. Combine flour and raisins in bowl; mix until raisins are coated. Add cinnamon, cloves and salt; mix well. Add to creamed mixture; mix well. Mix soda with applesauce. Add to raisin mixture; mix well. Pour into greased 9x9-inch cake pan. Bake at 350 degrees for 30 to 35 minutes or until cake tests done. Yield: 9 servings.

Approx Per Serving: Cal 318; Prot 2.9 g; Carbo 55.6 g; T Fat 10.5 g; Chol 27.6 mg; Potas 182.0 mg; Sod 418.0 mg.

NOBBY APPLE CAKE

6 tablespoons butter,
  softened
2 cups sugar
2 eggs, beaten
2 cups sifted flour
2 teaspoons soda
1 teaspoon salt
1 teaspoon cinnamon
1/2 cup milk
2 teaspoons vanilla extract
6 cups chopped peeled
  apples
1/2 cup pecans

Cream butter and sugar in mixer bowl until light and fluffy. Add eggs; beat well. Sift flour, soda, salt and cinnamon together. Add to creamed mixture alternately with milk and vanilla, mixing well after each addition. Stir in apples and pecans. Pour into greased 9x13-inch cake pan. Sprinkle with additional sugar and cinnamon if desired. Bake at 350 degrees for 40 to 45 minutes or until cake tests done. Yield: 15 servings.

Approx Per Serving: Cal 272; Prot 3.3 g; Carbo 47.1 g; T Fat 8.6 g; Chol 50.1 mg; Potas 104.0 mg; Sod 304.0 mg.

Toni Stanton
Carthage, New York

A TO Z CAKE

1 1/4 cups bran flakes
1 1/2 cups flour
2 teaspoons baking
  powder
1 teaspoon soda
1 teaspoon pumpkin pie
  spice
1 1/2 cups packed brown
  sugar
1 cup melted butter
3 eggs
2 teaspoons vanilla extract
1 cup chopped peeled
  apple
1/2 cup shredded carrot
2 cups shredded zucchini
3 ounces cream cheese,
  softened
1/4 cup butter, softened
2 cups confectioners'
  sugar

Combine bran flakes, flour, baking powder, soda and pumplin pie spice in bowl; set aside. Combine brown sugar, melted butter, eggs and vanilla in mixer bowl; beat until smooth. Add bran mixture; mix well. Stir in apple, carrot and zucchini. Pour into 2 greased and waxed paper-lined 9-inch cake pans. Bake at 350 degrees for 40 to 45 minutes or until cakes test done. Cool. Combine cream cheese, softened butter and confectioners' sugar in mixer bowl; beat until creamy. Spread between layers and over top and side of cake. Garnish with sprinkle of additional bran flakes and chopped pecans. Yield: 16 servings.

Approx Per Serving: Cal 345; Prot 3.5 g; Carbo 45.5 g; T Fat 17.5 g; Chol 96.0 mg; Potas 174.0 mg; Sod 280.0 mg.

PERFECT BIRTHDAY CAKE

1 cup baking cocoa
2 cups boiling water
2³/4 cups sifted flour
2 teaspoons soda
1/2 teaspoon salt
1/2 teaspoon baking
 powder
1 cup butter, softened
2¹/2 cups sugar
4 eggs, at room
 temperature
1¹/2 teaspoons vanilla
 extract
Whipped Cream Filling
Chocolate Frosting (see
 page 187)

Combine cocoa and boiling water in bowl; mix well. Let stand until cool. Sift flour, soda, salt and baking powder together. Cream butter, sugar, eggs and vanilla in large mixer bowl at high speed for 5 minutes or until light and fluffy. Add flour 1/4 at a time alternately with cocoa mixture 1/3 at a time, beating well at low speed after each addition. Spread batter in 3 greased and floured 9-inch layer cake pans. Bake in preheated 350-degree oven for 25 to 30 minutes or until layers test done. Cool in pans on wire rack for 15 minutes. Invert onto wire racks to cool completely. Spread Whipped Cream Filling between layers. Spread Chocolate Frosting over side and top of cake. Chill for 1 hour or longer before serving. Yield: 10 servings.

Approx Per Serving: Cal 1002; Prot 9.1 g; Carbo 116.0 g; T Fat 60.3 g; Chol 258.0 mg; Potas 257.0 mg; Sod 644.0 mg.

WHIPPED CREAM FILLING

1 cup whipping cream,
 chilled
1/4 cup confectioners'
 sugar
1 teaspoon vanilla extract

Whip cream with confectioners' sugar and vanilla until soft peaks form. Chill if desired.

CHOCOLATE FROSTING

1/2 cup cream
1 cup butter
6 ounces semisweet
 chocolate chips
2¹/2 cups confectioners'
 sugar

Combine cream and butter in saucepan. Cook over low heat until butter melts. Add chocolate chips. Cook until chocolate chips melt, stirring to mix well. Remove from heat. Pour into mixer bowl. Place in larger bowl of crushed ice. Add confectioners' sugar. Beat until frosting is of spreading consistency.

Scott Elliott

BLUEBERRY-SOUR CREAM CAKE

1/2 cup butter, softened
1/2 cup sugar
1 egg
1 teaspoon vanilla extract
1 1/2 cups flour
1 1/2 teaspoons baking
   powder
3 to 4 cups blueberries
2 cups sour cream
2 egg yolks
1/2 cup sugar
1 teaspoon vanilla extract

Cream butter and 1/2 cup sugar in mixer bowl until light and fluffy. Add 1 egg and 1 teaspoon vanilla; mix well. Add mixture of flour and baking powder gradually, mixing well after each addition. Pour into well-greased 9x9-inch cake pan. Spread blueberries over batter. Combine sour cream, egg yolks, 1/2 cup sugar and 1 teaspoon vanilla in bowl; mix well. Spoon over blueberries. Bake at 350 degrees for 1 hour or until brown around edges. Yield: 10 servings.

Approx Per Serving: Cal 379; Prot 5.1 g; Carbo 44.6 g; T Fat 20.9 g; Chol 127.0 mg; Potas 150.0 mg; Sod 164.0 mg.

BUTTERMILK CAKE

2 1/2 cups plus 2
   tablespoons flour
6 tablespoons cornstarch
1/8 teaspoon salt
1 cup shortening
1 cup buttermilk
1/4 teaspoon soda
6 egg yolks
3 cups sugar
1 teaspoon vanilla extract
6 egg whites, stiffly
   beaten

Sift flour, cornstarch and salt together; set aside. Combine shortening, buttermilk, soda, egg yolks, sugar and vanilla in mixer bowl; beat until smooth. Add flour mixture; mix well. Fold stiffly beaten egg whites into batter gently. Pour into greased and floured tube pan. Bake at 350 degrees for 1 1/4 hours or until cake tests done. Cool in pan on wire rack for 10 minutes. Invert onto serving plate to cool completely. Garnish with sprinkle of confectioners' sugar. Yield: 10 servings.

Approx Per Serving: Cal 606; Prot 8.0 g; Carbo 90.3 g; T Fat 24.4 g; Chol 164.0 mg; Potas 106.0 mg; Sod 110.0 mg.

MOCK BLACK FOREST CAKE

1 2-layer package
   chocolate cake mix
1 21-ounce can cherry
   pie filling
2 eggs
1 teaspoon vanilla extract
2 cups whipping cream,
   whipped

Combine cake mix, pie filling, eggs and vanilla in mixer bowl. Beat until well mixed. Pour into greased and floured 9x13-inch cake pan. Bake at 350 degrees for 35 minutes or until cake tests done. Cool completely. Frost generously with whipped cream just before serving. Yield: 12 servings.

Approx Per Serving: Cal 387; Prot 3.9 g; Carbo 50.9 g; T Fat 19.2 g;
   Chol 100.0 mg; Potas 79.9 mg; Sod 314.0 mg.

CHOCOLATE PUDDING CAKE

$1/2$ cup flour
1 teaspoon baking powder
$1/2$ teaspoon salt
$1/3$ cup sugar
1 tablespoon baking cocoa
1 tablespoon melted
   margarine
$1/4$ cup milk
$1/2$ teaspoon vanilla extract
$1/4$ cup chopped pecans
$1/2$ cup packed brown
   sugar
2 tablespoons baking
   cocoa
$2/3$ cup boiling water

Sift flour, baking powder, salt, sugar and 1 tablespoon baking cocoa into bowl. Add margarine, milk and vanilla; mix well. Stir in pecans. Pour into buttered 1-quart casserole. Sprinkle brown sugar and 2 tablespoons baking cocoa over batter. Drizzle boiling water over top. Bake at 350 degrees for 35 minutes. Serve warm with whipped cream or ice cream. Yield: 4 servings.

Approx Per Serving: Cal 319; Prot 3.5 g; Carbo 59.1 g; T Fat 9.3 g;
   Chol 2.1 mg; Potas 209.0 mg; Sod 402.0 mg.

FOUR-DAY CHOCOLATE AND COCONUT CAKE

1 2-layer package devils
   food cake mix
3 eggs
1 cup water
1/3 cup oil
2 cups sour cream
1 cup sugar
3 cups coconut
3 cups whipped topping

Combine cake mix, eggs, water and oil in mixer bowl; beat at medium speed for 2 minutes. Pour into 2 greased and waxed paper-lined 9-inch round cake pans. Bake at 350 degrees for 35 minutes or until cakes test done. Cool. Split each layer into 2 layers. Blend sour cream and sugar in bowl. Fold in coconut and whipped topping. Spread between layers and over top and side of cake. Chill, covered, for 4 days before serving. Yield: 12 servings.

Approx Per Serving: Cal 548; Prot 4.8 g; Carbo 68.7 g; T Fat 29.1 g; Chol 55.8 mg; Potas 127.0 mg; Sod 356.0 mg.

FRUIT COCKTAIL CAKE

1 16-ounce can fruit
   cocktail
1 cup flour
1 cup sugar
1 teaspoon baking powder
1/2 teaspoon soda
1/8 teaspoon salt
1/2 teaspoon almond
   extract
1 tablespoon melted
   butter
1 egg
1/2 cup packed brown
   sugar
1 cup chopped pecans

Combine undrained fruit cocktail, flour, sugar, baking powder, soda, salt, almond extract, butter and egg in bowl; mix well. Pour into greased and floured 8x11-inch cake pan. Sprinkle with brown sugar and pecans. Bake for 30 minutes or until cake tests done. Serve warm or cold with whipped topping. Yield: 8 servings.

Approx Per Serving: Cal 368; Prot 3.8 g; Carbo 63.6 g; T Fat 12.4 g; Chol 38.1 mg; Potas 180.0 mg; Sod 157.0 mg.

GREEK CAKE (EKMEK)

8 eggs
1 cup plus 6¹/₂
  tablespoons sugar
1¹/₄ cups uncooked cream
  of wheat
1¹/₃ cups flour
1 teaspoon nutmeg
2 cups water
2 cups sugar
1 slice lemon
2 4-ounce packages
  pistachio instant
  pudding mix
4 cups milk
2 envelopes whipped
  topping mix
¹/₂ cup chopped pistachios

Combine eggs and 1 cup plus 6¹/₂ tablespoons sugar in mixer bowl. Beat for 10 minutes. Add cream of wheat, flour and nutmeg. Beat for 5 minutes longer. Pour into ungreased 10x24-inch cake pan. Bake at 325 degrees for 45 minutes. Cool slightly. Combine water, 2 cups sugar and lemon slice in saucepan. Bring to a boil. Boil for 5 to 10 minutes. Discard lemon slice. Pour syrup over warm cake. Let stand until cooled to room temperature. Prepare pudding mix with milk using package directions. Chill until thickened. Spread over cooled cake. Prepare whipped topping mix using package directions. Spread over pudding layer. Top with pistachios. Store in refrigerator.
Yield: 10 servings.

Approx Per Serving: Cal 616; Prot 12.6 g; Carbo 113.0 g; T Fat 14.1 g; Chol 237.0 mg; Potas 331.0 mg; Sod 272.0 mg.
Nutritional information does not include cream of wheat.

Joy M.J. Karam
Ottawa, Ontario, Canada

POLISH HOLIDAY CAKE

12 egg whites
2 cups sugar
12 egg yolks, slightly
  beaten
1 pound finely ground
  walnuts
8 ounces confectioners'
  sugar
¹/₂ cup margarine,
  softened
¹/₄ cup baking cocoa
1 teaspoon vanilla extract

Beat egg whites in mixer bowl until stiff peaks form. Fold in sugar and egg yolks gently. Fold in walnuts gently. Spread in thin layers in greased 8-inch round cake pans. Bake at 350 degrees for 25 minutes. Cool. Combine confectioners' sugar, margarine, cocoa and vanilla in bowl; beat until smooth and creamy. Spread between layers and over top and side of cake. This is a traditional Polish dessert used for celebrations, especially Easter. Yield: 16 servings.

Approx Per Serving: Cal 446; Prot 9.0 g; Carbo 45.2 g; T Fat 27.7 g; Chol 204.0 mg; Potas 207.0 mg; Sod 114.0 mg.

Phyllis Wendt
Constableville, New York

HUMMINGBIRD CAKE

1¹/₂ cups honey
3 eggs
1 cup oil
1¹/₂ teaspoons vanilla
  extract
1¹/₂ cups whole wheat
  flour
1¹/₂ cups all-purpose flour
1 teaspoon soda
1 teaspoon cinnamon
1 8-ounce can juice-pack
  crushed pineapple
2 bananas, chopped
1 cup coconut
1 cup chopped pecans

Combine honey, eggs, oil and vanilla in mixer bowl; beat until blended. Sift flours, soda and cinnamon into bowl. Add honey mixture; mix well. Fold in pineapple, bananas, coconut and pecans. Pour into greased and floured 9x13-inch cake pan. Bake at 350 degrees for 45 minutes or until cake tests done. Serve warm with whipped topping. Yield: 15 servings.

Approx Per Serving: Cal 432; Prot 5.2 g; Carbo 55.8 g; T Fat 23.1 g; Chol 54.8 mg; Potas 212.0 mg; Sod 83.8 mg.

CHOCOLATE OATMEAL CAKE

1 cup quick-cooking oats
1¹/₂ cups boiling water
¹/₂ cup shortening
1¹/₂ cups sugar
2 eggs
1 cup sifted flour
¹/₂ cup baking cocoa
1 teaspoon soda
¹/₂ teaspoon salt
1 teaspoon vanilla extract

Combine oats and boiling water in bowl. Let stand until cool. Cream shortening with sugar and eggs in mixer bowl until light and fluffy. Add oats mixture, flour, cocoa, soda, salt and vanilla; beat until smooth. Pour into greased 8x12-inch cake pan. Sprinkle with a small amount of additional sugar if desired. Bake at 350 degrees for 35 minutes or until cake tests done. Frost with favorite frosting if desired or serve with whipped cream. Yield: 8 servings.

Approx Per Serving: Cal 387; Prot 5.7 g; Carbo 58.7 g; T Fat 16.0 g; Chol 68.5 mg; Potas 130.0 mg; Sod 256.0 mg.

COCONUT-TOPPED OATMEAL CAKE

1 cup quick-cooking oats
1¹/₂ cups boiling water
1 cup sugar
1 cup packed brown sugar
¹/₂ cup margarine,
  softened
2 eggs, beaten
1¹/₃ cups flour
1 teaspoon soda
1 teaspoon cinnamon
¹/₂ teaspoon nutmeg
¹/₂ teaspoon salt
1 cup packed brown sugar
6 tablespoons margarine
¹/₄ cup cream
1 teaspoon vanilla extract
1 cup coconut
1 cup pecans

Combine oats and boiling water in bowl. Let stand for 20 minutes. Cream sugar, 1 cup brown sugar, ¹/₂ cup margarine and eggs in mixer bowl until light and fluffy. Add oats mixture; mix well. Sift in flour, soda, cinnamon, nutmeg and salt; mix well. Pour into greased and floured 9x13-inch cake pan. Bake at 350 degrees for 35 to 45 minutes or until cake tests done. Combine 1 cup brown sugar, 6 tablespoons margarine and cream in saucepan. Bring to a boil, stirring constantly. Boil for 3 minutes; remove from heat. Stir in vanilla, coconut and pecans. Spread warm topping over warm cake. Bake for 5 minutes longer or until topping is golden brown. Yield: 15 servings.

Approx Per Serving: Cal 404; Prot 3.3 g; Carbo 55.7 g; T Fat 19.8 g; Chol 40.9 mg; Potas 186.0 mg; Sod 313.0 mg.

BRANDY POUND CAKE

3 cups sugar
1 cup butter, softened
6 eggs
1 cup sour cream
¹/₂ cup apricot Brandy
¹/₂ teaspoon rum flavoring
1 teaspoon orange extract
1 teaspoon vanilla extract
¹/₄ teaspoon almond
  extract
¹/₂ teaspoon lemon extract
3 cups flour
¹/₄ teaspoon soda
¹/₂ teaspoon salt

Cream sugar and butter in mixer bowl until light and fluffy. Add eggs 1 at a time, mixing well after each addition. Combine sour cream, Brandy and flavorings in bowl; blend well. Add to creamed mixture alternately with mixture of dry ingredients, mixing well after each addition. Pour into greased and floured tube pan. Bake at 325 degrees for 1 hour and 10 minutes or until cake tests done. Cool in pan for 5 to 10 minutes. Invert onto serving plate to cool completely. Garnish with sprinkle of confectioners' sugar. Yield: 12 servings.

Approx Per Serving: Cal 545; Prot 7.1 g; Carbo 78.2 g; T Fat 22.5 g; Chol 187.0 mg; Potas 96.8 mg; Sod 282.0 mg.

BROWN SUGAR POUND CAKE

1 pound light brown sugar
1 cup sugar
1½ cups shortening
5 eggs
3 cups flour
1 teaspoon baking powder
½ teaspoon salt
1 cup milk
1 teaspoon vanilla extract

Cream sugars and shortening in mixer bowl until light and fluffy. Add eggs 1 at a time, mixing well after each addition. Sift flour, baking powder and salt together 3 times. Add to creamed mixture alternately with milk and vanilla, mixing well after each addition. Pour into greased and floured bundt pan. Bake at 375 degrees for 1 hour or until cake tests done. Cool in pan for 10 minutes. Invert onto serving plate. Garnish with sprinkle of confectioners' sugar or drizzle with a small amount of lemon juice and confectioners' sugar glaze. Yield: 12 servings.

Approx Per Serving: Cal 591; Prot 6.5 g; Carbo 78.1 g; T Fat 28.9 g; Chol 117.0 mg; Potas 215.0 mg; Sod 171.0 mg.

CREAM CHEESE POUND CAKE

1½ cups butter, softened
3 cups sugar
8 ounces cream cheese, softened
6 eggs
3 cups flour
Almond flavoring to taste

Cream butter, sugar and cream cheese in mixer bowl until light and fluffy. Add eggs and flour alternately, beating well after each addition. Blend in flavoring. Spoon into greased and floured 10-inch tube pan. Bake at 350 degrees for 10 minutes. Reduce temperature to 325 degrees. Bake for 1 hour to 1 hour and 10 minutes or until cake tests done. Cool in pan for 10 minutes. Remove to wire rack to cool completely. This is delicious served with fresh strawberries like a shortcake. Yield: 16 servings.

Approx Per Serving: Cal 461; Prot 6.0 g; Carbo 55.8 g; T Fat 24.5 g; Chol 165.0 mg; Potas 70.5 mg; Sod 214.0 mg.

Inie-Mae Testa
Groveland, New York

PINEAPPLE UPSIDE-DOWN CAKE

1/2 cup melted butter
1 cup packed brown sugar
1 16-ounce can crushed
   pineapple
3 eggs
1 1/2 cups sugar
1 teaspoon vanilla extract
1 1/2 tablespoons melted
   butter
1 1/2 cups flour
1 1/2 teaspoons baking
   powder
1/8 teaspoon salt
3/4 cup milk

Combine 1/2 cup butter, brown sugar and pineapple in cast-iron skillet; mix well and spread evenly in skillet. Cream eggs and sugar in mixer bowl. Add vanilla and 1 1/2 tablespoons butter; beat until light. Add mixture of flour, baking powder and salt alternately with milk, beating well after each addition. Pour over pineapple mixture. Bake at 350 degrees for 45 minutes or until cake tests done. Invert onto serving plate. Yield: 8 servings.

   Approx Per Serving: Cal 540; Prot 5.7 g; Carbo 94.4 g; T Fat 16.7 g;
      Chol 142.0 mg; Potas 233.0 mg; Sod 258.0 mg.

RHUBARB CAKE

1 1/2 cups packed brown
   sugar
1/2 cup butter, softened
2 eggs
1 teaspoon vanilla extract
2 cups flour
1/2 teaspoon salt
1 teaspoon baking powder
1 teaspoon soda
1/2 cup milk
2 cups finely chopped
   rhubarb

Cream brown sugar and butter in mixer bowl until light and fluffy. Beat in eggs and vanilla. Sift dry ingredients together. Add to creamed mixture alternately with milk, beating well after each addition. Stir in rhubarb. Pour into greased 9x13-inch cake pan. Bake at 350 degrees for 45 minutes to 1 hour or until cake tests done. Yield: 15 servings.

   Approx Per Serving: Cal 216; Prot 3.0 g; Carbo 35.1 g; T Fat 7.4 g;
      Chol 54.2 mg; Potas 160.0 mg; Sod 223.0 mg.

June Griffin
Russell, New York

DELICIOUSLY DIFFERENT FROSTING

1 cup margarine, softened
1 cup shortening
2 cups sugar
1½ cups hot milk
2 teaspoons vanilla extract

Combine margarine, shortening and sugar in mixer bowl; beat until creamy. Add hot milk about 1 tablespoon at a time, beating constantly. Beat in vanilla. Frosting will be runny at first but will thicken as it cools. Yield: 15 servings.

Approx Per Serving: Cal 347; Prot 0.9 g; Carbo 27.8 g; T Fat 26.6 g; Chol 3.3 mg; Potas 40.0 mg; Sod 154.0 mg.

Phyllis Wendt
Constableville, New York

FAVORITE FROSTING

5 tablespoons flour
1 cup milk
1½ cups sugar
1 cup shortening
2 teaspoons vanilla extract

Place flour in 1-quart saucepan. Stir in milk gradually. Bring to a boil over medium-high heat, stirring constantly. Cook for 2 minutes, stirring constantly. Pour into mixer bowl. Let stand until cool. Add sugar, shortening and vanilla. Beat at high speed for 10 minutes or until of spreading consistency. This frosting has been used for every birthday cake in our house for the past 25 years. It is very easy to handle and is especially good with lots of coconut added. Yield: 12 servings.

Approx Per Serving: Cal 217; Prot 0.8 g; Carbo 22.6 g; T Fat 14.2 g; Chol 2.2 mg; Potas 25.0 mg; Sod 7.4 mg.

Phyllis Wendt
Constableville, New York

APPLE BROWNIES

2/3 cup margarine,
  softened
1 cup packed brown sugar
2 eggs
1 teaspoon vanilla extract
1 1/2 cups flour
2 teaspoons baking
  powder
1/4 teaspoon salt
1 cup chopped apples
1/2 cup chopped pecans

Cream margarine, brown sugar, eggs and vanilla in mixer bowl until light and fluffy. Add flour, baking powder and salt; mix well. Stir in apples and pecans. Spread in greased 9x9-inch baking pan. Bake at 350 degrees for 35 minutes or until edges pull from sides of pan. Cool. Cut into squares. Yield: 16 servings.

Approx Per Serving: Cal 200; Prot 2.4 g; Carbo 24.2 g; T Fat 10.9 g; Chol 34.2 mg; Potas 93.6 mg; Sod 178.0 mg.

CHOCOLATE DROPS

2 1/3 cup unbleached flour,
  sifted
1/2 teaspoon soda
1/8 teaspoon salt
1/2 cup butter, softened
1 cup packed brown sugar
1 egg, beaten
1/2 cup baking cocoa
1/2 cup sour milk
1 teaspoon vanilla extract
1/2 cup chopped pecans

Sift flour, soda and salt together. Cream butter, brown sugar, egg and cocoa in mixer bowl until light and fluffy. Add sour milk and vanilla. Add sifted dry ingredients; mix well. Stir in pecans. Drop by teaspoonfuls onto greased cookie sheet. Bake at 375 degrees for 12 to 15 minutes or until cookies spring back when lightly touched. Cool on wire rack. Yield: 36 cookies.

Approx Per Cookie: Cal 90; Prot 1.3 g; Carbo 12.5 g; T Fat 4.0 g; Chol 15.0 mg; Potas 42.4 mg; Sod 46.5 mg.

Deloris "Lorie" Okusko
Gouverneur, New York

DEVIL'S FOOD SANDWICH COOKIES

1/2 cup shortening
1 cup sugar
1 egg
1 teaspoon vanilla extract
1 3/4 cups flour
1/2 cup baking cocoa
1 1/4 teaspoons soda
1/8 teaspoon salt
1 cup buttermilk
1/4 cup butter, softened
1/4 cup shortening
1 cup marshmallow creme
1 1/2 teaspoons vanilla
extract
1 1/4 cups confectioners'
sugar

Cream 1/2 cup shortening and sugar in mixer bowl until light and fluffy. Beat in egg and 1 teaspoon vanilla. Add mixture of flour, cocoa, soda and salt alternately with buttermilk, mixing well after each addition. Drop by teaspoonfuls 2 inches apart onto cookie sheet. Bake at 375 degrees for 8 to 10 minutes or until cookies spring back when lightly touched. Cool on wire rack. Cream butter and 1/4 cup shortening in mixer bowl. Beat in marshmallow creme gradually. Add 1 1/2 teaspoons vanilla and confectioners' sugar; beat until fluffy. Spread 1 tablespoon filling on flat side of half the cookies. Place remaining cookies flat side down on filling. Yield: 18 cookies.

Approx Per Cookie: Cal 275; Prot 2.6 g; Carbo 41.0 g; T Fat 12.1 g; Chol 22.6 mg; Potas 69.8 mg; Sod 121.0 mg.

GINGERSNAPS

3/4 cup shortening
1/4 cup molasses
1 cup sugar
1 egg
2 cups flour
2 teaspoons soda
1/2 teaspoon salt
1 teaspoon cinnamon
1 tablespoon ginger

Combine shortening, molasses, sugar and egg in bowl; mix well. Add flour, soda, salt, cinnamon and ginger; mix well. Shape into small balls; roll in additional sugar. Place on cookie sheet; press to flatten. Bake at 325 degrees for 6 to 8 minutes; do not overbake. Cool on wire rack. Yield: 36 cookies.

Approx Per Cookie: Cal 91; Prot 0.9 g; Carbo 12.0 g; T Fat 4.5 g; Chol 7.61 mg; Potas 73.7 mg; Sod 79.5 mg.

HELLO DOLLY BARS

10 tablespoons margarine
1¹/₂ cups graham cracker
  crumbs
1 cup chocolate chips
1 cup coconut
1 15-ounce can
  sweetened condensed
  milk
¹/₂ cup chopped pecans

Melt margarine in 9x13-inch baking pan. Press graham cracker crumbs into margarine. Add layers of chocolate chips and coconut. Pour condensed milk over top; sprinkle with pecans. Bake at 350 degrees for 30 minutes. Cool. Cut into squares. Yield: 20 servings.

Approx Per Serving: Cal 238; Prot 3.1 g; Carbo 25.7 g; T Fat 14.7 g; Chol 7.2 mg; Potas 158.0 mg; Sod 160.0 mg.

ICE CREAM KOLACHES

2 cups butter
4 cups flour
1 pint vanilla ice cream,
  softened

Cut butter into flour in bowl until crumbly. Stir in ice cream. Chill overnight. Roll on surface sprinkled with confectioners' sugar; cut as desired. Make indentation in center; fill with favorite jam. Place on cookie sheet. Bake at 350 degrees for 15 minutes. Cool on wire rack. Sprinkle with confectioners' sugar. Yield: 60 cookies.

Approx Per Cookie: Cal 94; Prot 1.1 g; Carbo 7.4 g; T Fat 6.7 g; Chol 18.5 mg; Potas 18.5 mg; Sod 55.6 mg.
Nutritional information does not include confectioners' sugar or fruit filling.

LACY SEE-THROUGH COOKIES

¹/₄ cup margarine,
  softened
1 cup sugar
3 tablespoons flour
1 egg, beaten
1 teaspoon baking powder
1 teaspoon vanilla extract
¹/₄ teaspoon cinnamon
¹/₄ teaspoon salt
1 cup oats

Cream margarine and sugar in mixer bowl until light and fluffy. Add flour, egg, baking powder, vanilla, cinnamon, salt and oats; mix well. Drop by teaspoonfuls onto foil-lined cookie sheet. Bake at 350 degrees for 7 to 10 minutes or until golden brown. Yield: 36 cookies.

Approx Per Cookie: Cal 46; Prot 0.6 g; Carbo 7.6 g; T Fat 1.6 g; Chol 7.6 mg; Potas 11.3 mg; Sod 40.9 mg.

Marilyn K. Adams
Watertown, New York

LEMON CHEESE BARS

1 2-layer package yellow
   cake mix with pudding
1 egg
1/3 cup oil
8 ounces light cream
   cheese, softened
1/3 cup sugar
1 teaspoon lemon juice
1 egg

Combine dry cake mix, 1 egg and oil in bowl; mix until crumbly. Reserve 1 cup crumb mixture. Press remaining crumb mixture lightly into ungreased 9x13-inch baking pan. Bake at 350 degrees for 15 minutes. Combine cream cheese, sugar, lemon juice and 1 egg in mixer bowl. Beat until smooth. Spread over baked layer. Sprinkle with reserved crumb mixture. Bake for 15 minutes. Cool. Cut into bars. May substitute lemon cake mix for yellow cake mix. Yield: 16 bars.

Approx Per Bar: Cal 258; Prot 3.2 g; Carbo 32.5 g; T Fat 12.8 g;
   Chol 49.7 mg; Potas 25.3 mg; Sod 255.0 mg.

Barbara H. Haller
Dexter, New York

MINCEMEAT SQUARES

3/4 cup butter, softened
3 tablespoons
   confectioners' sugar
1 1/2 cups flour
1/3 cup butter, softened
1/2 cup packed brown
   sugar
2 eggs, beaten
1 1/2 cups mincemeat
3/4 cup coconut
1/3 cup chopped walnuts

Combine 3/4 cup butter, confectioners' sugar and flour in bowl; mix well. Pat into greased 9x13-inch baking pan. Bake at 350 degrees for 10 minutes. Cool. Cream 1/3 cup butter and brown sugar in large bowl until light and fluffy. Add eggs; mix well. Add mincemeat, coconut and walnuts; mix well. Spread over baked layer. Bake at 350 degrees for 20 to 25 minutes. Cool. Cut into squares. Yield: 32 squares.

Approx Per Square: Cal 112; Prot 1.3 g; Carbo 9.4 g; T Fat 7.9 g;
   Chol 33.9 mg; Potas 35.2 mg; Sod 62.8 mg.
   Nutritional information does not include mincemeat.

NUT SMACKS

1/2 cup sugar
1/2 cup butter, softened
2 egg yolks
1 teaspoon vanilla extract
1/8 teaspoon salt
11/2 cups flour
1 teaspoon baking powder
2 egg whites
1 cup packed brown sugar
1 cup finely chopped
  pecans

Combine sugar, butter, egg yolks, vanilla and salt in bowl; mix well. Add mixture of flour and baking powder; mix well. Spread in 9x9-inch baking pan. Beat egg whites in glass bowl until very stiff. Fold in brown sugar and pecans gently. Spread over batter. Bake at 350 degrees for 30 minutes. Cool on wire rack. Cut into squares. Yield: 16 servings.

Approx Per Serving: Cal 228; Prot 2.8 g; Carbo 30.3 g; T Fat 11.9 g; Chol 49.5 mg; Potas 91.1 mg; Sod 91.0 mg.

Mrs. Burton Grass
Kingston, Ontario, Canada

LEMON OATMEAL COOKIES

1/2 cup shortening
1/2 cup packed brown
  sugar
1/2 cup sugar
2 tablespoons lemon juice
1 tablespoon grated
  lemon rind
1 egg, beaten
3/4 cup flour
1/2 teaspoon salt
1/2 teaspoon soda
21/2 cups quick-cooking
  oats
1/2 cup chopped walnuts

Cream shortening, brown sugar and sugar in mixer bowl until light and fluffy. Beat in lemon juice, lemon rind and egg. Sift in mixture of flour, salt and soda; mix well. Stir in oats and walnuts. Drop by large spoonfuls onto greased cookie sheet. Bake at 375 degrees for 12 to 15 minutes or until brown. Cool on wire rack. Yield: 36 cookies.

Approx Per Cookie: Cal 80; Prot 1.1 g; Carbo 9.8 g; T Fat 4.2 g; Chol 7.6 mg; Potas 33.5 mg; Sod 71.0 mg.

ONE-CUP COOKIES

1 cup margarine, softened
1 cup sugar
1 cup packed brown sugar
3 eggs
1 cup peanut butter
1 cup flour
1 tablespoon soda
1 cup oats
1 cup coconut
1 cup chopped walnuts
1 cup raisins
1 cup chocolate chips

Cream margarine, sugar and brown sugar in mixer bowl until light and fluffy. Add eggs 1 at a time, mixing well after each addition. Add peanut butter; mix well. Add mixture of flour and soda; mix well. Add remaining ingredients 1 at a time, stirring well after each addition. Drop by heaping teaspoonfuls onto cookie sheet. Bake at 350 degrees for 10 minutes. Cool on wire rack. Yield: 60 cookies.

Approx Per Cookie: Cal 137; Prot 2.5 g; Carbo 14.8 g; T Fat 8.3 g; Chol 13.7 mg; Potas 98.2 mg; Sod 103.0 mg.

PECAN BARS

1/2 cup butter, softened
1/2 cup packed brown
  sugar
1/2 teaspoon salt
1 cup flour
2 tablespoons milk
1 tablespoon vanilla
  extract
2 eggs, beaten
1 cup packed brown sugar
2 tablespoons flour
1/2 teaspoon baking
  powder
1 cup chopped pecans

Cream butter, 1/2 cup brown sugar and salt in mixer bowl until light and fluffy. Add 1 cup flour alternately with milk, mixing well after each addition. Pat mixture into bottom of greased 9x9-inch baking pan. Bake at 325 degrees for 20 minutes. Beat vanilla, eggs and 1 cup brown sugar in bowl. Add 2 tablespoons flour, baking powder and pecans. Pour over baked layer. Bake at 325 degrees for 30 minutes. Cool. Cut into bars. Yield: 24 bars.

Approx Per Bar: Cal 147; Prot 1.6 g; Carbo 18.7 g; T Fat 7.8 g; Chol 33.4 mg; Potas 80.8 mg; Sod 96.0 mg.

RICE KRISPIE DELIGHTS

3 cups sugar
3 cups light corn syrup
3 cups peanut butter
6 cups Rice Krispies
1 cup chocolate chips

Bring sugar and corn syrup to a boil in saucepan, stirring constantly; remove from heat. Stir in peanut butter. Add cereal; stir until coated. Press into baking pan with wooden spoon. Sprinkle chocolate chips over top. Let stand until chocolate chips are soft. Spread with knife to frost top. Yield: 36 servings.

Approx Per Serving: Cal 310; Prot 6.6 g; Carbo 47.3 g; T Fat 12.7 g; Chol 0.0 mg; Potas 174.0 mg; Sod 157.0 mg.

Mrs. Ken Hollister
Owego, New York

SNICKERS BAR COOKIES

1   24-ounce package refrigerator chocolate chip cookies
5 or 6 Snickers candy bars, sliced 1/4-inch thick

Slice cookie dough. Press slices into 9x11-inch baking pan. Bake using package directions or until almost golden brown. Arrange candy over baked layer. Bake until candy is softened; spread evenly over baked layer. Cool. Cut into squares. Yield: 36 squares.

Approx Per Square: Cal 137; Prot 2.0 g; Carbo 18.7 g; T Fat 6.7 g; Chol 8.7 mg; Potas 59.2 mg; Sod 96.5 mg.

GALETTE

1 1/2 cups flour
1/2 cup unsalted butter
5 to 6 tablespoons cold water
5 or 6 apples, peeled, sliced
1/4 cup sugar
Cinnamon to taste
Nutmeg to taste
1/2 cup apricot jam

Place flour in bowl. Cut butter into flour, leaving lumps of butter; do not cut until crumbly. Add enough water to shape mixture into ball. Chill in refrigerator. Roll into large circle on lightly floured surface; fit into 9-inch pie plate, leaving overhanging pastry. Place apples in pie plate; sprinkle with sugar, cinnamon and nutmeg. Fold pastry over apples. Bake at 400 degrees for 1 hour. Spread jam over hot pie. Yield: 6 servings.

Approx Per Serving: Cal 433; Prot 3.9 g; Carbo 71.7 g; T Fat 16.1 g; Chol 41.4 mg; Potas 218.0 mg; Sod 6.6 mg.

Joy M.J. Karam
Ottawa, Ontario, Canada

APPLE PRALINE PIE

6 cups sliced peeled
  apples
3/4 cup sugar
1/4 cup flour
1 teaspoon cinnamon
1/4 teaspoon salt
1 recipe 2-crust pie pastry
2 tablespoons margarine
1/2 cup melted margarine
1/2 cup packed brown
  sugar
1 tablespoon milk
1/2 cup chopped pecans

Combine apples, sugar, flour, cinnamon and salt in bowl; toss lightly. Place in pastry-lined pie plate. Dot with 2 tablespoons margarine. Top with remaining pastry, sealing edge and cutting vents. Bake at 350 degrees for 50 minutes or until lightly browned. Blend 1/2 cup melted margarine, brown sugar and milk in small saucepan. Bring to a boil, stirring constantly; remove from heat. Stir in pecans. Spread over pie. Bake for 5 minutes longer or until bubbly. Yield: 6 servings.

Approx Per Serving: Cal 819; Prot 5.2 g; Carbo 89.0 g; T Fat 44.0 g;
    Chol 0.3 mg; Potas 282.0 mg; Sod 689.0 mg.

EASY WONDERFUL CHEESECAKE PIE

1 9-inch graham cracker
  pie shell
8 ounces cream cheese,
  softened
1/2 cup sugar
1 envelope whipped
  topping mix, prepared
1 21-ounce can
  blackberry pie filling

Bake graham cracker pie shell using package directions. Cool. Beat cream cheese and sugar in mixer bowl until light and fluffy. Add whipped topping; blend well. Spread in prepared pie shell. Top with pie filling. Chill for 3 hours or longer. May substitute any favorite pie filling for blackberry. Yield: 6 servings.

Approx Per Serving: Cal 563; Prot 5.4 g; Carbo 76.6 g; T Fat 27.7 g;
    Chol 41.3 mg; Potas 208.0 mg; Sod 460.0 mg.
    Nutritional information does not include prepared whipped
    topping mix.

Blanche Selke
Nepean, Ontario, Canada

SUPER CUSTARD PIE

1 14-ounce can
   sweetened condensed
   milk
1¹/2 cups hot water
¹/2 teaspoon salt
¹/2 teaspoon vanilla extract
3 eggs, well beaten
Nutmeg to taste
1 baked 10-inch graham
   cracker pie shell

Combine condensed milk, water, salt and vanilla in bowl; blend well. Add eggs; mix well. Pour into pie shell. Sprinkle with nutmeg. Bake at 425 degrees for 10 minutes. Reduce oven temperature to 300 degrees. Bake for 20 to 25 minutes longer or until knife inserted near center comes out clean. Cool to room temperature. Chill until serving time. Yield: 8 servings.

Approx Per Serving: Cal 193; Prot 6.3 g; Carbo 27.8 g; T Fat 6.5 g; Chol 120.0 mg; Potas 211.0 mg; Sod 228.0 mg.

Amanda Flanagan
Watertown, New York

LEMON TARTS

4 cups flour
1 teaspoon salt
1³/4 cups shortening
¹/2 cup cold water
Juice of 2 lemons
2 cups sugar
¹/2 cup butter
4 eggs, slightly beaten
Grated rind of 2 lemons
2 cups whipping cream,
   whipped

Combine flour and salt in bowl. Cut in shortening until crumbly. Add water gradually, mixing with fork until mixture forms ball. Roll thinly on floured surface; cut with small round cutter or glass. Fit into 1¹/2-inch tart pans. Prick with fork. Bake at 400 degrees for 10 minutes or just until golden. Remove from pans; place on wire rack to cool. Combine lemon juice, sugar and butter in double boiler. Heat over hot water just until butter is melted. Add eggs; mix well. Cook for 20 to 30 minutes or until thickened, stirring frequently; remove from heat. Stir in lemon rind. Cool. May store in refrigerator for up to 3 weeks. Spoon filling into shells just before serving. Top with dollop of whipped cream, sweetened if desired. Yield: 48 tarts.

Approx Per Tart: Cal 177; Prot 1.7 g; Carbo 16.5 g; T Fat 11.8 g; Chol 34.8 mg; Potas 21.6 mg; Sod 68.6 mg.

Mary Laidlaw
Ottawa, Ontario, Canada

Substitution Chart

	Instead of	Use
Baking	1 teaspoon baking powder	1/4 teaspoon soda plus 1/2 teaspoon cream of tartar
	1 tablespoon cornstarch (for thickening)	2 tablespoons flour or 1 tablespoon tapioca
	1 cup sifted all-purpose flour	1 cup plus 2 tablespoons sifted cake flour
	1 cup sifted cake flour	1 cup minus 2 tablespoons sifted all-purpose flour
	1 cup dry bread crumbs	3/4 cup cracker crumbs
Dairy	1 cup buttermilk	1 cup sour milk or 1 cup yogurt
	1 cup heavy cream	3/4 cup skim milk plus 1/3 cup butter
	1 cup light cream	7/8 cup skim milk plus 3 tablespoons butter
	1 cup sour cream	7/8 cup sour milk plus 3 tablespoons butter
	1 cup sour milk	1 cup milk plus 1 tablespoon vinegar or lemon juice or 1 cup buttermilk
Seasoning	1 teaspoon allspice	1/2 teaspoon cinnamon plus 1/8 teaspoon cloves
	1 cup catsup	1 cup tomato sauce plus 1/2 cup sugar plus 2 tablespoons vinegar
	1 clove of garlic	1/8 teaspoon garlic powder or 1/8 teaspoon instant minced garlic or 3/4 teaspoon garlic salt or 5 drops of liquid garlic
	1 teaspoon Italian spice	1/4 teaspoon each oregano, basil, thyme, rosemary plus dash of cayenne
	1 teaspoon lemon juice	1/2 teaspoon vinegar
	1 tablespoon mustard	1 teaspoon dry mustard
	1 medium onion	1 tablespoon dried minced onion or 1 teaspoon onion powder
Sweet	1 1-ounce square chocolate	1/4 cup cocoa plus 1 teaspoon shortening
	1 2/3 ounces semisweet chocolate	1 ounce unsweetened chocolate plus 4 teaspoons granulated sugar
	1 cup honey	1 to 1 1/4 cups sugar plus 1/4 cup liquid or 1 cup corn syrup or molasses
	1 cup granulated sugar	1 cup packed brown sugar or 1 cup corn syrup, molasses or honey minus 1/4 cup liquid

Equivalent Chart

	When the recipe calls for	Use
Baking	1/2 cup butter	4 ounces
	2 cups butter	1 pound
	4 cups all-purpose flour	1 pound
	41/2 to 5 cups sifted cake flour	1 pound
	1 square chocolate	1 ounce
	1 cup semisweet chocolate chips	6 ounces
	4 cups marshmallows	1 pound
	21/4 cups packed brown sugar	1 pound
	4 cups confectioners' sugar	1 pound
	2 cups granulated sugar	1 pound
Cereal – Bread	1 cup fine dry bread crumbs	4 to 5 slices
	1 cup soft bread crumbs	2 slices
	1 cup small bread cubes	2 slices
	1 cup fine cracker crumbs	28 saltines
	1 cup fine graham cracker crumbs	15 crackers
	1 cup vanilla wafer crumbs	22 wafers
	1 cup crushed cornflakes	3 cups uncrushed
	4 cups cooked macaroni	8 ounces uncooked
	31/2 cups cooked rice	1 cup uncooked
Dairy	1 cup shredded cheese	4 ounces
	1 cup cottage cheese	8 ounces
	1 cup sour cream	8 ounces
	1 cup whipped cream	1/2 cup heavy cream
	2/3 cup evaporated milk	1 small can
	12/3 cups evaporated milk	1 13-ounce can
Fruit	4 cups sliced or chopped apples	4 medium
	1 cup mashed bananas	3 medium
	2 cups pitted cherries	4 cups unpitted
	3 cups shredded coconut	8 ounces
	4 cups cranberries	1 pound
	1 cup pitted dates	1 8-ounce package
	1 cup candied fruit	1 8-ounce package
	3 to 4 tablespoons lemon juice plus 1 tablespoon grated lemon rind	1 lemon
	1/3 cup orange juice plus 2 teaspoons grated orange rind	1 orange
	4 cups sliced peaches	8 medium
	2 cups pitted prunes	1 12-ounce package
	3 cups raisins	1 15-ounce package

	When the recipe calls for	Use
Meats	4 cups chopped cooked chicken 3 cups chopped cooked meat 2 cups cooked ground meat	1 5-pound chicken 1 pound, cooked 1 pound, cooked
Nuts	1 cup chopped nuts	4 ounces shelled 1 pound unshelled
Vegetables	2 cups cooked green beans 2 1/2 cups lima beans or red beans 4 cups shredded cabbage 1 cup grated carrot 8 ounces fresh mushrooms 1 cup chopped onion 4 cups sliced or chopped potatoes 2 cups canned tomatoes	1/2 pound fresh or 1 16-ounce can 1 cup dried, cooked 1 pound 1 large 1 4-ounce can 1 large 4 medium 1 16-ounce can

Measurement Equivalents

1 tablespoon = 3 teaspoons
2 tablespoons = 1 ounce
4 tablespoons = 1/4 cup
5 1/3 tablespoons = 1/3 cup
8 tablespoons = 1/2 cup
12 tablespoons = 3/4 cup
16 tablespoons = 1 cup
1 cup = 8 ounces or 1/2 pint
4 cups = 1 quart
4 quarts = 1 gallon

1 6 1/2 to 8-ounce can = 1 cup
1 10 1/2 to 12-ounce can = 1 1/4 cups
1 14 to 16-ounce can = 1 3/4 cups
1 16 to 17-ounce can = 2 cups
1 18 to 20-ounce can = 2 1/2 cups
1 20-ounce can = 3 1/2 cups
1 46 to 51-ounce can = 5 3/4 cups
1 6 1/2 to 7 1/2-pound can or Number
   10 = 12 to 13 cups

Metric Equivalents

Liquid	Dry
1 teaspoon = 5 milliliters 1 tablespoon = 15 milliliters 1 fluid ounce = 30 milliliters 1 cup = 250 milliliters 1 pint = 500 milliliters	1 quart = 1 liter 1 ounce = 30 grams 1 pound = 450 grams 2.2 pounds = 1 kilogram

NOTE: The metric measures are approximate benchmarks for purposes of home food preparation.

Plant	Description	Meats
Basil	Strong aromatic herb Good salt replacer Main ingredient in pesto sauce	Use with meat loaf, meat balls, spaghetti, pizza, chili & hamburgers
Chives	Mild Onion flavor Use fresh or frozen	Use on any meat that needs a mild onion flavor
Parsley	Most popular herb Carrot-like flavor	Delicious in lasagna & in stews Add to roast lamb
Marjoram/Oregano	Milder flavor than oregano; Salt replacer for all dishes ——— Pizza herb	All Italian dishes, meat loaf, pork & lamb; Add to hamburger, casseroles, chili & fried chicken
Sage	Strongly aromatic with a slight taste of nutmeg	Roast pork, ham loaf, goose & duck Try on veal, baked ham, pork, & sausage
Savory	(Summer & Winter) Strong with pepper-like taste The "bean herb"	Roast duck & game Use in stews
Thyme	One of the most versatile herbs Very fragrant	Lamb, beef, pork, game & barbeque sauces Add to meat loaf

Fish/Poultry	Vegetables/Soups/Salads	Eggs/Cheese/Sauces, Etc.
All fish dishes & poultry dishes	Use with all vegetables Good on tomato dishes Especially good on squash; Add to salad dressings; Sprinkle over tomato soup	Omelets Scrambled eggs Cheese soufflé Good in quiche
Use in sauce for fish Sauté with chicken Try in tuna salad or tuna casserole	Sprinkle on baked potatoes & salads Cook with rice & new potatoes; Use in soups & mashed potatoes	Sprinkle over eggs & cream cheese sandwich Add to biscuit dough or corn muffins
Sprinkle over chicken & fish dishes Use in chicken salad	Toss with new potatoes Cut for fresh salads & soups Add to potato salad	Good in omelets & sandwiches Add to gravies, sauces & quiche
All baked fish & crab dishes; Good in chicken cacciatore Add to poultry casseroles	Blend in butter to season all vegetables Add to salad dressings Use in potatoes	Sprinkle over cheese in grilled cheese sandwich Try in white sauce, omelets & marinades
Add to bread stuffing for poultry & for fish	Add to baked onions Sprinkle over beans	Add to cheese sauce Try in gravies All cheese dishes
Use sparingly with fish Mix with other herbs in tuna salad	Any green vegetable & salads; Good in soups	Blend with other herbs in eggs
Baked or broiled fish, shrimp, chicken, & turkey Add to tuna casseroles	Sauté with butter & pour over vegetables Use in clam chowder Good on peas, carrots & onions; Sprinkle over baked potatoes	Use on spanish omelet Add to salad dressing, soufflé & quiche

Index

APPETIZERS
Artichoke Squares, 21
Asparagus Roll-Ups, 21
Cheese
  Balls
    Taco, 23
    Three, 22
  Brie, Baked, 22
Chicken
  Bits, 23
  Wings, Peanutty, 24
Cocktail Sauce, 24
Crab
  Dip, Cheesy Hot, 25
  Muffin Toasties, 24
Dip
  Crab, Cheesy Hot, 25
  Dill, 25
  Fiesta, Layered, 26
  Fruit, Tropical, 25
  Salmon, 26
  Spinach, 26
Salmon
  Dip, 26
  Log, 27
  Pâté, 27
Sausage Bites, Sweet and Sour, 28
Seviche, 28
Snacks, Yummy, 28

BEEF
Brisket, Peppered, 81
Catalan, 84
Reuben Casserole, 86
Roast
  Company, 82
  Fruited, 81
  Pot, with Coffee Gravy, 82
  Sauerbraten and Noodles, 85
Sirloin Tips, Braised, 84
Steak
  Flank, Rice-Stuffed, 83
  Grilled, with Wine Sauce, 83
  Sirloin Tips, Braised, 84
Stew
  French, 85

Greek, and Onion, 86
BREADS
Biscuits, Sausage and Sour Cream, 151
Coffeecake
  Monkey, 166
  Overnight, 152
  Poppy Seed, 152
Corn, Jalapeño, 153
Loaves
  Quick
    Apricot, 153
    Avocado, 154
    Lemon, 154
    Orange and Pecan Honey, 155
    Pear, 155
    Poppy Seed, 156
    Pumpkin and Raisin, 156
    Strawberry, 157
  Yeast
    Egg Braid, 158
    French, Food Processor, 158
    Honey, 157
    Monkey, 166
    Oatmeal, Refrigerator, 159
Muffins
  Apple Spiced, Sugary, 159
  Banana and Walnut, 160
  Cheddar Bran, 160
  Christmas, 161
  Gingerbread, 161
Pancakes
  Apple, 162
  Multi-Grain, 162
Rolls
  Butterhorns, 164
  Cheese
    Filled Squares, 166
    Herbed, 166
  Cream Cheese, 164
  Mashed Potato, 165
  Yeast Bread Sweet, 165
Scones with Mock Devonshire
    Cream, 151
Waffles
  Best-Ever Henderson, 163
  Mexican, 164

CAKES
A to Z, 177
Apple, Nobby, 177
Applesauce, Old-Fashioned, 176
Birthday, Perfect, 178
Black Forest, Mock, 180
Blueberry-Sour Cream, 179
Buttermilk, 179
Chocolate
  Pudding, 180
  Four-Day, and Coconut, 181
  Frosting, 178
  Oatmeal, 183
    Coconut-Topped, 184
Filling, Whipped Cream, 178
Frosting
  Chocolate, 178
  Deliciously Different, 187
  Favorite, 187
Fruit Cocktail, 181
Greek, 182
Holiday, Polish, 182
Hummingbird, 183
Pineapple Upside-Down, 186
Pound
  Brandy, 184
  Brown Sugar, 185
  Cream Cheese, 185
Rhubarb, 186

CHICKEN
Baked, Garlic, 104
Breasts, Supreme, 106
Broiled, and Rice, 102
Cacciatore, 104
Cherry, 102
Dijon, 105
Fried, Italiano, 103
Golden Glazed, 103
Junk, 105
Kiev, Mexican, 105
Spaghetti for-a-Crowd, 107
Supreme, 107
Tipsy, 106

COOKIES
Apple Brownies, 188
Chocolate Drops, 188
Devil's Food Sandwich Cookies, 189
Gingersnaps, 189
Hello Dolly Bars, 190

Ice Cream Kolaches, 190
Lacy See-Through Cookies, 190
Lemon Cheese Bars, 191
Mincemeat Squares, 191
Nut Smacks, 192
Oatmeal, Lemon, 192
One-Cup, 193
Pecan Bars, 193
Rice Krispie Delights, 194
Snickers Bar, 194

DESSERTS
Apples, Honey-Crunch Baked, 169
Butter Brickle, Frozen, 173
Cheesecake
  Mocha, Frozen, 171
  Pumpkin, 172
  White Chocolate, Microwave, 171
Cherry Dump, 170
Chocolate
  Death by, 172
  Ice Cream, Cherry, 173
Fruit Pizza, 175
Ice Cream
  Chocolate-Cherry, 173
  Roll, Crispy, 173
Lemon Lush, 174
Peach Crisp, 174
Pudding
  Banana, Deluxe, 169
  Bread, Surprise, 170
  Poor Man's, 176
Pumpkin
  Cheesecake, 172
  Delicious, 175
Raspberry Jubilee, 176

FISH
Baked, 47
  Cottage, 48
  Fillets with Tomato, 52
  Fry, 47
  Haddock, 54
  Perch, 54
  Simply Delicious, 49
  Stuffed, 48
  Trout in Cream, 63
Bass, Norwegian, 53
Batter for-a-Gang, Hank's, 78
Boneless, Fillets, 49
Carp, Cakes, 53

Deep-Fried, 49
Fritters, 50
Haddock, Baked, 54
Loaf, 50
Patties, 51
Perch
    Baked, 54
        Italian, 54
    Nuggets, 55
    Pizza, 55
Pike
    Broiled Northern, 56
    Dilled, and Pea Pods, 56
Roll-Ups, Lively Lemon, 51
Salmon
    Appetizers. *See Appetizers*
    Baked
        King, 57
        Lorrie's, Fillet, 56
    Balls, 59
    Barbecued, 58
    Canned, 58
    in Herb Sauce, 57
    with Lemon-Mushroom Sauce, 59
    Loaf, 60
    Pie, and Potato, 60
    Planked, 61
    Poached, 61
    Poor Man's Shrimp, 58
    Scallop, Crunchy, 62
    Steaks, Teriyaki, 61
Sauce for, 78
Trout
    Baked, in Cream, 63
    Crispy Brown, 64
    Garlic, 63
    Pan-Fried Brown, 64
    Quiche, 65
    Savory Lake, 62
in Sour Cream, 51
Walleye, Lime and Wine, 65
in Wine Sauce, 52

GAME
Bear Roast, 115
Porcupine Stew, 121
    Sausage, 118
    Schnitzel, Paprika, 118
    Stew, 119
        with Dumplings, 119
    Stroganoff, 120

Supreme, 120
Venison
    Big Bob's Shoulder, 115
    Chili, 116
    Marinated, 116
    Meatballs, 117
    Roast, 117

GAME BIRDS
Dove, Monterey-Style, 121
Duck
    with Apple Dressing, 122
    Barbecued, 122
    Cassoulet, Crock•Pot, 123
    Charcoal-Broiled, 123
    Gumbo, 124
    Oriental, with Snow Peas, 124
    Wild, in Sweet and Sour Sauce,
        Baked, 125
Goose
    Stew, Savory Wild, 126
    Stir-Fry, Oriental, 125
Grouse
    and Wild Rice, 126
Partridge Cordon Bleu, 127
Pheasant
    Casserole, 128
    Chili, 127
    Roast, in Applejack and Cream
        Sauce, 128
Quail
    Baked in Mushroom Sauce, 130
    Crock•Pot, 129
    with White Grapes, 129
Wild Turkey, Stuffed, 130

GROUND BEEF
All-in-One, Casserole, 92
Cornish Pasties with Mushroom
        Sauce, 91
Lebanese Lubi, 93
Loaf, 89
    Italiano, 90
    Miniature Mexicali, 90
Meatballs
    Cranberry, 87
    and Yorkshire Pudding, 88
Patties Cordon Bleu, 88
Pie, and Broccoli, 92
Roll, Deluxe, 89
Stew, Baked Stew, 93

Tagliarini, Favorite, 94
Wellington, 91

HAM
Baked, with Stuffing Supreme, 99
Horseradish-Glazed, 99
Loaf, Glazed, 100
Omelet Roll, and Cheese, 101
Quiche Olé, 101
Strata, Ham and Broccoli, 100

MEATLESS MAIN DISHES
Black Beans and Rice, 109
Chili, Vegetarian, 110
Eggplant Parmesan, 110
Eggs Florentine, 109
Pasta
Fettucini Alfredo Verde, 11
Spaghetti
Vegetable, 111
Zucchini, 112
Rice and Zucchini, 112

PIES
Apple Praline, 195
Cheesecake, Easy Wonderful, 195
Custard, Super, 196
Galette, 194
Lemon Tarts, 196

PORK
Canadian Bacon and Egg Bake, 97
Chops
Oriental, Grilled, 95
Pizza-Style, 95
and Sauerkraut, 96
Ribs, Crock•Pot, 96
Roast, Saucy, 94
Sausage
Stew
Hot, 97
Mediterranean Irish, 98
Stuffed French Toast, 98

SALADS
Fruit
Cranberry Freeze, 35
Cup, Frozen, 36
Grape Ring with Creamy
Dressing, 37
Peach, 37

Pineapple
Congealed, 38
and Cottage Cheese, 37
Poppy Seed, 36
Main Dish
Chicken and Fruit, Curried, 38
Ham, 39
Salmon, 39
Shrimp Louis, 40
Tortelini, 40
Tuna, Supreme, 41
Rice, Cold, 43
Vegetable
Garden, Loaf, 41
Pea, Peanutty, 42
Potato, Confetti, 42
Slaw, Favorite, 44
Spinach, Layered, 43
Summer, 44
Tomatoes, Marinated, 44

SEAFOOD
See also Fish, Shellfish
Linguine with, Sauce, 77
Paella, 76
Seasoning Mix, 77

SHELLFISH
Clam
Risotto with, 66
Spaghetti, 66
Crab
Cakes, 67
Divan, 67
Imperial, Easy, 68
Lobster
Cantonese, 68
Florentine, 70
Newburg, 69
Spanish, 69
Oysters
Casino, 70
Rockefeller, 71
Scallop
Casserole, 71
Coquilles St. Jacques, 72
Shrimp
Cacciatore, 72
Creole, 73
Curry, 73
Etouffée, 74

and Pasta Casserole, 75
Punjabi, 74
and Red Rice, 75
and Rice Special, 76

SIDE DISHES
Dressing
  Crock•Pot, 143
  Potato, 144
Fruit
  Cranberry Relish, Easy, 141
  Curried, 141
  Pineapple Bake, 141
Grits Casserole, 144
Macaroni, Party, 144
Noodles
  Neapolitan, 145
  Pudding, 146
Pasta with Pesto, 145
Pickles
  Best Bread and Butter, 142
  Dills, Candied, 143
  Vegetable, Overnight, 142
Rice
  Brown, 146
  Casserole, 146
  Green, 147
  Herbed, 147
  Pilaf, 148
  Primavera, 147
Sauces
  Cocktail, 24
  Creamy Cheese, 148
  for Fish, 78
  Horseradish, 148
  Special, 163

SOUP
Bean, 29
Carrot, Cold, 29
Chicken Vegetable, 30
Chowder
  Clam, 30
  Fish, 31
    Creamy, 31
    Maritime, 32

and Vegetable, 32
Turtle, 35
Fish, 33
Gazpacho, Easy, 33
Potato, Sour Cream, 33
Strawberry, Cold, 34
Tomato, Old-Fashioned, 34

TURKEY
Loaves, Individual, 108
Pie, Deep-Dish, 108
Wild, Stuffed, 130

VEAL
Cutlets with Mustard Sacue, 87
Medallions, 86

VEGETABLES
Asparagus
  Deluxe, 133
  Microwave Cheesy, 133
Beans
  Baked, Greatest, 135
  Black, and Rice, 109
  Nippy Green, Casserole, 134
  Seven, Casserole, 134
Broccoli and Noodles, 135
Buffet, Bake, 140
Carrot
  and Apple Casserole, 136
  and Rice Bake, 136
Chili, 110
Colcannon, 137
Corn, Scalloped, 136
Eggplant Parmesan, 110
Green and Gold Casserole, 140
Onions, Baked, 137
Potato Casserole, 138
Ratatouille, 138
Spaghetti, 111
Squash, Stir-fried, 139
Sweet Potato Bake, 139
Tomatoes, Fried Green, 139
Zucchini
  Rice and, 112
  Spaghetti, 112

Recipes for Hookin' & Cookin'

Mail to:
Rod & Reel
P.O. Box 125
Watertown, New York 13601-125

Please send _____ copies of *The Rod & Reel Cookbook* at $12.95 per copy plus $2.50 per book ordered for shipping and handling.

Name _____

Address _____

City _____ Province _____ State_____ Zip/Postal _____

Enclosed you will find names and addresses for gift cookbooks. I understand you will enclose a gift card with name for each gift cookbook.

Recipes for Hookin' & Cookin'

Mail to:
Rod & Reel
P.O. Box 125
Watertown, New York 13601-125

Please send _____ copies of *The Rod & Reel Cookbook* at $12.95 per copy plus $2.50 per book ordered for shipping and handling.

Name _____

Address _____

City _____ Province _____ State_____ Zip/Postal _____

Enclosed you will find names and addresses for gift cookbooks. I understand you will enclose a gift card with name for each gift cookbook.